Explorations in the Politics

Issues in Sociology, Politics and Education

Explorations in the Politics of School Knowledge

Edited and Introduced by
Geoff Whitty and Michael Young

Nafferton Books
Studies in Education, Nafferton, Driffield, England

First published 1976 by
Studies in Education Ltd.
Nafferton, Driffield, England, YO25 OJL
Reprinted 1977.
Third print 1980

ISBN paperback 0 905484 05 3

Printed in Great Britain by
Cheshire Typesetters Ltd, Chester

Contents

Introduction:
The politics of school knowledge

This book attempts to explore the possibilities and problems of transforming the nature of educative activity. By including within the same volume discussion of this issue by sociologists and radical teachers, we hope to examine the relationship between a sociological perspective on the school curriculum and the problems which face teachers who attempt to transform the nature of educational experience for themselves and their pupils. Although recent work in the sociology of education has made an important contribution to the development of many of the ideas discussed here, it is not our intention in undertaking this project to establish the sociology of school knowledge as yet another area of academic study. Rather, as our title implies, we are concerned to explore the *politics* of school knowledge, and these papers are collected together in the hope that they will contribute to an understanding of the political character of schooling and of the possibilities for change. From their various perspectives, our contributors share with us a profound dissatisfaction with the prevailing circumstances and definitions of schooling, and see a need to redefine the sorts of experiences which have come to be regarded as 'educational'. Recent developments in the sociology of education seem relevant to these concerns, only because, unlike a great deal of educational theory, they have often been sceptical of attempts to justify current definitions of 'education' as intrinsically worthwhile and because they have attempted to examine the interests which underlie the persistence of the very educational practices which we wish to change. At the same time, each of the competing fashions which have recently characterized the world of academic sociology has tended to present an oversimplified view of the real world of schooling and to generate either a naive optimism or a fatalistic pessimism about the possibilities for educational change.[1]

Sociology can perhaps best be regarded as an attempt to 'name that which secretly keeps society going'.[2] In some cases, the work of sociologists seems to suggest that human beings have very little part in that process. Thus, for example, one of the implications of much of the earlier work in the sociology of education seemed to be that, whatever organizational changes were introduced into the system of schooling, 'society' would continue to distribute 'life chances' to individuals in the same way, and assign them to the same preordained position in the social scientist's sets of statistics. The minutiae of day-to-day activities within educational institutions seemed irrelevant to the analysis, and a number of sociologists seemed to devote their time to creating models of educational systems whose relationships to the real-life activities of individuals within

1

schools was, to say the least, somewhat tenuous. Partly as a reaction against the limitations of this emphasis, the so called 'new direction' sociology of education [3] has tended to focus instead upon the ways in which teachers and pupils make sense of their everyday classroom experiences, and on how educational 'reality' is continuously reconstructed in the interaction of individuals, rather than imposed upon them by mysterious external forces. Linked to this change of emphasis has been a refusal to regard definitions of what counts as 'education' as somehow neutral and irrelevant to the way in which inequality is produced in school and society. From such a perspective, what secretly keeps society going is crucially the practices of individual teachers and pupils, and the assumptions about knowledge, ability, teaching, and learning, which are embedded in them. Something of the value of such a perspective can be glimpsed in the contributions to Parts 1 and 2 of this volume, which explore some of the assumptions which underlie both the explicit and the hidden curricula of schooling and the contribution which they make to the maintenance of the *status quo* in society. They show how it is both the values embodied in current conceptions of curricular knowledge and the styles of pedagogy and assessment adopted by teachers, which help to sustain existing social hierarchies.

However, as a number of the contributors to these sections explicitly recognize, there was an important weakness in some of the earlier 'new direction' sociology.[4] The implication that an invitation to teachers to suspend their taken-for-granted assumptions and to examine critically their own practices would produce a transformation in the nature of their activities was ludicrously naive. Thus while most of our contributors go beyond a critique of existing practice to consider possible strategies for change, they do not suggest that the implementation of their proposed alternatives will be without its difficulties. They recognize that the practices which keep society going and hide the ideological dimensions of prevailing notions of knowledge from public view are not just those of the classroom, but take place within a context as wide as capitalist society itself. Tulloch's paper therefore illustrates some interesting parallels between school knowledge and the conceptions of knowledge sustained by the mass media, while other contributors make reference to the ways in which the definitions of 'knowledge' and 'competence' which characterize life in schools must be seen as related to those of other institutions of capitalist society. Chapter 5 on marking and Chapter 6 on the keeping of school files, for example, make very explicit the links between the everyday activities of teachers and the division of labour in society, and pose in a particularly stark manner the difficulties and dilemmas facing those teachers whose conception of society differs radically from that in which prevailing educational practices are grounded.

It would, however, be unfortunate if the need to explore the relationship between schooling and other aspects of capitalism were to lead us to ignore the complexities of the contexts in which we as teachers work. This seems to be a real danger in the various forms of analysis which have very recently become influential amongst sociologists of education. Some of these approaches [5] tend to produce accounts which make it difficult to see much scope for radical teachers within the 'educational' institutions of capitalist society. Although it is

2

clearly crucial to analyse the role of education in the reproduction of the existing division of labour, such analyses are often too general to be meaningful to anyone seeking to comprehend the nature of his or her work situation and of the possibilities for transforming it. There is also a danger that a narrow emphasis upon the political economy of schooling [6] will tend to obscure the ideological significance of prevailing definitions of curricular knowledge and their contribution to the maintenance of a quiescent work force. In both these respects the recent experiences of Chris Searle [7] are perhaps an illustration of the way in which the activities of practising teachers point to complexities and contradictions within the institutions of schooling which are sometimes neglected in theories generated within academic circles. Thus the political potency of Searle's work, which is largely an attempt to change the overt rather than the hidden curriculum, is evidenced by the hysterical reaction to it in both the conservative and the liberal press. Yet, at the same time, he is able to survive (albeit with difficulty) as a teacher in a school within the state system of education. This is not to suggest that the alternative curriculum content devised by Searle presents, of itself, a model for transforming the nature of education, but rather that any critique of schooling in capitalist society cannot afford to neglect such efforts to exploit its contradictions, whether they attempt to redefine what counts as school knowledge or to develop alternative pedagogies. The various contributions to the third section of this book are illustrative of the extent to which alternative approaches to education can begin to be developed, even within our existing society. They show how, in small yet potentially significant ways, the overt and hidden curricula of schooling may be challenged by those who reject the social consequences of existing practice. Our examples span both the state school system and the free school movement and range from an alternative approach to the teaching of O level physics to the introduction of a new subject, media studies, into the school curriculum. It is probably inevitable that accounts of such practical attempts to explore alternatives will at times seem contradictory, but it is part of our argument that such explorations are a necessary part of the struggle to develop a more coherent strategy for educational change.

It is nevertheless quite clear that, for the radical potential of such alternatives to achieve broader significance, they must become more than isolated experiments. An analysis of the wider political context of schooling must therefore be part of the attempt to assess both the importance of particular alternatives and the broader possibilities for change. We have already implied that definitions of what counts as education and knowledge are sustained, not merely by the assumptions and activities of teachers but by the ideas and actions of a whole variety of other interests in society. Given the inadequate and abstract nature of many broad theories about the relationship between education and society, it becomes important to identify quite precisely the institutional practices which produce and sustain the constraints within which teachers work. It is only in the context of such work that we will be able to develop a more adequate understanding of the nature of that relationship and generate appropriate strategies for change. The contributions to Part 4, which are amongst the most exploratory in this volume, illustrate ways in which the existing possibilities for teachers and pupils to take control of their own worlds are severely limited. They point to the importance of teachers' actions to transform the nature of education going beyond the confines of a particular classroom or school to challenge the activities of those who place constraints upon educational change. Among the particular examples discussed are curriculum development agencies, school examination boards, and educational publishers, although it is not suggested that these are the only, or even the most important, ones. Such examples are, of course, relatively easy to locate but, as the chapter on examiners suggests, attempts to challenge their right to define the nature of educative activity may well expose less tangible and probably more significant constraints. Thus, while it is important to point, as we do in Part 3, to the sort of alternative educational practices which have flourished, or at least survived, it is equally important to point to instances where those who appear to have made progress in transforming the nature of educational experience have met with dismissal. The cases of Duane, Mackenzie and German, [8] and the earlier experiences of Searle, [9] are only the most publicized examples but they are indicative of the way in which the defenders of the *status quo* (and even apparently 'liberal' ones) are able to impose limits on the nature of educational innovations.

There remain considerable numbers of teachers who struggle for change in isolated situations and probably many more who, in the light of the constraints imposed upon them, can see no way in which it is possible to continue that struggle. For the first group, the 'new direction' sociology of education may offer some support; to the second, a political economy of education may offer the consolation that their failure is not a personal one. Yet the blindly optimistic activism or the resigned defeatism, which such a division implies, are not the only alternatives. Insofar as schooling is by no means the only institution of ideological control to sustain a view of knowledge which facilitates the presentation of the ideas of the ruling class as correct and absolute, it is unlikely that the struggle against such ideas will be fought and won within the world of education alone. Both from within the institutions of schooling and from outside them, radical teachers face the institutionalized power of those for whom their conceptions of education and society pose a real threat, and it is only in the context of an organized challenge to that power that progress will be made. This need not, however, be seen as an argument for quietism but for a recognition that unless radical teachers are prepared to link their struggle to transform the nature of educational experience to broader struggles to transform the distribution of power and privilege in society, there may be some force in the charge that they do a disservice to their pupils. In such a situation, pupils will probably remain as resistant to radical alternatives as they were to the innovation which Spradbery describes in Chapter 19, and continue to demand just that 'proper' education which ensures that the vast majority of them enter the outside world as 'failures'.

To recognize this is not, we maintain, to conclude that the struggle to transform the experience of schooling must await the transformation of society. Even in the context of education cuts, too narrow a concentration on the politicization of the teacher unions via economistic issues is, we believe, mistaken. [10]

The efforts of teachers like those who describe their work in this book are a vital element in any broader struggle to create an alternative future. Economic and political transformation in the narrow sense will prove to be an empty reality, if radical teachers do not exploit the contradictions of capitalist society to develop a cultural critique of that society and create the elements of a genuinely socialist education for the future. Wright's contribution, which concludes the volume, illustrates the importance of collective action by teachers to transform the nature of education, and points to the weakness of the NUT and its internal pressure group, Rank and File, in this respect. It also points to a lesson which can equally well be learned from recent events at the William Tyndale School in London.[11] As long as radical teachers remain isolated within their schools, and fail to develop links of solidarity with other teachers or work out ways of concretely identifying themselves with the broader working class movement for the transformation of society, they will lack both the support and understanding of those groups upon whose power their capacity to resist the establishment will ultimately depend. In the context of broader collective action, however, the exploration of possibilities may itself serve to transcend the existing limits to change.[12]

Perhaps the greatest weakness of radical educators has been their tendency to try to redefine education only within the contexts which those they oppose have characterized as 'educational institutions'. The papers in this volume do not escape from that weakness, but they do begin to recognize it. While acknowledging the tremendous task which faces those who wish to change the nature of educational practice so that it contributes to the transformation rather than to the maintenance of existing social relations, we hope that the papers collected here will begin to make some contribution to that end. We have tried throughout to avoid the extremes of the resigned pessimism or the naive optimism which seem to characterize the various competing sociological perspectives on the possibilities for change in schools. We hope that such sociology as is contained in this volume will be seen as relevant to the real contexts of change, though we are only too aware that some of us who work as sociologists have been less than successful in escaping from the jargon of our discipline. We trust, however, that these papers will not be treated merely as a body of knowledge to be learned for a degree or diploma but hope that they will be seen instead as a meaningful contribution to efforts being made in a whole variety of contexts to create a socialist future.

Notes

1 This point will be explored at greater length in M. Young and G. Whitty (eds), *Society, State and Schooling* (Brighton, Falmer Press, 1976)

2 This phase is borrowed from Adorno's characterization of 'critical theory'.

3 See, for example, M. F. D. Young (ed), *Knowledge and Control: New Directions for the Sociology of Education* (London, Collier Macmillan, 1971).

4 See, for example, D. Gorbutt, 'The New Sociology of Education' in *Education for Teaching* (1972). See also the critique of this position by Whitty in M. Young and G. Whitty (eds), op. cit.

5 See, for instance, parts of S. Bowles and H. Gintis, *Schooling in Capitalist America* (London, Routledge, 1976), a book which has been a major influence upon the new Open University course, *Schooling and Society*. A similar point is being made about an Althusserian Marxist perspective on education by M. Erben and D. Gleeson in their paper in M. Young and G. Whitty (eds), op. cit. and ,to a lesser extent, it is also applicable to the mode of theorizing adopted by R. Sharp and A. Green in *Education and Social Control* (London, Routledge, 1975). In making this criticism we do not wish to deny the important contribution which these various forms of Marxist theorizing have made to the sociology of education.

6 See, particularly, S. Bowles and H. Gintis, op. cit. The analysis of school experience they offer concentrates almost exclusively on the 'hidden' curriculum of schooling.

7 For details of Searle's recent work, see C. Searle, *Classrooms of Resistance* (London, Writers' and Readers' Cooperative, 1975), and the interview with Searle, together with the editorial comment, in *Teaching London Kids*, No 7 (1976). We share the concern expressed there that Searle has so far had little to say about his *methods* of teaching.

8 The best known account of Duane's experiences at Risinghill is L. Berg, *Risinghill: Death of a Comprehensive* (Harmondsworth, Penguin, 1968). The dismissals of Mackenzie and German were described by Peter Wilby in *The Observer* on 6 April 1974 and 19 January 1975, respectively.

9 Searle offers an account of his dismissal from Sir John Cass and Redcoat School, Stepney, in C. Searle, *This New Season* (London, Calder & Boyars, 1973).

10 This has increasingly been the policy of the Rank and File group within the NUT. The development of this policy can be traced in the pages of *Rank and File*, first published in 1968. The Socialist Teachers' Conference which first met in 1975 was, in some respects, a response to the narrowness of the Rank and File perspective.

11 See the pages of the national and educational press during the autumn of 1975. For a useful comment on the shortcomings of the William Tyndale experiment, see 'Triumph Meriden, Scottish Daily News . . . William Tyndale' in *Teachers' Action* (January 1976).

12 For a fuller discussion of the relationship between radical educators and the labour movement, see S. Frith and P. Corrigan, 'The Politics of Education', in M. Young and G. Whitty (eds), op. cit.

Part 1: The politics of school subjects

It is often claimed that, in some sense, school subjects represent the universal concerns of humanity. There are certainly, within them, elements of the universal human concern to express experience and collectively transform the social and natural environment. However, as in the examples of English, music, science and social studies which we include in this section, the ways in which prevailing conceptions of these subjects represent the world express particular values and interests, both through what they include and exclude and what relations between teachers and pupils they presuppose. School subjects tend to represent education as relatively discrete bodies of knowledge, largely independent of the social relations between teachers and taught, and experienced as a set of hurdles through which pupils have to pass, directed and assessed at each stage by the repository of knowledge, the teacher. In 'What *is* English?' (Chapter 1) Hand describes the variety of fashions which have characterized English teaching in the last decade. While not denying the importance of the problems they focus on, he argues that each particular approach has become invested by its supporters with the status of a total world view. They have, thus, in effect served to fragment that concern for the totality of experience, to which many of those involved in English teaching express a commitment. In 'What Counts as School Music?' (Chapter 2) Vulliamy describes how, in the particular case of music teaching, the very conceptions of music which music teachers share have also succeeded in closing off whole areas of musical expression, which are often part of the culture that pupils bring to school. In the process, music teachers have actually created, albeit unwittingly, the widespread sense among pupils that 'being good at music' is some peculiar innate quality that a very few people are born with. Given the narrow cultural basis for current conceptions of school music, it is scarcely surprising that those few who appear 'good at it' tend to be drawn from a particular social background.

The two chapters in this section by Whitty and Young, examine how, in the process of becoming accepted within the existing assumptions and social relations of school and society, particular conceptions of social and natural science teaching have come to prevail. Despite the intentions of some of those concerned, the social and natural sciences have become 'things to learn', or 'steps on the way to becoming a scientist'. With a few important exceptions, the possibility that they could become opportunities for pupils and teachers to engage critically with the largely taken-for-granted knowledge of the social and natural world that they bring to school has, in the process of schooling, been systemati-

7

cally denied or devalued. In their chapters, both Whitty and Young make the point that is implicit in those by Hand and Vulliamy — that the schooling of knowledge cannot be understood, let alone transformed, by critique and practice within school contexts alone. The process is inextricably linked to the emerging contradictions within wider political and economic relations in our society, and to the way these are expressed in the conceptions of knowledge that characterize our schools.

Chapter 1

What *is* English?

Nigel Hand

A certain healthy imperialism characterizes most, if not all, teachers of English —
a long-standing belief that they, more than anyone else, are concerned with 'the
whole child'.[1] In fact some concept of wholeness or totality underpins, explicitly or implicitly, most writing about English teaching. Strange, then, that no
subject in the curriculum presents, in practice, a more fragmented appearance.
How are we to understand this paradox?

I would like to put the argument in terms of my own experience. During the
last ten years I have taught English (from junior school to college of education)
as high culture, children's literature, vocational skill, existentialism, creative
writing, and drama. If this is representative experience of a decade, so too, I
think, is a reaching through it all for a promised wholeness. After ten years I put
the argument to myself roughly as follows. Each fragmented version of English
offers a compartmentalized view of language, or literature, or both. But each of
these one-eyed outlooks then proposes itself as the promised whole. I see each
definition as highlighting certain values and practices, while masking other incon-
venient aspects of reality. In particular I shall develop in concrete terms the
theoretical view that each version of English teaching either universalizes its
contents and conceals its form, or universalizes its form and conceals its content.
The problem, then, is to see these practices and definitions of English for what
they are. Or, as some would say, here is a case for a little demystification.

1

Perhaps the strongest and most energetic claims to totality have been made by
the high cultural tradition which has been the backbone of most, if not all, enlightened English teaching for a number of decades. The roots of the assumptions
which sustain contemporary English teaching spread wide and deep, both
socially and historically. High cultural English teaching, for instance, is modelled
on the practices which sustained the nineteenth century novel. Aphoristically
put, the critical assumption is that the word is the thing.[2] The nineteenth
century novel apparently takes itself to be continuous with the real world. The
reader is expected to take a created world as both given, and even total, reality.
It is the acceptance of this assumption which marks not only the Victorian reading public, but the practice of much English teaching today. There is a direct
continuity.

Perhaps the most striking and familiar instance of this cultural practice, and of its pervasiveness, is the treatment of 'character' in literature. We have all 'described the character of . . .' – as if the 'character' could be isolated from the text and talked about as if he were a 'real' person. This practice appears at all levels of literature teaching and is massively sustained by the examination system, as we all know. Let me develop an illustration of the way this cultural practice works, and of the kind of consequences it has. The fate of George Orwell's last works gives us a profoundly representative case. Both *Animal Farm* and *1984* have been much used in schools, and very frequently prescribed in examination syllabuses. Thousands of young people carry away from their study of these works the summary conclusion that Orwell, from the inside, pronounced the decisively adverse judgement on socialism in this century. How many readers of Orwell would credit, then, that he wrote this of *Animal Farm?*

> Nothing has contributed so much to the corruption of the original idea of socialism as the belief that Russia is a socialist country and that every act of its rulers must be excused, if not imitated. And so for the past ten years I have been convinced that the destruction of the Soviet myth was essential *if we wanted a revival of the Socialist movement.*[3]

Or that he wrote this of *1984?*

> My recent novel is *not* intended as an attack on Socialism or on the British Labour Party (of which I am a supporter) but as a show-up of the perversions to which a centralized economy is liable and which have been partly realized in Communism and Fascism.[4]

In other words, each book was written out of a *positive* concern for the promotion of socialism. *Animal Farm* enacts the perversion of a revolution, but the *form* of the book – the medium in which the story moves – is a critical irony embodying not a sense that revolutions are wrong and should not take place, but a sense of what, by comparison, a true revolution would be like. However, in the course of its mediation through the educational and social system, *Animal Farm* undergoes a sea change. The true irony embodied in the form of the book is eliminated – the story reduced to a crude content illustrating a bourgeois theme. How is the elimination achieved? By the demand for, say, a description of the 'character' of Napoleon, or Squealer, or Boxer, or for an account of the Battle of the Cowshed – as if they were real people (!) and events; so that the form, the mode of presentation, is side-stepped – the critical and liberating consciousness of the book is denied. There is despair in *Animal Farm,* but despair is not the whole communication. However, despair about the possibility of revolutionary change in society is a doctrine which comes very conveniently to hand, and the point has not been missed. In fact no books are more widely used in schools than those such as *Lord of the Flies* and *The Day of the Triffids* which despair of man's capacity for constructive social action. These books are crude rationalizations of the given. It is George Orwell's tragedy to have been absorbed into this tradition.

What is strange is that even in terms of literary history the character approach is an anachronism. Early in this century writers such as Joyce and Eliot made an apparently decisive break with the 'realist' tradition when they began to write the act of creation *into* their work. The major works of Joyce and Eliot *enact* their creation. Joyce's *Portrait of the Artist as a Young Man* embodies the creation of the central character in the developing and changing content *and* form of the book. However, although there have been some attempts to follow this, it is not clear that there have been any decisive steps forward. Actually, if 'reflexivity' means that a sociologist or artist embodies in his work a sense of his own identity and location, and of his relationship to his subject, then it is very arguable that, after Joyce and Eliot, reflexivity went into criticism. This would begin to explain why Leavis so often seems like the creative writer of our time (and why so many off-the-peg judgements of his work are wide of the mark: the slackly conventional judgement that Leavis 'writes badly' only reveals a failure to perceive not only the distinction of his style, but of his work as a whole – its self-searching integrity). The runners up, as it were, such as William Empson, on the one hand, and Raymond Williams on the other, could be understood in very much the same way. Perhaps that is why their work is exciting in a way which one doesn't even begin to associate with the general run of literary criticism – or sociology. Moreover, we have here some profound implications for education. Perhaps the true source of our creative inspiration should not be the thousands of bourgeois novels that continue to be written (the higher gossip), nor those slim volumes of poetry (privatized worlds), but that really self-reflecting and generously creative criticism which is our contemporary literature. Fundamentally, this gives us a model for the humanities in which the child is enabled to see, and experience, active relationships both between society and its works, and between himself and those works.

Meanwhile, even books like Joyce's *Portrait* are given the realist-character treatment in schools – undermining the patient integrity of the artist's creation. Shakespeare suffers in the same way. It is extraordinarily difficult to get students, character-study ingrained in them throughout their schooldays, to read a Shakespeare play as anything but a realistic novel – even though a 'character' may soliloquize, in blank verse, in the presence of six others. The students are aware neither of the premises of their own thought nor of those of Shakespearian drama. All this despite the fact that Shakespeare is quite as 'reflexive' in his own terms, as Joyce; indeed, he is profoundly more so.

To take another instance, on teaching practice students commonly feel that they ought to make a show of teaching poetry. What sort of poetry do they choose, and in what terms do they deal with it? In my observation, the poetry chosen is of the 'descriptive', 'narrative' variety – poetry with 'good descriptive phrases', or incidents from 'real life'. The student discusses with the children how far the poet has succeeded in creating a scene or event which conforms to everyday reality. Moreover, when progressive teachers use material which, also, is documentary – but in a controversial or even sensational way – they are by no means necessarily doing anything more helpful. For in the end this practice often ratifies a *way of seeing* which takes the world as given, just as much as does the traditionally descriptive. At any rate, it is clear that, outside the context of the parroted essay, most students can't, when it matters, handle poetry which refuses to take the world for granted. In their academic courses, students may study such poets as Wordsworth, Yeats, and Eliot, whose best work is always designed to thwart the assumptions of common sense realism. Yet there is no pay-off from this study to the student's own teaching. Instead we see a retreat to the same second-rate anthology pieces which the student did at school! The reason is not far to seek. The great poets are taught in colleges as a body of knowledge to be learnt. Prevented from realizing the poetry as inquiry, the students never come into real possession of what they have studied. Consequently they abandon it in the classroom – and in their own lives.

The pervasiveness of the realist-character approach indicates that it is not a fortuitous mistake, a simple failure here and there to respect the conventions of different kinds of works of art. On the contrary, *this* mistake is formative of the cultural suzerainty of the middle class. The 'character' moves unimpeded between the world and the book because the two are (apparently) continuous – parts of a universal documentary reality. To ask who wrote the 'document' is to reveal how the high cultural version of English teaching engineers its claims to wholeness. The act of writing the document, and hence its particular *form,* is eliminated. Content is universalized. It is clear that, here, all those Marxist pejoratives – false, contradictory, mystifying, and so on – have an obvious application.

2

Of course there are those who have begun to feel that the reading public and the bourgeois novel aren't what they used to be. In fact both are now seen from time to time, and with good reason, as 'corrupt' and 'debased'. One result of this state of affairs has been the rise of children's literature, and an attempt in education to reconstruct a modified version of high culture (with new claims to wholeness) in terms of a literature written specifically for children. What is the significance of this lively vogue, with its ever-increasing coverage in newspapers and journals, its promotion not only in the classroom but through conferences, journals, children's book groups, and exhibitions?

At a time of prolonged crisis and change, when values are shifting and unstable, individuals and groups who, consciously or unconsciously, have axes to grind will compete for the allegiance of the confused and uncommitted. Children, in particular, will be canvassed incessantly. Moreover, the same sort of claim to wholeness which I have attributed to English teachers will be an obvious strategy. In fact the children's literature movement commonly goes forward under just such a banner. Psychologically (and reductively) conceived, the claim is to the fostering of the complete personal development of the individual. A well-known writer for children, Joan G. Robinson, remarks: 'I am only interested in books which . . . may help children in their own inner growing up.'[5]

Now this programme would be unexceptionable – if it were informed by a sense that children's 'inner growing up' doesn't take place in a social vacuum. But in fact it is just this realization that is notably missing. What is the outcome?

The programme of the children's literature movement reveals itself as *adjustment*. A recent article on Nina Bawden, a mediocre writer for children, was entitled 'Getting Used to Things as They Are'.[6] Just how socially blinkering and reductive is children's literature as a contemporary cultural and educational practice is seldom disclosed so blatantly as in the justification of this writer simply because she encourages the reader to accept the given reality.

Some of these realities are, however, now beginning to be noticed. Women's Lib has begun to observe 'sex stereotyping' in books for children. Radical and anti-racialist groups have begun to point to similar racial stereotyping. Extraordinarily 'colonial' attitudes are here and there beginning to be seen for what they are — as in the nauseous best-seller *Charlie and the Chocolate Factory* (which is much used in junior schools). But it is the treatment of social class in children's books which is most revealing. All the way from the Victorian classic *Froggy's Little Brother* to the contemporary best-selling school series 'Nippers', children's writers have patronized the working class. Some books, such as *The Family from One End Street,* have become classics purely by virtue of the consistent energy with which they have done so.

But it is not fundamentally this or that 'attitude' that makes children's literature in education oppressive, but the whole shape of the cultural and educational practice by which it is sustained. The notion of 'inner growth' translates into 'learning to accept reality' — into 'adjusting' to things as they are. Seen in this way the enterprise is manifestly anti-rational, though insofar as thought can be trapped at the level of the individual, then we have a plausible wholeness. Thus the children's literature movement is another confused version of realist individualism — a-historical, a-social, and contradictory. Again, *forms* which have a particular social meaning, which shape a particular social experience, are dissolved into content; so that content is once more taken for the total reality, the universal.

3

On the face of it, it is curious that in the teaching of reading as a 'skill' we have a situation which is apparently the opposite of what I have so far described. That is, content virtually disappears, and nothing is seen but form. And the case seems to be the same with the teaching of writing as a skill. I shall try to account for this strange reversal, and to show how it relates to the state of affairs I have already described.

Now all that vast and dreary slough of mediocre English teaching done in the name of reading and writing — and speaking — as 'skills' — the graded reading schemes, the tests of 'reading age', the lessons on how to write a business letter, and how to conduct yourself at a job interview — all these have a manifest political significance. As the Newsom Report pleasantly remarked:

A wide and generous course of English should do much to prepare these pupils for life in an adult society; it is vocational in the best possible way. Such a course should provide a good foundation for *workmanlike* English in that it will enable boys and girls in later life to *read instructions* or *pass on messages,* or write a letter, or jot down a record.[7]

Here is another momentarily plausible concept of wholeness. What sustains the teaching of reading and writing as skills is a concept of citizenship. The aim is to prepare the individual 'for his place in society' — so that he can 'play a *useful* part in the adult world'. In such formulations a profoundly revealing metaphor frequently appears: language as tool. Now, in the first place, there are obviously those who use tools and those who don't. And, in the second place, this whole body of educational thought enshrines a view of language as pure form which is alienation itself. It is a concept appropriate to those who will not create the content of their own working lives, but will have it supplied to them by others.

On the one hand, then, high culture and children's literature develop an apparently universal content concealing form; on the other, the teaching of reading and writing as skills embodies a view of language as form without content. Actually, of course, there is no paradox here. High culture is for, and shaped by, the middle class; instrumental language skills are for (but not shaped by) the working class. The middle class child really learns to read at home. He learns through bedtime fairy tales, family story books, and so on — content and skill form one growing experience. Thus, from the first, reading comes naturally as a way of understanding and enlarging one's individual world. The working class child learns to read — if at all — at school. In toiling through the reading schemes he learns that reading is a mechanical task unrelated to anything he can understand. Thus he is prepared for a role in which reading is relevant only to the accomplishment of tasks ordained by others. For other purposes — apart from the reading of newspapers — he abandons it as quickly as possible.

It is notable in another way that while high culture and children's literature, within an apparently unchanging reality, point to a certain degree of *inner* freedom — the middle class freedom to imagine and adjust — language as instrument, on the other hand, eliminates inner personal content — the worker is a depersonalized tool in an apparently unchanging system. *His* adjustment is purely external. As in *1984* no one cares what the proles *think*; they merely function. But the members of the Party — the managers of the corporate state — they, at all costs, must *think right*. Nowhere is the nature of our divided society more apparent than here — in these fissures that run through our educational system. No concept of wholeness which fails to confront them can be taken seriously. It must result in contradiction.

4

Of course, some English teachers define themselves not as conservative or utilitarian — but progressive, even 'existentialist'.

Our emphasis is upon the present moment and its value, irrespective of the value of the past. Our concern with life, our interpretation of life in the classroom, our concern to present the meaningful present to our pupils is properly an existentialist concern.[8]

What does this mean in practice? Of all the vague ideas in progressive education the notion of 'starting from the children's own experience' seems to me the most naive. No idea is made more play with, or receives less intelligent examination. If, as seems obvious, we cannot start with the total experience of the pupil, let alone that of the entire class, how does one part of that experience rather than another become the content of education? Now in practice, at the everyday level, the teacher has 'to get something going' – to establish, as they say, a relationship. At this point the situation seems to me uncannily similar to that described by Leslie Farber in a perceptive essay about the psychotherapist and the schizophrenic patient.[9] Farber's subtle argument loses a great deal in summary, but the process he describes goes roughly as follows.

In order to provoke relationship the therapist identifies with the patient ('I'm on your side, kids!'). As a result, he 'comes to view himself as a victim, acted upon by the force of nature, society, or the family. . . . His story will be the familiar one of hero as victim, irreversibly oppressed by the will of others' ('It's the system that's killing us, kids'). But then, 'should the therapist forget the degree to which he has supplied meaning to a patient unable to provide any for himself, he may come to regard the schizophrenic as a sort of oracle with whom he sits each day . . .' ('They really make you see things as they are, those kids, if you listen to them'). And finally, 'the therapist, by virtue of the prolonged apprenticeship he has served in the most indulgent kind of self-expression, may be led towards the posture and ultimately the belief, that he, too, is an oracle' ('English for salvation, come and get it!').

In other words the 'existentialist' approach offers an alluring temptation to self-dramatization. The content of the work, apparently open ended, is in the end caught up and trapped in the form – the 'relationship'. The current which energizes, and constantly has to re-energize the relationship – keeping the teacher's brightly burnished charisma aglow – never gets released into real creative work. The imagination is never released to transform reality. The teacher cannot afford, ironically, the pupil's autonomy – the autonomy which derives from a mature relationship in which both parties share an experience but do not possess it.

The political and educational significance of all this is part of the long history of the radical intellectual, in which tradition the English teacher undoubtedly places himself. Centrally significant here is the radical teacher's obsessive preoccupation with working class life. The 'working class' novels which are so much used, the course book material on working class life, the social surveys of the working class family – what exactly does it all add up to? Certainly – or so my experience suggests – working class children would prefer to read something other than this. Or, if they accept it, they do so – as with television programmes of the same order – feeling that it refers to other people than themselves. Both these intuitive responses are very sensible, prompted as they are by the instinctive knowledge that what is being offered are limited and limiting images of themselves. So what's in it for the progressive teacher? At the heart of the matter, I suspect, is the radical teacher's deep uneasiness about his own *relationship* to the working class – to his pupils. The obsessiveness with which this theme runs

15

through progressive education is accounted for by the unresolved and always un-examined tensions which lie hereabouts. The knot that is tied is complicated. At odds with his own middle class background, bearing a sense of guilt about those less favoured than himself − yet unable really to enter into a form of life which can never be his, the radical teacher's sense of community is deeply frustrated.

The determining factor, then, is form − unresolved and contradictory relation-ship. If it were not so, if in a really open sense *all* contemporary social life were the 'existentialist' content, then we should obviously see just as much attention given to middle class life. Now in one sense middle class life is the subject of plenty of literary material used in schools. But how often is it brought into focus as an object of study − bracketed for consideration as a particular social pheno-menon? Very rarely, if ever, of course. Thus in the midst of the apparent radicalism, or existentialism, middle class life remains the taken for granted norm, the universal by which working class life is seen as the problem, the particular.

As George Gissing put it: 'I identified with the poor and ignorant; I did not make their cause my own, but my own cause theirs.'

5

I suppose that if you asked some schoolchildren what they thought English was all about, the least unsatisfactory answer you would get would be: 'It's for developing your imagination'. The children who proposed this definition would be those who had learnt to see 'creative writing' as lying at the heart of English. In the last few decades this version of English has undoubtedly built up the most positive achievement to be observed on the current educational scene. This has to be remembered. But if this programme is to realize its potential there is a problem which remains to be confronted.

The roots of the difficulty lie in what 'being a writer' means in our culture. [10] Towards the end of the nineteenth century a cultural dissociation took place which may be initially characterized by pointing to the appearance of the 'social novel' and the 'psychological novel' as separate categories. In the 'social' tradition, running from Wells (in his realistic vein) to Orwell's journalistic works and the working class realist, the kind of interest suggested by the term 'docu-mentary' became paramount. 'Content' was what mattered, while 'form' was written off as the plaything of the dilettante. In the 'psychological' tradition, beginning with Henry James and running finally to seed in such writers as Iris Murdoch, the defining characteristic is not exactly a preoccupation with the inner life, but the artist's 'handling' of his 'material' − the way in which he mani-pulates his characters to reveal how they work. The doctrines of 'Significant Form' and 'Art for Art's Sake' signalled an increasingly specialized view of art as having to do with no more than the manipulation of a medium. This doctrine has been the legacy of English as a subject. English participates in the history of the 'privatization' of imagination. In English, then (English isolated as a subject), imagination becomes what you can do with words 'as a medium'. Imagination becomes an isolated faculty bearing only on the specialized treatment of certain given areas and kinds of experience. To illustrate the point by contrast, how often do we come across writing by schoolchildren on this sort of subject? I came across it in a nine-year-old's rough book:

Silence

Silence, silence, said my teacher.
Read in silence, he said aloud.
Read in silence, little ones.

Silence, silence, said my teacher.
Do your English in silence.
Write down the words and work in silence.

Silence, silence, that's what I said.
Work in silence.
Silence, little children, silence.

The fact is that there are certain kinds of experience which are in practice seen as natural and legitimate subjects for creative writing, while writing itself is reduced to certain appropriately 'imaginative' ways of treating them. What it's really like being a schoolchild belongs in a second category — the unsuitable. Of course it is the mark of a really creative mind to encompass new areas of experience in art.

All perception is creative; we make the world we live in. But what children finally learn from the existence of English as a separate subject is that creativity is, apparently, the 'handling' of certain more or less 'personal' experiences within a specialized medium. 'Being a writer' is apparently a private affair.

However, in so far as we have here *some* marrying of content and form, and therefore a real approach to wholeness, we have seen genuine educational achievement.

6

For my own part I have most nearly realized a sense of wholeness in teaching drama. If drama is commonly seen as part of English, its great strength is nevertheless that in a number of important senses it is not a subject at all. To begin with, it lacks many of the features by which the structure of a subject may be recognized — markable work, textbooks, homework, examinations, indeed any commodity as end-product. But more fundamentally, in drama (meaning the kind of thing suggested by the word 'improvization', rather than the learning of scripts, and so on — though that has its place), form and content are one. Teacher and class *make* the subject. Form and content together are the 'subject' of the 'lesson'. Moreover, in the process of *making,* drama work evolves its own standards.[11] Children often become so much more involved in drama than in any other school work because teacher and class create and therefore *possess* their own standards. To put it another way, in a drama lesson the children are both

17

actors and audience. *Creativity begins to regain its public purpose.* Often, therefore, there is a sense of shared experience, of collective insight and growth — which should be a fundamental educational dynamic throughout the curriculum, but isn't.

When, in English and drama, the making and evaluation of experience become one, a further and profound educational alienation — of thought from feeling — begins to be eliminated. In such a context, thankfully, the question 'What does this *mean* to us?' makes no sense considered in purely 'cognitive' or 'emotive' terms. Both categories are transcended. In the sense that it organizes at the same time both thought and feeling, drama work shares in the nature of the poetic symbol, ordering experience as a whole.

But drama's transcendence goes beyond the integration of thought and feeling. It has in fact a Utopian significance. It embodies the human capacity to create new worlds. Thus drama distinguishes itself from the purely mindless 'happening' — which, lacking intention, is no more than a more or less random rearrangement of the *actual*. Shared and self-evaluating creativity, drama points beyond the actual to new human possibilities.

Finally, however, 'Utopian' is an ambiguous word, and nowhere more so than here. It attracts the word 'merely', as 'play' attracts the word 'mere'. Herein lies the explanation why the System (as we have got into the habit of calling it) can tolerate and control drama, and similar manifestations. Precisely because it lacks the credentials of a 'subject', drama can be defined as not 'serious' — not 'real'. Here we have a case which is profoundly representative of the present state of things. The more significant, the less 'serious'; the more liberating, the less 'real'. It is this appalling tangle which is at the heart of the fragmentation of English and which makes the vision of wholeness so desperately hard to realize.

Notes

1 Some of the points I make in this chapter were first expressed in an article in the *Use of English* (May 1975). I would like to thank Geoff Whitty, Michael Young and Pete Thompson for their helpful comments on various drafts of the work.

2 I am developing here, for my own purposes, a point made by Gabriel Josipovici in his very interesting study *The World and the Book* (London, Paladin, 1973).

3 Quoted by Raymond Williams, *Orwell* (London, Fontana, 1971), p. 70. My italics. Readers of Williams's book will see how far I have plundered from it in this section.

4 Ibid., p. 76.

5 *Children's Literature in Education,* No. 6 (1971), p. 23.

6 Nicholas Tucker, *Children's Literature in Education,* No. 13 (1974), p. 35.

7 *Half our Future* (the Newsom Report) (London, HMSO, 1963), p. 159, para. 483. My italics.

8 Brian Hollingworth, *Use of English*, vol. 21, No. 2 (1969).

9 In *Laing and Anti-Psychiatry*, (Harmondsworth, Penguin, 1972).

10 I am making use of a point made by Raymond Williams, as for instance in *The English Novel, from Dickens to Lawrence* (London, Chatto & Windus, 1970).

11 A comment of Richard Winter's prompts me to add that judgement — criticism in the 'reflexive' sense mentioned earlier — is of the essence of this enterprise. Creativity and criticism are inseparable.

Chapter 2

What counts as school music?

Graham Vulliamy

My aim in this chapter is to apply some of the insights of contemporary sociologists of education to a particular area of the curriculum – namely, music – which has rarely been examined hitherto other than from the perspective of 'academic' musicians themselves.* A major focus of recent work in the sociology of education has been a critical consideration of the school curriculum and what counts as valid knowledge in educational institutions. Such an analysis necessarily involves a questioning of the 'absoluteness' of many of the educator's assumptions about knowledge; by illustrating the social origin of such assumptions, the way is open for the possibility of alternative definitions and assumptions. The case of music is interesting precisely because the existence of competing definitions of music is explicitly recognized by music educators. The Newsom Report noted that 'out of school adolescents are enthusiastically engaged in musical self-education', [1] but one might suggest that, because of the assumptions on which music teaching in schools is based, this involvement by teenagers in their own type of music (called 'pop' music by the teacher) is taken by most music teachers as an additional hindrance to what they are trying to achieve. Here I hope to show that, by suspending the traditional assumptions on which music teaching is based, a number of interesting questions and possibilities are opened up.

How, then, do most music teachers view their subject? Until quite recently the main components of class music (as opposed to extracurricular musical activities in the school) were some combination of singing, history of music, music appreciation, the teaching of notation and theory and, in some cases, the playing of a simple instrument like a recorder or a harmonica. This conception has, however, been challenged by a group of music teachers who stress the importance of practical music making in the classroom. One of the early influences of this recent approach to class music was the work of Carl Orff, the German composer. He developed the use of simple, tuned percussion instruments (such as the glockenspiel) which enabled large numbers of children actually to play instruments in the classroom. In addition, the emphasis which Orff placed on the role of improvization has led to the possibility of children composing their own music. Such an approach has been extended in different ways by recent music teachers who reject the main aims and emphases of traditional class music teaching. Many of these teachers are themselves composers of 'serious'

* Parts of this paper first appeared in G. Vulliamy and E. Lee (eds), *Pop Music in School* (Cambridge University Press. 1976). We are grateful to Cambridge University Press, who hold the copyright on this material, for permission to reproduce it here.

19

music (in the field of what is generally referred to as the *'avant garde'*) and they are concerned to acquaint pupils with the 'serious' music of today.[2] Emphasis is therefore placed on the different techniques that today's *avant garde* composers themselves use. An attempt is made to get away from the traditional approaches to the more recent *avant garde* approaches stressing practical music been developed which has something in common with that used by a number of today's *avant garde* composers, and the shift in such an approach is away from teaching pupils to play instruments the 'right' way and towards the actual composition of music and the creative manipulation of sounds.

Thus school music teaching is characterized by a variety of approaches (ranging from what might be called, purely for convenience of comparison, traditional approaches to the more recent *avant garde* approaches stressing practical music making in the classroom), but what is common to all of them is the fact that the content of the music lessons tends to be restricted to one particular type of music – namely music in the European 'serious tradition'.[3] This is a reflection of the music establishment's conceptions of serious music, which might now be examined by reference to the work of the music critic Henry Pleasants.

In a series of books, culminating in *Serious Music and all that Jazz,* Pleasants suggests that this century has witnessed a momentous musical revolution but one which, for various historical and sociological reasons, has gone almost unnoticed by the music establishment.[4] The revolution in music derives from what has come to be called Afro-American music – that is, those types of music (jazz, blues, rock and soul would be examples) that can be traced, in some of their aspects at least, to the merging of a West African tradition of music with that tradition of music, European in origin, which thrived in the southern states of America in the nineteenth century. With jazz came the development of a new musical language and a language that was to shape not only jazz but much of the popular music of the twentieth century. The main features of this new musical language have been analysed at length elsewhere.[5] They include a differing conception of rhythm from that in the European 'serious' tradition, the use of the blues scale, which leads to the violation of traditional 'classical' melodic and harmonic practices, the extended use of musical improvization and different conceptions of the sonorities that instruments produce between the Afro-American and European 'serious' music traditions. Here is a black aesthetic with respect to music, but what has happened is that a large section of the western world (namely youth) has taken over the aesthetic and used it in its own music. Prior to 1956 'pop' was either watered down 'classical' music or watered down jazz and, whilst the famous ballad crooners of yesteryear (Sinatra, Johnny Ray, etc.) were to some extent influenced by the jazz tradition, Afro-American musical criteria were not in the forefront of their music. This all changed in 1956 with the birth of rock and roll, where Negro rhythm and blues records were put out by white musicians for the first time. Such Afro-American music became more and more popular with young people, in the styles of rock music, blues, soul, Tamla Motown and others – so much so that Charles Keil, the ethnomusicologist, writing in 1966 stated that:

It is simply incontestable that year by year American popular music has come to sound more and more like African popular music. The rhythmic complexity and subtlety, the emphasis on percussive sound qualities, the call and response pattern, the characteristic vocal elements (shout, growl, falsetto and so on), blues chromaticism, blues and gospel chord progressions, Negro vocabulary, Afro-American dance steps — all have become increasingly prominent in American music.[6]

It is Afro-American musical criteria and the electronic amplification of instruments that underpin the principal *musical* differences between music in the European 'serious' tradition and the mushrooming rock music culture which has taken such a hold of the musical tastes of young people. There are, of course, in addition important extra-musical differences between the musical culture of rock music and the European 'serious' tradition; as many commentators have noted, rock music is much more than just *music* for many of its devotees; it has taken on the status of a subculture involving changing attitudes and values in a social and political sense.

It is when we observe the variety of musical styles in the field of so-called 'pop' music which are directly influenced by Afro-American musical criteria, together with the international scope of these styles, that we can see the force of the views expressed by Henry Pleasants. Himself a music critic trained in the 'classical' tradition, he believes that this century will be seen by future historians as being dominated by Afro-American music in the same sense as one might associate the Romantic period in music with Germany or the Baroque period with Italy.

Pleasants makes some poignant comments on the debate which has been raging within the musical establishment during this century concerning the exhaustion of possibilities of further development within the traditional framework of tonality and the responses of 'serious' composers to this situation, ranging from the twelve-tone and serialist developments of Schoenberg to aleatory music and electronic music. The terms of the debate, as it has been discussed by 'serious' musicians, have been such that the future of music can only be conceived of in terms of 'serious' music in the tonal idiom or music in the atonal idiom. Pleasants suggests that 'serious' musicians have been led to such a view only because they have been blinkered by their own terms:

Historians, critics and composers have made the mistake of thinking of the main stream of musical evolution solely in terms of serious music, as if there were *a* serious music and *a* popular music instead of simply various qualities of music.[7]

The important change of this century is not to be seen, Pleasants suggests, as the move from a tonal to an atonal language, but rather as the change from a music based on theme and harmony to one based on melody and rhythm. The latter change has, however, gone largely unobserved by the musical establishment because it has taken place in an area of music (jazz and 'popular') which was not, until quite recently, normally recognized as music at all.

21

Why, briefly, was there this total neglect of Afro-American music by the establishment? The reaction to the growth of jazz in America from the 1920s onwards has been well documented.[8] Jazz was resisted because of its identification with the Negro, a low status group in society, and because of further identifications with crime, vice and greater sexual freedom (probably because the earliest jazz was played in brothels for want of anywhere else where the Negro musicians were allowed to play). In addition, traditionally trained 'classical' musicians opposed jazz because it appeared to violate both 'classical' music standards and 'classical' cultural standards, since it was not performed in concert halls. The reactions of the musical establishment to the 'rock revolution' were similar in that not only was the 1950s rock and roll seen as a gross violation of traditional musical values, but also as a moral threat to the young people who represented the major part of its audience.

One result of these reactions is that the standards of criticism by which Afro-American music is usually judged and discussed derive from that tradition of music which has been dominant in Europe – in the latter the adoption of the 'tempered' scale by J. S. Bach led to the primacy of harmony and the formal structure of music. Whilst this point must remain undeveloped here, musical analyses of both Afro-American musical styles and of so-called primitive musics which judge the latter from criteria derived from the European 'serious' music tradition fail to 'understand' the musical bases of these other styles of music.[9]

Thus in its reactions to various types of Afro-American musical styles the music establishment has used inappropriate critical canons which have led to highly restricted notions of 'serious' music. In particular it has operated with an assumed dichotomy between 'serious' music and 'popular' music, where all varieties of Afro-American music are grouped under the latter label. Thus the whole field of Afro-American music is dismissed as non-music by Routh in his lengthy survey of contemporary British music since 1945:

> The term music is taken to include as many aspects of the composer's work as fall under the heading of art-work. An art-work is one which makes some claim on our serious attention. This implies a creative, unique purpose on the part of the composer and an active response on the part of the listener; it implies that the composer possesses and uses both vision and technique, and that the listener in return is expected to bring to bear his full intelligence. This excludes non-art music, such as pop music, whose purpose is chiefly if not entirely commercial. Pop groups are big business; they are socially significant; there is no question that they form a remarkable contemporary phenomenon – but this does not make the result into an art-work, and to consider it as if it were is an illogical affectation.[10]

This is illustrative of the prevalent establishment ideology concerning the nature of 'pop' music – 'ideology' being used in the Marxist-derived sense to refer to a system of beliefs which give a distorted picture of the 'real' world in the interest of those dominant social groups sharing such beliefs. There are three aspects of this ideology:

1 'Pop' music is a homogeneous product.

2 'Pop' music's sole motivation is a commercial one.

3 The musical tastes (and emotions) of young people are thus manipulated by commercial exploiters who aim their product at a mass
market.

Such an ideology has been criticized at greater length elsewhere;[11] here, concerning the first point, it must be emphasized that the term 'pop' music is a
thoroughly misleading one, in that it covers many different types of music, some
of which are popular and some of which are not, some of which are found on LP
records (which since 1968 have outsold singles in absolute terms) and some on
singles records. Various types of so-called 'pop' music (soul, Tamla Motown,
teenybopper pop, rock, folk, reggae, 'progressive' music, to name but a few) not
only have very different musical origins and qualities but also appeal to widely
different social groups.

The argument that all 'pop' music is commercial is a considerable over-
simplification. Certainly some musicians' primary motivation is a financial one
but the main concern of many others is to create what they consider to be
serious artistic music. But, unlike 'classical' musicians, serious jazz or rock musicians who want to create music which, because of its complex or experimental
nature, is unlikely to be commercial get little or no help from the establishment
in terms of financial subsidies or media exposure. The BBC's policy of excluding
practically all serious jazz and rock music from the radio has become something
of a national scandal. Radio 1, which is supposed to be the 'popular' music programme, is a constant object of ridicule amongst rock musicians and many
young people, geared as it is almost entirely to commercial 'pop' singles, whilst
the two categories of music – namely 'progressive rock' and 'reggae and soul'
– which a recent Schools Council survey [12] found to be among the most
popular with schoolchildren are conspicuous by their absence.

In addition the expenses involved in running a rock group are enormous and
it is only the smallest minority of such groups who ever recoup enough money
to pay back the initial outlay. Whilst some 'pop' musicians are strongly motivated by commercial factors, many others try to make no concessions to the
commercial pressures of recording companies even to the extent of living at
income levels which would be considered an outrage by any trade union. Merely
because some authors write primarily for the money does not mean we can dismiss all books as non-art and the product of big business – and the same goes for
music. The further assumption, implied in Routh's definition – that popularity
or commercial gain leads inevitably to inartistic results – is also highly dubious.
Who would suggest, for example, that Mozart's symphonies are less artistic
simply because they were composed in order to make a living?

The questionable nature of the third aspect of the music establishment's
ideology concerning the nature of 'pop' music follows largely from what I have
already said. Those who argue that 'pop' music exploits the tastes of young
people never make clear what type of 'pop' music they have in mind; nor do
they make clear who is supposed to be doing the exploiting. The major record

23

companies who have attempted to impose 'pop' music tastes have been continually outflanked by smaller independent companies who have reflected the pre-existing tastes of different groups of young people. Numerous surveys of the rise of recent pop music forms demonstrate this.[13] Rather than the recording companies imposing their tastes on young people, there is now a tendency for record companies to do as much as they can to identify the tastes of young people and then reflect them back in their records — hence the rise of the 'company freak' [14] whose job it is to provide a liaison between the young audience and the older record company executives. Other critics see the exploiter as the radio (usually Radio 1), but this fails to recognize that, as I suggested earlier, this is not an accurate reflection of the musical tastes of young people. Consequently, many commentators are unaware that young people are listening to good music — termed 'popular' music despite the fact that in many cases it is not popular at all — which rarely finds its way to the radio (or television).

I have argued that the music establishment's ideology concerning 'pop' music contains many highly misleading assumptions. These assumptions are perpetuated, not only by selective financial subsidies and by certain media policies, as I have mentioned, but also by means of the educational system, where there has been an almost total neglect of both jazz and rock music in music education both in America and Britain. 'Academic' music in this country is totally dominated by music in the European 'serious' tradition; neither O nor A level consider Afro-American music at all in any of its forms, whilst an examination of the syllabuses of nearly all university music degree courses shows the same pattern. Since most class music teachers have their initial training either in a university or in a conservatory, at no point in their training will they have been required either to listen to or to play any style of music other than European 'serious' music. Such an educational background is likely to produce not only ignorance of the musical criteria of Afro-American musical styles, but also the kinds of attitudes to such music that have been shown to be associated with members of the music establishment. Thus Brocklehurst, in a popular book used in the training of music teachers, argues that:

> The primary purpose of musical appreciation is to inculcate a love and understanding of good music. It is surely the duty of teachers to do all they can to prevent young people falling ready prey to the purveyors of commercialized 'popular' music, for these slick, high-pressure salesmen have developed the exploitation of teenagers into a fine art.[15]

These key features of the subject perspective of music teaching can now be related to a sociological analysis of the school curriculum utilizing Young's concept of the 'stratification of knowledge'.[16] In any society at any point in time some knowledge is defined as high status (approved by dominant groups) and some as low status (for example, not taught or not examined) and this power of some to define what is 'valued' knowledge leads to problems of assessing how 'stratified' knowledge is and by what criteria. My analysis of the subject perspective of music teaching suggests that with music we have a rigid stratification of knowledge and perhaps the clearest example in the school curriculum of a rigid distinction between subject-based knowledge ('serious' music), which is the musical culture of the school, and everyday knowledge ('pop' music), which is the musical culture of most of the school pupils. As with other cases of cultural clashes between teacher and taught, in order to preserve the rigid hierarchy between them, the culture of the pupils has to be regarded as 'deprived' or 'deficient'.[17] In the case of music this involves maintaining highly misleading assumptions concerning the nature of 'pop' music, which is why I am at pains to expose the ideological view of it that is held by the music establishment.

It has been argued by Young and others that one of the unfortunate consequences of much traditional work in the sociology of education, which tended to be carried out within a structural-functional framework where 'education' itself was taken as given, was that the explanation of the failure of the predominantly working class pupils placed all the emphasis on the characteristics of those who failed rather than considering also the nature of what they failed at. Recent approaches to the sociology of education point to the social nature of educational categories and the necessity of looking at the social assumptions underpinning teachers' definitions of knowledge and ability in the context of interaction in the classroom. The fruitfulness of such an approach in an analysis of the social assumptions underpinning various styles of music teaching suggested itself to me after limited periods of participant observation study in different educational institutions where 'what counted as music' differed radically. I was interested in the music teachers' perspective [18] concerning, in particular, their definition of music and musical ability and their identification of the main problems in music teaching.

In one large comprehensive school that I observed, which had a very high reputation for the standard and scope of its instrumental extracurricular work, the main orientation of the music staff was to produce 'good all-round musicians' with a thorough grounding in the discipline of music, sight reading and so on.[19] Class music in the school was taught for two periods a week up to the fourth year; in one period the intention was to teach all pupils to play the recorder and at the same time the basis of musical theory and notation, whilst the other period was to be devoted to either singing or music appreciation – the latter incorporating listening to music, the history of music and the provision of information about music such as details of the instruments of the orchestra or of the lives of famous composers. Each year group was fairly rigidly streamed into top, middle and low ability groups and these groups remained the same for the teaching of all subjects including class music. In the context of extracurricular music, which featured an unusually wide variety of music groups, including an orchestra, a dance band, a military band and a choir, the equation of 'playing the instrument well' and sight reading meant that there was a corresponding emphasis on music that is notated rather than on predominantly improvized music.

The prevailing definition of 'what counts as music' in the school with its emphasis on musical literacy, the provision of information about music, and the teaching of musical theory (all of which were strongly emphasized at A and O level, and to a lesser extent at CSE) makes the 'discipline' of music not unlike other 'academic' disciplines with their emphasis on literacy, abstract theory and so on. It was not surprising to find, therefore, that the music teachers should assume that those pupils (in the upper streams) who were good at other academic subjects might be good at the 'discipline' of music, whilst those pupils who had failed in other academic subjects (that is, those in the lower streams) would also 'fail' at music. This assumption clearly influenced the ways in which the different streams were taught. Whilst the top streams were taught the academic aspects of music, there was a general feeling amongst the music staff that there was little one could do with the lower streams in terms of teaching them music. It also affected which pupils were encouraged to take up playing musical instruments, since it was the Head of Music's view that a pupil in a lower stream would have neither the ability nor the perseverance to play an instrument well and take full benefit from the peripatetic instrumental tuition provided.

Such observations, together with an examination of the literature on music education, tend to support the view that music educators with what I have called the 'traditional' paradigm of music teaching make the false assumption that only a limited number of people are 'musical' and that, as Long puts it:

> The paramount aim in grammar school music is to discover the talented and to provide the conditions in which they can develop their talents as fully as the school pressures will allow.[20]

The assumptions of music educators holding what I have called the *'avant garde'* paradigm of music teaching tend to be very different, as are their criteria of success. Their main emphasis is on developing pupils' musical creativity, rather than on producing good instrumental musicians (I am speaking here of their aims in class music) and this involves them in making different assumptions concerning the nature of 'musicality'. One of the pioneers of 'creative' music in the classroom, Carl Orff, has said:

> I do not think of an education for specially gifted children. . . . My experience has taught me that completely unmusical children are very rare and that nearly every child is at some point accessible and educable.[21]

In such a paradigm, definitions of what constitutes valid music are far more open-ended:

> A pupil of the school once told me (and this epitomizes George Self's attitude towards what constitutes a potentially musical sound) that if an accidental noise was made in the classroom (the squeaking of a chair or a ruler 'flicked' upon a desk) the child, instead of being admonished for the interruption, was encouraged to incorporate the sound into whatever musical activity was in progress.[22]

This also illustrates the very different criteria of success under such a paradigm (for example, no learning of conventional notation or of facts about music and music history).

It is likely that with such an orientation towards music teaching, very different assumptions will be made by the teacher concerning the relationship between the pupils' musical ability and their 'academic' intelligence as perceived by other teachers and the organizational processes of the school. During observation of another comprehensive school with a predominantly *'avant garde'* paradigm associated with creative music in the classroom, I found that one of the music groups performing an 'experimental' composition by one of the teachers at a school concert consisted entirely of pupils in the lower streams. In addition, the emphasis on 'creativity' led to the possibility of pupils composing music, which is practically unheard of at schools where the traditional paradigm of music teaching is dominant.

Whilst these two paradigms are radically different in terms of both the teachers' assumptions concerning what constitutes 'valid' music and the criteria of success, they shared one aspect in common — namely, a rigid separation of the musical culture of the school and that of the pupils. The principal musical influences behind the pedagogical approach to the *avant garde* style of music teaching lie in the world of contemporary 'serious' music and pupils utilizing, for example, the simplified notation developed by the contemporary composer George Self will be producing music in the classroom which bears many similarities to the works of certain contemporary 'serious' composers. This music is likely, however, to seem to be even more alien to the pupils' conception of music than that music emphasized in the traditional paradigm of music teaching. This is because *avant garde* 'serious' music, unlike traditional 'classical' music and most jazz and 'pop' music, does not use the diatonic scale and such music is rarely heard outside the concert hall.

Yet another radically different conception of 'what counts as music' in an educational institution was suggested to me by my observations in a highly unusual music department in a technical college, where music was taught both in the context of class music (in the college's liberal studies programme) and as an extracurricular activity. What was unusual about the music in the college was that it seemed to be the aim of the Head of Music not to lay down a musical policy based on his own preferences. Instead he would start with the interests of the students whom he then encouraged to follow whatever directions they found most appealing, there being no attempt to 'sell' any particular type of music. The musical activities of the college were as a result a very close reflection of the types of music most often associated with young people today. A very large number of music groups took part in the extracurricular musical activities of the college. During the period of my observation these groups included two rock groups, a large jazz-rock group, a rock and roll group, a modern jazz trio, two folk groups, a solo folk singer (in the style of Bob Dylan — guitar and harmonica), a large dance band, a traditional jazz band and a seventy-five voice choir (then rehearsing Mozart's *Requiem*). There was no attempt to teach musical notation unless the students themselves wanted to learn it in connection with the particular instruments they were learning. The Head of Music stressed in conversation with me that trying to teach notation to students who had not learned it earlier was 'at this stage' most likely to 'just put them off music altogether'. He felt that if a student wanted to master a particular instrument he would want to learn the notation and then would find it quite easy. He explained that 'there's no point in teaching it if they're unmotivated and anyway some instrumentalists don't

27

need it or want it — they can perform exciting creative music without being able to read music'.

Class music lessons placed much emphasis on listening to music to illustrate certain aspects of its 'construction' and most of the music selected to illustrate these points (during the period of my observation at least) was from the field of 'pop'. The very large record collection contained (in addition to extensive 'classical' and jazz sections) numerous 'pop' records covering a very wide field from soul music, through folk-rock to the music of 'progressive heavy rock' bands. The main music room was equipped with a very expensive hi-fi system and, in addition, twelve Garrard SP twenty-five record turntables, each with its own pair of stereo headphones. The Head of Music explained to me that this system not only allowed students to hear their records at whatever volume they desired (and he recognized that much contemporary rock music has to be played loud for full effect) but also allowed them to hear whatever music they liked without disturbing other people. Many of the music groups rehearsed on a Wednesday afternoon in the 'music block' (consisting of two 'special' music rooms and a number of ordinary classrooms). What was most apparent to this particular observer on attending such afternoon sessions was that the conventional barriers both between different types of music (for example, jazz and rock) and between teacher and taught were broken down to a considerable extent. Lecturers from both the music department and other departments were members of different music groups and musicians of different types (for example, jazz and rock musicians who are often very snobbish towards each other) 'jammed' freely with each other. Criteria of success were not measured in terms of playing instruments 'correctly' or being able to sight read well, but in terms of whether the musician, either playing together with other musicians in a group or playing by himself, created music that communicated with other people (and the Head of Music could judge this by the reactions of other students who were watching the groups rehearse). By these criteria a number of the department's most talented musicians, particularly guitarists and drummers, were students who had left the lower streams of their schools having been defined as both 'unmusical' and 'less able'. Like most rock musicians they could not read music and had learned all their music outside the school by playing in apprentice groups with friends and by listening to rock records.

A view of music teaching which, as in this technical college, takes seriously the musical culture of the students, necessarily involves profound changes in the nature of the teaching situation. In addition to the criteria of success changing, the teacher, instead of being an 'expert', is more a guide and an organizer, with the teaching and learning situation becoming a two-way process between teachers and students. In relying on the students for knowledge about particular styles of music with which they are more familiar than the teacher, the latter is constantly having to reappraise the assumptions that he and his colleagues are tempted to make concerning the musical culture of the young.

It should be clear from this account that my own feeling is that schools would benefit from this more 'open' approach to music teaching, where the musical tastes and interests of the pupils are taken seriously. However, I am also aware that many sociologists, in their enthusiasm for looking critically at commonly accepted assumptions concerning the nature of curricula and schooling, too easily skirt over the real problems of how change towards a more desirable situation might be effected. On a theoretical level it seems clear that redefining the relationship between high status 'serious' music and low status 'pop' music is not bedevilled by the same epistemological problems that have confronted sociologists attempting to look critically at more 'academic' subjects. Whilst relativizing human knowledge, especially in the field of the natural sciences, is a controversial exercise, as is shown for example by Pring's critique of Young's application of a sociology of knowledge perspective to the school curriculum, the relativity of aesthetic judgements is much more acceptable.[23] Thus the assumption derived from the later philosophy of Wittgenstein that different 'language games' are associated with different public truth criteria is applicable more obviously, and less controversially, to issues of aesthetic judgements than to those of scientific judgements. It can thus be argued that different types of music necessitate different criteria for aesthetic judgement and the 'objectivity' of such judgements is relative to public truth criteria within that particular type of music. In terms, therefore, of Whitty's discussion of the parameters within which redefinitions of knowledge may be feasible in schools, music would seem to be an area where change could take place as a result of a shift in the 'subject perspective' of music teachers.[24]

How likely is such a shift in the subject perspective of music teachers and, even if there was some shift, are there not further obstacles to changing school music teaching towards a more 'open' approach? Much of the earlier part of this chapter was concerned to illustrate how, as Young puts it, 'contemporary definitions of culture have consequences for the organization of knowledge in the school system',[25] and in particular, in this case, how the ideological nature of the 'serious'/'popular' music dichotomy, which it has been shown is perpetuated by the music establishment and the cultural élite, permeates the dominant attitude to music teaching. Just as Whitty [26] argues that it is difficult for sociologists to counteract the widespread 'culture of positivism', it is also difficult for music teachers to counteract the dominant ideology concerning the relationships between music and culture. That this is by no means impossible, however, is illustrated by the contributors to the book *Pop Music in School,*[27] where a number of heads of school music departments discuss how they became committed to what I have called 'open' approaches to music teaching and the problems and possibilities of effecting such changes.

A number of contributors became interested in varieties of Afro-American music via an early teenage interest in jazz. For another an interest in various types of 'pop' music emerged as a result of a switch in instrument from piano to guitar together with listening to an extremely talented school pupil who composed and played numbers in a folk-rock style. For the Head of Music at Countesthorpe College, a comprehensive school near Leicester, it was not so much a love of Afro-American musical styles that led to the development of 'open' music teaching but rather an educational philosophy, backed by the rest of the school, that it is pupils who should as far as possible initiate things themselves. In all these cases the teachers' initial moves to incorporate varieties of 'pop' music into teaching resulted in such positive responses by the pupils that any qualms the teacher might originally have had about such an approach were soon dispelled.

But even where teachers are committed to such an approach (and one might expect the numbers so committed to increase as more young music teachers, who have been exposed in their adolescence to the rock music subculture, enter the profession) the structure and organization of schools provide constraints. The major problems can be summarized in one phrase – 'limited resources'. The teachers contributing to *Pop Music in School* found that, when given a totally free choice, the most popular instruments that school children choose to play are percussion (drum sets rather than timpani), guitars, bass guitars and keyboards – in addition, of course, to singing. This was also reflected at the technical college where the music department provided a drum set, bass and lead guitars with amplification and speakers and a PA (public address) system for vocalists. At the school level this would necessitate a radical redistribution of financial resources. Far too many schools insist on purchasing, say, timpani because they are a conventional orchestral instrument and then find trouble finding a pupil motivated to play them, whilst half a dozen or more are only too keen to learn the drums.

Another aspect of the 'limited resources' problem is that of staffing. Peripatetic teachers capable of helping pupils with rock music instruments are often not available even when a school music department wants them. Sometimes this reflects a real shortage, but more often it reflects the local authorities' conservative attitudes in the appointments of peripatetic teachers which are often made only in the sphere of orchestral instrumental tuition; whilst this may benefit those children who enjoy playing in youth orchestras or brass bands, it does nothing for those who seek other forms of individual or corporate music making. Some progress has been made in recent years and a number of jazz musicians are now employed teaching peripatetically in a few London schools, although rock musicians employed in this way are very few and far between. But even if, for whatever reason, the head of music cannot get outside help, he can always turn to staff members of other departments in his school. There must be very few schools which do not have a competent folk guitarist on the staff if only we are prepared to seek him out. But this willingness to delegate teaching and organizational commitments to other teachers, some of whom are not even in the music department, does run against a widely held attitude of many heads of music, that they should run (and be seen to run) the show almost single-handed.

A further problem associated with 'limited resources' is providing the time and space for groups to practice. In this respect the volume at which rock groups can play obviously creates problems (though school orchestras and choirs rehearsing are also quite loud!). As much soundproofing as possible of practice rooms is essential; so also is careful timetabling so that flautists are not competing with rock guitarists next door. Finally, headphones can be used, not only to listen to records, but also for guitarists, organists, etc., when practising.

The music teacher committed to an 'open' approach to music teaching may also have to contend with widespread prejudices against the use of 'pop' music in schools. Many teachers hold the view that high culture is in some sense threatened by the pervasiveness of 'pop' culture and that it is the school's duty to fight the latter. This view, which I have criticized at length elsewhere,[28] assumes that young people are a captive and defenceless audience who are totally uncritical in their response to mass media products. Somewhat refreshingly, the evidence from a recent Schools Council survey [29] shows that, on the contrary, many young people are extremely critical in their appreciation of various types of 'pop' music and approach the latter with clear sets of criteria concerning the relative worth both of various styles and of various records within one style.

The point that needs stressing here is that there are critical standards in varieties of 'pop' music by which we can evaluate say a good rock or soul record as against a poor one, but these musical standards are derived predominantly from an Afro-American tradition of music rather than from that of the European 'serious' tradition. In this sense not only are many musical critiques of 'pop' music highly misleading, but so also are some highly sympathetic critical appraisals of the work of 'pop' groups by academically trained musicians. For example, Mellers's analysis of the Beatles,[30] whilst fulfilling the valuable role of communicating to the music establishment that even by the latter's criteria the Beatles were fine musicians, nevertheless provides only a very limited and misleading perspective on the Beatles' work. This is because the musical criteria used are, as Mellers puts it, the accepted musical terminology which 'has been evolved by professional musicians over some centuries'.[31] Such musical criteria are those derived from the European compositional tradition which stresses the importance of form and harmonic relationships in creating musical tension and release. This leads to an overemphasis on the harmonic structure of the Beatles' songs at the expense of a consideration of those characteristics of Afro-American music such as the bending, shaping, distorting and colouring of notes together with highly complex rhythmic inflections. It is such ornamentation in rock music which, unlike the use of ornamentation in 'classical' music, forms the main musical argument and has the same function of building up and releasing tension that harmony has in 'classical' music. Thus in Mellers's book many facets of the Beatles' music, which the rock music lover untutored in academic music finds the most musically satisfying, are completely neglected.[32]

A final point that needs stressing to combat the worries that many teachers (and headmasters!) have concerning a more 'open' approach to school music teaching is that it is not being argued that the use of 'pop' music should replace the use of 'classical' music. To concentrate solely on varieties of 'pop' music to the exclusion of other types of music would be as educationally limiting as the reverse procedure where 'pop' music is entirely rejected. The process of musical education should be concerned with expanding pupils' horizons, and the best way to achieve this is by encouraging all forms of musical expression without as far as possible holding preconceived ideas about which forms of music are intrinsically better or worse than others. One of the striking aspects of the 'open' approach in both the technical college and in the Countesthorpe College school

31

music department already mentioned is that many pupils are led to enlarge on their musical interests (in many cases to areas of 'classical' music) as a result of their present musical tastes being taken seriously and incorporated into teaching.

In surveying the varieties of ways in which what counts as school music can be defined, I have attempted to show that differences in the latter are likely to be associated with different criteria of success, different relations between teacher and taught and different assumptions concerning the musical abilities of pupils. It might be suggested that assumptions concerning the limited number of people who can either play musical instruments well or who are motivated to appreciate good music depend more on the way in which both 'musical instruments' and 'good music' are defined than on the innate musical potential of the people themselves. A similar point is made by John Blacking, the ethnomusicologist:

> If, for example, all members of an African society are able to perform and listen intelligently to their own indigenous music, and if this unwritten music, when analysed in its social and cultural context, can be shown to have a similar range of effects on people and to be based on intellectual and musical processes that are found in the so-called 'art' music of Europe, we must ask why apparently general musical abilities should be restricted to a chosen few in societies supposed to be culturally more advanced. Does cultural development represent a real advance in human sensitivity and technical ability or is it chiefly a diversion for the élite and a weapon of class exploitation? Must the majority be made 'unmusical' so that a few may become more musical? . . . I have met some people who did not understand how an anthropologist, trained in Western 'art' music, could study the traditional music of a small African society and then say, after two years' fieldwork and twelve years' analysis, that he was only beginning to understand the system. And yet my own experience of music in Venda society and the experiences of ethnomusicologists in many other parts of the world, have produced abundant evidence of the complexity of 'folk' music systems and of the role of the social and cultural environment in the development of musical capacities.[33]

That there are problems concerning music in schools is widely recognized — as a recent Schools Council paper has put it, 'To put the situation plainly, many teenage pupils, especially those in the 14 to 16 age group, are indifferent and even hostile towards curriculum music'.[34] Just as Keddie [35] shows that by treating classroom knowledge as problematic critical questions are raised in relation to the assumptions that teachers make concerning notions of educational success and failure, I have tried to illustrate here, by making what counts as music in schools problematic, that questionable assumptions are implicit in the formulation of the music teacher's problem. My aim has been to show not only how the problem is rooted more in the teacher's definition of music than in supposed deficiencies of pupils, but also how in practice this situation might be changed.

Notes

1 Quoted in Standing Conference for Amateur Music, *Music and the Newsom Report* (London, National Council of Social Service, 1966), p. 7.

2 See, for example. G. Self, *New Sounds in Class* (London, Universal Edition, 1967), p. 2.

3 The term 'European serious tradition' is used in H. Pleasants, *Serious Music and all that Jazz* (London, Gollancz, 1969). Many other terms are sometimes used to cover the range of music in the European non-jazz tradition, from the Baroque through the Romantics to twentieth century 'serious' music – for example, this range is sometimes called 'Western art music' or, more loosely, simply 'classical' music.

4 H. Pleasants, op. cit.

5 See particularly G. Schuller, *Early Jazz* (New York, Oxford University Press, 1968), ch. 1.

6 C. Keil, *Urban Blues* (Chicago, University of Chicago Press, 1966), p. 45.

7 H. Pleasants, *The Agony of Modern Music* (New York, Simon & Schuster, 1955), p. 167.

8 See, for example, M. Berger, 'Jazz: Resistance to the Diffusion of a Culture Pattern', *Journal of Negro History*, vol. 32 (1947), and N. Leonard, *Jazz and the White Americans* (Chicago, University of Chicago Press, 1962).

9 See, for example, the excellent critique of L. B. Meyer, 'Some Remarks on Value and Greatness in Music', *Journal of Aesthetics and Art Criticism*, vol. 17 (1959), by C. Keil, 'Motion and Feeling through Music', *Journal of Aesthetics and Art Criticism*, vol. 24 (1966). This particular point, in addition to a number of others in this chapter, is considered at greater length in G. Vulliamy, 'Definitions of Serious Music' in G. Vulliamy and E. Lee (eds), *Pop Music in School* (London, Cambridge University Press, 1976). It is also a central theme of J. Shepherd, P. Virden, G. Vulliamy and T. Wishart, *Whose Music? A Sociology of Musical Languages* (London, Latimer New Dimensions, forthcoming).

10 F. Routh, *Contemporary British Music* (London, English Universities Press, 1972), p. x.

11 See G. Vulliamy 'Music Education: Some Critical Comments', *Journal of Curriculum Studies* (May 1975), and G. Vulliamy, 'Definitions of Serious Music' in G. Vulliamy and E. Lee, op. cit.

12 See G. Murdock and G. Phelps, *Mass Media and the Secondary School* (London, Macmillan, 1973).

13 See, for example, the excellent history of rock and roll by C. Gillett, *The Sound of the City* (London, Sphere, 1971) and the discussion of West Coast Rock by R. Gleason, *The Jefferson Airplane and the San Francisco Sound* (New York, Ballantine Books, 1969).

14 See D. Fields, 'Who Bridges the Gap between the Record Executive and the Rock Musician? I do', in J. Eisen (ed.), *The Age of Rock, Volume Two* (New York, Vintage Books, 1970).

15 J. B. Brocklehurst, *Music in Schools* (London, Routledge & Kegan Paul, 1962). p. 55.

16 M. F. D. Young (ed.), *Knowledge and Control* (London, Collier-Macmillan, 1971), p. 32.

17 See N. Keddie (ed.), *Tinker, Tailor . . . The Myth of Cultural Deprivation* (Harmondsworth, Penguin, 1973).

18 See H. S. Becker *et al., Boys in White: Student Culture in Medical School* (Chicago, University of Chicago Press, 1961), p. 34.

19 A full account of this participant observation study is given in J. Shepherd, P. Virden, G. Vulliamy and T. Wishart, *Whose Music? A Sociology of Musical Languages* (London, Latimer New Dimensions, forthcoming).

20 N. Long, 'Some Problems of Grammar School Music' in W. Grant (ed.), *Music in Education* (London, Butterworths, 1963), p. 148.

21 Quoted in J. Horton, 'Carl Orff', *Music Teacher* (April 1969), p. 25.

22 B. Dennis, 'Classroom Electronics', *Times Educational Supplement* (7 February 1969), p. 412.

23 R. Pring, 'Knowledge Out of Control', *Education for Teaching* (Autumn 1972).

24 That is the category (c) rather than (b) on p. 123 of G. Whitty, 'Sociology and the Problem of Radical Educational Change' in M. Flude and J. Ahier (eds), *Educability, Schools and Ideology* (London, Croom Helm, 1974).

25 M. F. D. Young (ed.), op. cit.

26 G. Whitty, 'Sociology and the Problem of Radical Educational Change' in M. Flude and J. Ahier (eds), op. cit.

27 G. Vulliamy and E. Lee (eds), op. cit. p. 10.

28 G. Vulliamy, 'A Reassessment of the "Mass Culture" Controversy: The Case of Rock Music', *Popular Music and Society*, vol. 4, No. 3 (1975).

29 See G. Murdock and G. Phelps, op. cit.

30 W. Mellers, *Twilight of the Gods: The Beatles in Retrospect* (London, Faber & Faber, 1973).

31 Ibid., p. 15.

32 A fuller discussion of the question of by what critical criteria 'pop' music can be judged, together with a consideration of how the pitfalls of an 'intellectualization of pop' stance can be avoided, will be found in G. Vulliamy, 'Pupil-Centred Music Teaching' in G. Vulliamy and E. Lee (eds), op. cit.

33 J. Blacking, 'Man and Music', *Times Literary Supplement* (19 November 1971), p. 1443.

34 Schools Council, *Music and the Young School Leaver* (London, Schools Council Publications, 1971), p. 8.

35 N. Keddie, 'Classroom Knowledge' in M. F. D. Young (ed.), op. cit.

Chapter 3

Studying society : for social change or social control ?

Geoff Whitty

Social studies courses are frequently criticized as a not-so-subtle means of keeping the masses in their place.* Usually designed for those who have already been labelled as 'failures' in terms of the conventional curriculum, they often concentrate upon the pupils' personal and local environment and have thus been seen as a way of limiting their horizons and presenting the known as the inevitable. In many such courses society is treated as something static and the 'awareness' which they often claim to encourage seems to involve an ability to find one's way around society as it is rather than to look at it critically. A glance down the contents pages of the many text and topic books produced for 'Newsom' and 'ROSLA' courses reveals the patronizing assumption that pupils on such courses will fit neatly into preordained slots in society and follow particular styles of life. Treatment of the work context and industrial relations abounds with references to the importance of the 'small cog' in the large wheel but rarely raises questions about why some cogs are bigger than others. The sexist assumptions are even more blatant, with one recent book for girls unashamedly including a chapter 'Making the Most of Yourself: Getting Married'. Time after time the *status quo* is presented as normal, unchanging and unchangeable, and there is no doubt that John White's charge that these courses amount to 'instruction in obedience' has considerable validity.[1] Social studies teaching often is a thinly disguised exercise in social control.

On the other hand, a view of social studies which seems to persist amongst both its staunchest advocates and its fiercest critics is that the subject has some sort of radicalizing potential. Many of the students who train to teach social studies claim that they are doing so because social studies is somehow 'different' from other school subjects, less divorced from the world outside school, more likely to encourage a critical attitude towards the *status quo* and hence more likely to contribute towards social change. Whilst there are certainly also those who advocate the teaching of social science 'for its own sake', and even those who positively celebrate its 'irrelevance',[2] supporters of a wide range of approaches to social studies teaching have, to some degree, seen their work as making an important contribution to change in school and society.[3] What is disturbing for those of us attracted by such a view is the way in which even these

* Some of the material in this chapter has already appeared in *Developments in Social Studies Teaching* by Denis Gleeson and Geoff Whitty (London, Open Books Publishing Ltd, 1976). An edited version of the paper first appeared in the *Social Science Teacher* (March 1976).

approaches have somehow seemed in practice to lose their radical promise and to make their own contribution to the maintenance of the *status quo*.

The fate of the social studies movement of the 1940s and 1950s has by now been chronicled many times.[4] This rather amorphous movement was heralded with extravagant claims which have, in fact, left precious little mark upon the English educational scene. Whilst it was certainly not a really radical movement, and one of its major obsessions was to develop education to fit the changing demands of British capitalism and democracy after the war, it did propose significant changes in our system of schooling. It opposed the prevailing élitism of the English educational system and proposed alternatives which would open the way for a more 'healthy' society. The argument was that social studies should form a backcloth to more specialist studies and allow every child to 'feel himself to be closely associated with the past and present struggles and achievements of mankind, and to have a personal contribution to make towards future progress'. [5] James Hemming explicitly argued that pupils following courses 'broadened by social studies carried on with plenty of project work' were 'adventurous in outlook, approachable and articulate, eager to give their minds to new problems'. Those who followed a curriculum composed entirely of formal subject courses had, on the other hand, 'a marked tendency to be parochial in outlook, reserved, conditioned *against* change'. Hemming's ideas had a lot in common with the American 'progressive movement', and there was a further parallel in the concern of two other influential writers of this time, Dray and Jordan, to ensure 'orderly change' in a society facing the dual threats of totalitarianism or anarchy.[6] It may well be argued that had the social studies movement succeeded in transforming the educational system to produce the creative, flexible and tolerant citizens envisaged by Hemming, they would have bolstered British capitalism more successfully than has in fact happened. It remains the case, however, that this movement fell foul of the traditionalism of the British school system even before its impact on the outside world could begin to be assessed. It failed to make headway in a world where its claimed relevance to grammar schools was treated as nothing but a joke and where the secondary modern schools in which it did make some progress increasingly came under pressure to compete with the grammar schools for examination successes in discrete, well-established academic subjects.

Thus it was that the 'liberal' (let alone any possible 'radical') promise of this early social studies movement was largely still born. Only the more explicitly conservative features of the tradition remained as a target for its successor, the 'New' Social Studies movement of the 1960s. The divisiveness by which such courses were restricted to the bottom streams of secondary modern schools ultimately served only to maintain the élitism of British schools and society. The concept of citizenship encouraged in most of the courses which survived was far from the active one which Hemming envisaged, but rather a passive one in which activity and involvement did not seem to go beyond the ability to fill in an income tax form, remember the name of the local mayor or decorate some old lady's kitchen without pausing to consider why she was permitted to exist in such squalor anyway. Small wonder that their critics dismissed such courses in 'life adjustment' as 'social slops' and sought for alternatives which encouraged pupils to look critically at society rather than passively accepting their lot in a society seemingly beyond their control. The earlier movement, although it had consciously challenged the prevailing social relations of the school, had ultimately made no significant impact even there – let alone in society at large.

The New Social Studies movement of the 1960s, with which the names of Charmian Cannon and Denis Lawton are closely associated, tried to avoid the pitfalls which had led to the demise of its predecessor.[7] Thus even those who were intensely critical of society at large adopted a strategy which accepted schools as they were. They accepted that high status subjects were derived from academic disciplines and merely argued for an additional subject to be placed alongside the other specialisms in the school curriculum – a social studies firmly grounded in the social sciences. There was still a demand for social relevance and indeed for a questioning attitude towards society but, where earlier approaches had failed to achieve such goals through ignoring traditional conceptions of curriculum, the New Social Studies was in danger of assuming that the traditional curriculum, and the view of knowledge implied by it, would by its very nature achieve them. Barry Dufour, for instance, argued that 'if we are trying to encourage critical and intelligent thought amongst pupils about human relationships, it seems self-evident that this can only come from a true knowledge of the social structure and the social processes.[8] The assumption seemed to be that the social science disciplines yielded 'true' knowledge which, if taught to pupils, would necessarily encourage such a critical stance towards the social world.

While this view of the radical potential of the New Social Studies was by no means shared by all its advocates, it was and still is an important strand of thinking amongst those who argue for a social-science-based social studies in schools. In its early forms, however, it often failed to look critically at the concept of knowledge upon which it was based, which was intensely conservative and implied a conservative view of the relationship between social scientists, teachers and pupils. Even though, for many of its supporters, the new subject was not academic knowledge 'for its own sake', but social science with a social purpose, many of us as teachers failed to look sufficiently critically at the social relations of our own practice. The New Social Studies movement and the parallel creation of sociology courses at A and O level took place at a time when curriculum theorists had a seemingly unbounded faith in the value of the knowledge and methods of inquiry associated with the academic disciplines – a case argued in its most extreme form by Philip Phenix.[9] At the same time social scientists were more prone than they are today to claim that their work produced 'facts' and yielded the 'truth' about social reality in an 'objective' and 'value free' way. It is therefore hardly surprising that the advocates of social science teaching in schools used such terms liberally in their writings but made little attempt to specify in what sense such expressions were being used. There was an overwhelming confidence amongst them that the knowledge yielded by the social sciences exhibited such characteristics and thus could not fail to be of value to everyone.

It was against this background that many people felt that the teaching of social science in schools would give pupils more understanding of the world in which they lived and hence a firm foundation of knowledge about social structure and social processes, upon the basis of which they could, if necessary, act to change it. Social science could be used to remedy 'half truths' and make pupils 'critically aware' of the extent to which their own commonsense ideas were distorted by bias and prejudice. In other words, teaching social science could help free pupils from the sorts of parochial concerns and assumptions which earlier social studies courses (with their narrow conceptions of 'relevance') merely served to reinforce. Unfortunately, though, this has often led in practice to a situation in which what is taught is decided in terms of its centrality to the discipline as conceived in academic circles, with all other conceptions of 'relevance' being lost in the reaction against the supposed 'parochialism' of earlier approaches. It has often also meant that pupils, far from gaining control over their own environment, as the rhetoric of education for 'autonomy' seemed to imply, find themselves in a situation where they depend upon social scientists and teachers for their understanding of it.

The view of knowledge embraced by the 'New Social Studies' effectively maintains a situation in which knowledge about the world is seen as something produced by scientists, and then transmitted to school pupils via teachers. Social science teaching – whether purely didactic in approach or employing some sort of 'discovery' method – thus becomes, almost by definition, a process of trans-mission. The professional social scientist is placed on a pedestal and, even at advanced level, the study of sociology largely involves the consumption of knowledge produced by these professionals. Even sociological 'methods' are generally something to be learnt *about* rather than experienced and, when pro-ject work was introduced into one A level sociology syllabus, it was accom-panied by this warning:

> Candidates can hardly be expected to make a distinctive contribution to knowledge. The rationale for including project work is to facilitate the learning process by giving greater insight and realism .... The emphasis should be on giving insight and realism – *not* on advancing knowledge and discovering unknown data. This should be left to qualified sociologists who will publish their findings. ...
>
> (AEB Notes for the Guidance of Teachers, April 1972)

Such findings will presumably be transmitted to the next generation of A level students, whilst the only recognition of the work of the current generation of students is encapsulated in a single grade upon an A level certificate.

Lower down the school, many social studies schemes have seemed to encourage more active participation of pupils in the production of knowledge. Here discovery and inquiry methods are a common feature of social studies teaching. Nevertheless, in practice, an emphasis on 'a freedom guided and dis-ciplined by the teacher's clearer perspective of the subject and of the problems' has often made such methods merely motivational devices whereby the pupil may be persuaded to accept the sense someone else has made of the world rather than actively struggling to develop his own. Given the inherent conservatism of much social theory, it is perhaps fortunate that many of our pupils are more sceptical and resilient than Berger and Pullberg feared when they suggested that a few generations of teaching about 'roles' would lead to a self-fulfilling prophecy in which people came to accept passively that they should occupy the social roles they had learnt about in school.[10] There is, however, some evidence that at least a provisional acceptance of the validity of the knowledge generated by the disciplines is a contributory factor to educational achievement and 'success' in terms of our prevailing social hierarchy. Certainly social science teachers sometimes express concern about their pupils being 'too critical for their own good'.

Many of the highly structured social studies courses which have been spawned by the New Social Studies movement lead, however, not to a critical approach but to either uncritical acceptance or uncritical rejection of the gospel according to Sociology. Whilst the former may, in many cases, ensure examination success, neither can be seen as the sort of liberating experience which some of the advocates of social science teaching in schools envisaged. By trying to avoid the so-called 'anarchy' of alternative methods, the worksheets produced by social studies teachers often serve to alienate pupils from their work context rather than giving them an increasing sense of control over their world. 'It's your (i.e. teacher's) work, not our work' was the comment I heard from one group of pupils following such a course. Ivor Goodson also reports some revealing discussions with pupils at Countesthorpe College about their work in courses designed to embrace 'the student's understanding of himself, of his relationships with those he works, plays and lives with, both [sic] past, present and future'.[11] Goodson reports asking a pupil who has shown his dislike of carrying out prescribed 'tasks from a worksheet, 'Do you like showing your work to people?' Chris responds:

If it's different from everybody else's, but if it's the same it's pointless. I mean I wouldn't have shown you these [i.e. poems he has written instead of answering the worksheets] if it were just full of answers like everybody else's. It's different.

Goodson suggests that worksheets denied Chris 'the possibility of "making the work his own". . . . Worksheets designed to stimulate individual autonomy were seen by most pupils as a complete denial of that right'. Whilst superficially the classroom differed substantially from the traditional one, 'the central assumptions of the Teachers' Curriculum remained substantially unchallenged'. The social and intellectual hierarchy between knowledge producers, transmitters and consumers remained intact.

Whatever the situation at Countesthorpe College, it is probably the case that in most schools pupils who rejected the teachers' courses of studies would be less prepared to articulate their reasons for doing so. It is probably also the case that they would be categorized as deviants and indeed as 'failures'. Whilst going along with work they do not feel engaged with will do little to enhance pupils' feelings of power and control over their own situation, outright rejection of it is unlikely to serve that purpose either — since it is likely to precipitate a situation in which their autonomy is constrained by forms of social control even less subtle than those entailed in accepting other people's ways of looking at the world. In Nell Keddie's study of teaching about the family and socialization in a multidisciplinary humanities programme, those who rejected sociologists' accounts of the world were seen as 'problems', whilst those who were prepared to accept sociologists' accounts on trust tended to be those who became successful in the school's terms.[12] On the one hand the course seemed in no sense to have enabled pupils to be critical of their own everyday assumptions, and on the other it seems to have encouraged 'sociology adjustment' or uncritical acceptance of the world as seen by sociologists – the New Social Studies equivalent to the 'life adjustment' of earlier approaches. Neither response seems to have entailed a marked increase in the pupils' belief in their power to transcend the *status quo* in school or society.

There is a sense, then, in which the New Social Studies can be seen as a means of social control as effective as that of earlier courses in social studies. The failure of the movement to challenge the existing social relations of school knowlege has meant that, as much as other subjects, social studies has become something which is done to pupils rather than something which they do. It has come to be perceived as just more 'normal school', much the same as other subjects and not noticeably more relevant to the world outside the classroom. Social studies has very quickly become part of a prevailing culture of schooling in which pupils feel alienated from their activities and their products. The views of these pupils half way through an A level sociology course, which has been preceded by a highly structured two-year course in social science, are not unrepresentative of those I have talked to. Their views suggest that the New Social Studies movement has not, in practice, fulfilled the hopes of its more radical advocates. Asked what they thought sociology was, these pupils responded as follows:

Carol: Back to our first essay (laughter).
David: An A level subject . . .
Geoff: Yes, that's the cynical answer, David. But have you any other . . .
David: It's the truth to a large extent. It *is* just another A level subject.
Jane: Something I thought I was going to be interested in but I find a bit boring . . .
Geoff: What do you find boring about it?
Jane: A lot of concepts . . .
Carol: You don't seem to get anywhere . . .
Jane: (untranscribable) ideas and you can't make any conclusions of your own, they've all been made for you.
Carol: There's all the things you've got to learn to learn other things.
Geoff: When you say it's an A level subject, you presumably have some means of distinguishing it from economics or any other A level subject?
David: Well, I mean, you've got to do as he says – you've got to do reading, you've got to go to lessons and you've got to take notes and, um . . . it seems you're inevitably bored . . .

Jane: . . . I mean the sheer fact of having to do the same lesson at the same time the same day every week bores me, because I know exactly what I'm going to do. . . . Once you've left the classroom you don't bother about it until the next lesson.

These comments, and others like them, suggest that Graham Vulliamy's view that a lot of social science teaching in schools conforms to Freire's 'banking' concept of education — and thus has little in common with education as 'the practice of freedom' — has some validity.[13]

Vulliamy is one of a growing number of critics who, in recent years, have criticized prevailing approaches to social studies teaching and begun to formulate an alternative and apparently more 'radical' concept of social studies teaching. Such views have emerged partly from the recent radical critiques of schooling and partly from critiques of positivism in the social sciences. It has thus been suggested that the approach to social studies teaching described here as typical of much of the practice of the New Social Studies has something in common with 'commodity' consumption and — in contrast to the hopes of some of its advocates — has become a process of domestication rather than liberation. Indeed as much has been suggested earlier in this paper. At the same time, the crudely positivistic conception of knowledge typical of so much school social studies teaching has been severely called into question by the so-called 'new directions' in sociological theory. Certainly the idea that knowledge generated by the academic disciplines is intrinsically superior to other forms of knowledge is argued with less conviction now than it was ten years ago and certainly the status of sociological method and the knowledge it generates is considerably more in question than is likely to be apparent to most pupils exposed to social science curricula in schools. This has led to the view that what has been wrong with social studies teaching has been its epistemological assumptions which in turn have necessitated a transmission mode of teaching and hierarchical relationships between teachers and pupils. For Vulliamy, amongst others, this has pointed to the conclusion that if we get our epistemology right we can transform social studies teaching so that it becomes truly 'the practice of freedom'.

Vulliamy argues that critiques of positivist social science relieve teachers of the necessity of teaching their pupils correct 'facts' about the social world or even, presumably, correct methods of studying it, if by that is meant methods which will produce the 'objective' account of that world. Any sociological account, he argues, 'must remain simply one particular interpretation of social reality'. This frees teachers to cooperate with their students in 'doing' sociology in the sense of 'thinking critically about their everyday assumptions (and about the assumptions their teachers make)'. Through this process Vulliamy predicts that students will become aware that alternative assumptions and alternative social structures are a possibility and that they can actually shape their world as opposed to being shaped by it. I want, however, to suggest that, for a number of reasons, the claim that such an approach will finally fulfil the elusive radical promise of social studies teaching should itself be looked at 'critically'.

For many teachers critiques of positivist sociology do not of course have these implications anyway. For some they imply that sociology should be cele-brated as one 'language game' amongst many which, 'like philosophy, would leave the world as it is' — and some embryonic attempts have been made to develop such courses based on an ethnomethodological sociology.[14] For others 'new directions' in sociology have been treated as incremental additions to existing content in social science courses — either generating new 'facts' about everyday life or new perspectives to be learnt *about* along with all the others. None of these approaches radically challenges the *status quo* in the way Vulliamy proposes, and none of them is likely to lead teachers into conflict situations in either school or society. More significantly, however, Vulliamy's own interpretation of these critiques may equally lose its radical potential within the contexts of schools as they are. The admittedly few attempts I have seen to operate with such a radical conception of social studies suggest that liberating the minds of pupils from the world-taken-for-granted and restoring to them a sense of subjective power to restructure reality is less easy than Vulliamy implies.

Whilst there certainly have been occasions where I have seen social studies generate a conscious excitement that the world might be different, there have been more instances where attempts by teachers and student teachers to operate in radically different ways have been met by 'What's he on about?' or 'So what?' The former response indicates the difficulty of challenging the tacit assumption that, whatever the theoretical niceties, schooling essentially involves the trans-mission of knowledge from teacher to pupil. The difficulties of challenging pre-vailing expectations of schooling and developing the understanding that the relationship between teacher, pupil, knowledge and classroom activity could be different are considerable — as this attempt by a student teacher to 'generate reflexive talk about classroom activity' suggests.

Ian: No? Yes? (murmurs) Sorry? I mean I'm sure you must have similar questions about what's the value of studying history, geography, maths, you know , . . . because I can't remember a thing from when I was at secondary school. I can't remember a thing of it . . . (Rising chatter) I mean this is the thing, you talk between yourselves, you never talk . . . like you don't talk openly. I mean you love secretly, if you know what I mean, you have your love letters under the desk and you sort of . . .

Pupil: They're for our friends.

Ian: Oh, I see, you don't want them to be public?

Pupil: No.

Ian: All right then, there's nothing you want to say about anything? Nothing . . . well that's a bit of a drag . . .

Pupil: Yes can we do something on drugs?
(Suggestion rejected by other pupils because 'it's what she's doing for her project').

Ian: O.K. You sit and have a conversation or something . . . as you like . . . because you've obviously dried up . . . all right?

Pupil: What?

Ian: I said 'You've obviously dried up'.
Pupil: What were you meant to be taking up for this term then? What . . .
Ian: What have I what?
Pupil: What have you *really* got to do with us this term?

If the difficulty of transcending the prevailing social relations in educational contexts is difficult enough, the power of classroom activity in returning to pupils a feeling of control over other social contexts must be viewed with some scepticism – and this is perhaps the foundation of the 'so what?' response. To recognize that the world *could* be different is not to feel confident of the power to *make* it different. Earlier in the conversation these pupils had made savage criticisms of school, suggesting alternatives they would have preferred, but, in practice, felt that there was an inevitability about what Ian *really* had to do with them.

The 'So what?' response recognizes that, despite the apparently liberating epistemology with which teachers of this 'alternative' social studies may be operating, the real world of existing social relationships is not so easily trans-formed. In a situation where the constraints of timetables, examination syllabuses and unsympathetic colleagues are placing severe limitations on the teacher's power to transcend what he feels ought to be different, it is difficult to feel that sort of 'insulated' radicalism which Vulliamy proposes will be sufficiently power-ful to achieve the ends which he foresees. Whilst the approach may meet some of the criticisms of conventional sociology teaching, as expressed by this A level student, it still fails to meet the central point:

> In . . . perhaps . . . in the real world, it's . . . you know, I mean, things happen immediately, possibly explosive – and you get it in such a canned form . . . [You learn about] proletarian, capitalist, and this sort of thing. Yet, you know, the place you learn about this is on the streets – not in the classroom . . . or from personal experience, or perhaps from meetings with really dedicated people . . .

To appreciate the real possibilities for transcending the *status quo,* one has to experience change as a collective endeavour, not *merely* as a theoretical possibility.

If, as seems likely, consciousness of the real possibilities for change will only develop in the context of a practical struggle to transform reality,[15] then this sort of 'alternative' social studies course may be less of a threat to the *status quo* than some of the more hysterical sociology bashers might suppose. If the aim of such courses is to 'raise' consciousness, we must look carefully at the way such activities are perceived by our pupils – even if this threatens our own sense of purpose as isolated subverters of the *status quo.* Schools are not unambiguously institutions of social control, but changing the social experience of schools for their pupils is an activity which will involve those of us committed to it in an active struggle with more than merely 'epistemological stances'. Some ideas which are suggestive of the sort of approach which might more genuinely contri-bute to the transformation of consciousness were generated by the Social Education Project at Nottingham.[16] This did seem to offer pupils the possi-bility of experiencing the power to transcend the *status quo* – to go beyond their existing understandings of social reality and experience that transcendence as something achieved by them in collaborative work with others. Unlike some of the pupils whose experiences were discussed earlier in this paper, they did not feel forced to accept (or indeed reject out of hand) someone else's way of looking at the world.

It is apparent from Williams and Rennie's various accounts of the Project that a particular piece of work on local redevelopment, which they carried out with a class of fourth-year pupils, came near to achieving their ideal of social education. The pupils involved had already spent two years on social education activities, creating 'profiles' of groups which they belonged to and developing skills of observation and communication. This work had been carried out both inside and outside the school. The work on problems of redevelopment began with a concern expressed by some of the boys about some plans they had studied. Williams and Rennie describe what happened next in the following terms:

> Today their class teacher and we have decided to introduce to them the problems which the redevelopment will create for their community. We do not give them a lecture; we do not outline the problems that we, or the sociologists, or the welfare services, think will be created. Simply we present to them two sets of figures:
> Present population of the area: 14,500
> Population after redevelopment: 5,750

This provoked a mass of question about the effects of the redevelopment and about the way in which decisions on rehousing would be made. Teachers and pupils together then devised a strategy for answering their questions and, in small groups, set about investigating particular aspects of the problem. Much of their work, which went on for two school terms (with two periods a week on the timetable), took them out of school into a variety of contexts to find out the costs of the redevelopment scheme and the reactions of various groups of people to it. They interviewed local inhabitants, the planning department and members of the city council, visited an exhibition and a public meeting on the plan, and studied various alternative proposals. For the project team, however, what was most important was that out of it, apart from the amassing of information, and the experience of this type of action survey work, came various proposals for action that they, as a group, would like to see initiated. Their suggestions included a mobile exhibition to show people what was happening, an alternative redevelopment plan with a higher density of population and a poster campaign based on a boy's cartoon of a bulldozer approaching a family at the breakfast table under the caption 'WAKE UP NOW!'

What was particularly interesting about this Project was the way in which, after taking control of their own learning situation, pupils had the desire and the opportunity to see if they could achieve change beyond the school. Of course, some of their early confidence was shattered, but it was shattered in a social context which could well contribute to a fuller understanding of the nature of the collective struggle for change. However, if this Project did make a serious effort to break down in practice the prevailing relations of 'dependency' which characterize so many schools, it was by no means an unqualified success.[17] It remained an isolated experiment even within many of the schools which showed an interest — it remained a way of keeping non-examination pupils amused. As such, it could be classed as a 'non-serious' or indeed 'non-educational' activity and, if it merely meant that previously disaffected youth smashed up less telephone boxes, it may well just be a further example of social education as social control. It must also be recognized that this Project has probably made less impact on the minds of teachers than many of the others and, since it neither produced packs of 'goodies' for pupils to consume nor told teachers how to do what they were already doing 'better', it will quite possibly remain marginal. Nevertheless it does seem to me that it points to some quite exciting possibilities for transforming the nature of teacher-pupil relationships and providing opportunities for experiencing the struggle for change rather than merely theorizing about it. However, unless teachers are at the same time prepared to engage in a parallel struggle with others to transform the social context within which such experiments take place, then such activities *will* continue to be characterized as less than 'serious' education and their radical promise will be lost as their less controversial aspects are assimilated into the life of schools as they are.

I am not arguing that those of us who retain the conviction that social studies has some radical potential should abandon the struggle to change our classrooms, but that we must also be involved in a broader struggle if we are to be anything but a safety valve to preserve the *status quo*. If we are realistic, we must be aware of the argument that places such as China, Tanzania and Cuba — where schools do seem to be making an important contribution to the changing of consciousness — are also places where the contexts of schooling have been radically transformed and the barriers between school and the outside world removed. At the same time, however, we should recognize that some of the constraints on our own activities are being removed by apparently contradictory influences — with the fragmentation of school experience typical of the traditional timetable being eroded by bureaucratic rationalization and the insulation of school from the outside world collapsing before the authorities' demands for cost effectiveness. These are all opportunities to transform the social contexts of social studies teaching which we must exploit if our work is ever to realize in practice that radicalizing potential which in theory it has so often seemed to offer.

Notes

1 J. White, 'Instruction in Obedience', *New Society* (2 May 1968).

2 For a recent example, see B. Anderson, 'Sociology and Social Studies: a Cautionary Note', *Social Science Teacher* vol. 4, No. 2 (1974-5).

3 Examples of various approaches to social studies teaching are explored at greater length in D. Gleeson and G. Whitty, *Developments in Social Studies Teaching* (London, Open Books, 1976).

4 The best account remains C. Cannon, 'Social Studies in Secondary Schools', *Educational Review*, vol. 7, No. 1 (1964).

5 J. Hemming, *The Teaching of Social Studies in Secondary Schools* (London, Longmans, 1949).

6 J. Dray and D. Jordan, *A Handbook of Social Studies* (London, Methuen, 1950).

7 Details of the development of the New Social Studies can be found in D. Lawton and B. Dufour, *The New Social Studies* (London, Heinemann, 1973). This handbook also shows that by the early 1970s the advocates of the New Social Studies were beginning to adopt a somewhat less narrow and rigid conception of the subject than that which characterized their earlier statements. Its central features were, however, retained intact.

8 B. Dufour, 'Society in the School', *Education and Social Science* vol. 1, No. 2 (1969).

9 P. H. Phenix, 'The Use of Disciplines as Curriculum Content' *Educational Forum*, 26 (1962).

10 P. Berger and S. Pullberg, 'Reification and the Sociological Critique of Consciousness', *New Left Review* (1966).

11 I. Goodson, 'The Teachers' Curriculum and the New Reformation', *Journal of Curriculum Studies* (November 1975).

12 N. Keddie, 'Classroom Knowledge' in M. Young (ed.) *Knowledge and Control* (London, Collier-Macmillan, 1971).

13 G. Vulliamy, 'Teaching Sociology: a New Approach', *New Society* (8 March 1973).

14 See I. Shelton, 'The Sociology of Everyday Life', *Social Science Teacher*, vol. 4, No. 1. (1974).

15 For a useful discussion of the relationship between practice and consciousness, see Mao Tse-tung, 'On Practice', in *Selected Works* (Peking, Foreign Languages Press, 1960-5).

16 W. Williams and J. Rennie, 'Social Education' in D. Rubinstein and C. Stoneman, *Education for Democracy* (Harmondsworth, Penguin, 1972).

17 See Schools Council Working Paper No. 51, *Social Education: An Experiment in Four Secondary Schools* (London, Evans/Methuen, 1974).

Chapter 4

The schooling of science

Michael Young

Despite a decade of unprecedented investment in curriculum innovation, school science displays many of the manifestations of a continuing 'crisis'.* Closure of degree and teachers' certificate courses through lack of applicants, and further education colleges with science departments which only remain viable by accepting an overseas student intake of up to 90 per cent are but two examples. At the school level we have fears expressed that one outcome of comprehensive reorganization could be that 'the teaching of physics in schools may be a dying activity . . . the subject could even disappear'[1] and that 'the shortage of good physics teachers [would] not be quite so alarming . . . [were we to] concentrate our scarce manpower on the older secondary school pupils who could better appreciate the intellectual content'.[2] The price that we are being asked to pay for preserving school physics then is a withdrawal from most junior and middle school science, and therefore, in effect, from any science at all for many pupils.

Another aspect of this crisis is considered by Matthews, who reviews the various attempts to attract more pupils to science by an emphasis on projects and the social implications of science. These can, he suggests, 'trivialize teaching with the attendant dangers of disturbing the supply of competent scientists'.[3] In other words, attempts to make science more 'relevant' merely confound the problem which is, according to Matthews, almost echoing the words of the Dainton and Swan Reports that 'it is vital that society maintains a supply of highly qualified scientists . . . and that . . . science education in schools represents an important stage in this process'. Thus problems in science education are not just problems of curriculum reform and more 'relevant' courses, nor of philosophical arguments about the nature of science, but problems which have their origins and their resolution in a particular kind of society and its transformation. In other words, the failure of science teaching to enable science, a major human activity, to become more than a minority pursuit, though related to the historical emergence and persistence of current practices in science education, cannot be understood in terms of them alone. This paper is divided into four parts:

1 A sketch of aspects of the way school science was established in the nineteenth century, and how contemporary curriculum innovations have been

* Part of the work reported in this paper was supported by a grant from the Social Science Research Council; the research on 'the social meanings of school science' developed into a collaborative project with John Porter, Barnet Senior High School. He was involved as teacher, researcher and critic, and whatever significance the work reported has for science teachers owes more to him than me; it is part of a continuing project and I am deeply grateful for his considerable contribution.

developed within that framework.

2 An attempt to indicate how prevailing traditions of school science are reflected in and reflect the much wider separation of science and technology in society as a whole.

3 An examination of some of the practices of teachers that sustain prevailing conceptions of school science, of alternatives to them, and possible constraints on the alternatives being realized.

4 Conclusions and implications.

1

Science emerged later as a branch of education and its assimilation into the existing institutions and structures was not achieved without some noticeable exercises of accommodation.[4]

This view of the incorporation of natural science into the school curriculum is taken by David Layton, who offers us a valuable account of this process of 'accommodation' in the late nineteenth century, complementary to his earlier study of the demise of 'the science of common things'.[5] In particular he describes how one conception of 'pure' laboratory science was established which enabled school science to be justified in terms of the prevailing tradition of liberal education and its devotion to 'the discipline of the mind, the attainment of habits of controlled attention and the exercise of reasoning powers and memory'. Thus Chemistry and Physics could comfortably claim a place alongside the Classics and Mathematics. Likewise, the purpose of introducing science into the secondary schools was never in doubt to such leading advocates as H. E. Roscoe, the first President of the Association of Public School Science Masters (the precursor of our Association for Science Education); school science was, for Roscoe, as Layton quotes him, to be 'the means of sifting out from the great mass of the people those golden grains of genius which now are too often lost amongst the sands of mediocrity'.

A consequence of this accommodation was, as Layton puts it, that 'the application of science to everyday life had (by the 1870s) disappeared . . . the learner [of course only those learners who experienced any science teaching at all — M.Y.] was slowly inducted into the ways of the scientist — a particular type of scientist also — the "pure" researcher'. Largely through the method of government recognition and financing of laboratories, the separation of school science into separate 'subjects', physics, chemistry, and biology, became firmly established before the end of the century, as did for quite other reasons the exclusion of geology. Furthermore, the models of 'subject' teaching which dominated (and in many ways still do) experimental work were part of this process. As Layton describes it, school chemistry became the 'easily organized and easily examined exercises in qualitative analysis . . . [in which] packets of powder were sent out [to the schools] and packets of paper were returned when the pupils had completed the routine of taking the solution through the charts'; if anyone asked 'why?', 'training of the faculties of observation and reasoning' would doubtless have been the reply.

Likewise in physics pupils were offered 'a starvation course on the precise measurement of physical quantities . . . [for, as an influential text of the time began] "Physics is essentially the science of measurements" '. Of course, many things have changed, but even in the Nuffield era 'the emphasis has remained on abstract . . . "technically sweet" science, dissociated from its applications and implications'.

Before turning to the attempts to revitalize science teaching which have emerged since the early 1960s, it is important to ask the question 'Why did school science emerge in the way it did?' Is it adequate to see it as an accommodation to existing educational structures, as Layton does? I suggest we need to try and grasp both the innovations Layton describes and the structures they confronted in terms of their wider political and economic significance. Alternative traditions of science education in which scientific knowledge was conceived, among other things 'as an instrument in the pursuit of political independence and social emancipation', had, Layton writes, become 'casualties in a process of natural selection as the educational environment had become progressively more sharply defined'.[6] The problem with this kind of social Darwinist view is that it treats a *social* process, selection, as *natural,* rather than as an outcome of certain activities and interests in particular historical contexts. This is indicated in Layton's reference to the views of science on the one hand in terms of 'the disinterested pursuit of truth', and on the other, particularly by those involved in the Great Exhibition, as 'the producer for the industrial market place (so that science was to be studied for the economic benefits it would yield)'. The question of economic benefits of science points to a concern with the character of the economy at the time and to the importance of considering the demise of the attempts to implement a science curriculum 'as. practice' and the success of the science curriculum 'as fact' [7] in the context of changes in Victorian capitalism.[8]

The political economy of school science remains to be written and in particular the response by the Nuffield Foundation to the ASE proposals in the early 1960s which were followed by the setting up of the Industrial Fund for the Development of science teaching in the private sector. All I want to do here is to suggest that, as in the nineteenth century contexts described by Layton, more recent curriculum innovations in science actually acted as a constraint on certain of the possibilities that science teachers might have developed. I am not suggesting that this was either intentional or always directly experienced by teachers, but that it can be seen as a way of looking at how certain possibilities get closed off, how certain frameworks for action become seen as almost in the order of things. The following are illustrative of some of the ways this process may work:

(*a*) In characteristically linking all the early projects to O and A level, the new materials sustained and affirmed an existing distinction between academic and non-academic science — the former claiming credibility from the professional scientific community, and the latter through notions of 'relevance' and immediate interest for pupils. 'Relevance' and intellectual credibility have come to be seen in opposition, so that courses concerned with glass making, ceramics, photography and the environment are either treated as 'for the non-examinable', or as only warranting at best a CSE grade 3.

(b) The corollary of this is that the one set of materials which at least makes some attempt to set its activities in a non-school, non-lab world — Secondary Science — is viewed as an unsuitable base for O level, even by its originator, 'as it lacks a strong enough chemical component' — echoing the dominance of a view of school science as 'knowledge to be transmitted'.

(c) The failure of academic science (pre- and post-Nuffield) for the majority is explained either in terms of its conceptual difficulties or in terms of the pupils' lack of ability. 'If one teaches science to average classes in a comprehensive school . . . one is unlikely to have met any pupils whose thinking goes beyond the concrete operations stage'.[9] An example Shayer gives is understanding density, though how one might identify such an understanding might tell us more about school physics than a pupil's ability; was it an ability to memorize a definition, or calculate from a ratio of mass to volume, or to know, for example, why one might put a hydrometer in a car battery? What is never considered is the 'non-subject' but scientific and technological knowledge which pupils often have (and teachers sometimes lack), or even more, the actual social relations between teacher and taught, and how they may 'produce' the lack of understanding that is attributed by many researchers as well as teachers to low ability.

(d) 'Innovations' in school science have confirmed it as laboratory knowledge and as distinct from technology as workshop or factory knowledge, despite their practical inseparability. It is only in the academy that so called 'pure' science is practised, and even there the claim of 'pure' science as disinterested has little foundation as university departments compete for a more generous allocation of government or business funds. The pure/applied distinction obscures the way in which the practice of scientists is inextricably linked to the productive labour upon which they depend for their livelihood. We have therefore the absurd situation of Project Technology, largely avoided except in ritual statements by school science educators, being set up as a separate attempt to upgrade craft, metal and woodwork, and thus somehow infiltrate the school knowledge order (we have no grounds for doubting parallel outcomes of the Nuffield 16+ Project, as it becomes incorporated into the no-man's-land of the Certificate of Extended Education). This helps to obscure the possibility that the very separation and hierarchy that the curriculum projects have sustained between science and technology may be responsible for the drop out of so many children from serious scientific work. The experiment described in Chapter 12 by Hoskyns calls into question the opposition between supposed interest or relevance and intellectual credibility — why else were regular truants turning up only for physics, learning the kinetic theory in working diesel engines, electronics in building hi-fi equipment, and optics through photography. As one boy said about building circuits: 'Building helps you understand. If you're just given a piece of paper, you wouldn't know, because you wouldn't know what went into building it'.

(e) Under the assumption of learning theories that emphasize how learning takes place through doing, most of the projects neglect the social character of learning and have failed to examine, except in a very superficial way, the activity of science teachers at all. All too easily *doing* becomes equated with following worksheet instructions *for* doing, and the emphasis on resources implies the teacher as a stimulus without whom nothing will take place. Thus pupils are assumed only to really *learn* when stimulated by a teacher, and the teacher's traditional didactic style has been replaced by a view of him as a kind of puppet master leading his pupils through the routines of the syllabus. Asked whether it helped to talk, a boy from the physics class referred to above replied 'If everybody talks about what they are doing and how they're figuring it out, everybody takes an interest in everybody else' — a view of learning very different from that espoused by most producers of curriculum project materials, and one rooted, albeit in a limited context, in a view of knowledge as men collectively objectifying their experience of the world, and taking responsibility for it.

(*f*)   In the one project (SCISP) that considers 'science and society' questions, these are raised primarily as debates about the uses and abuses of science and the pro- and anti-science lobbies. Science teaching in general has tended to close off the opportunity for pupils to grasp science as a social practice, rather than as a body of knowledge, through the selective nature of the assumptions and choice within syllabuses, and the form that topics take. These are presented as given and necessary (though sometimes revised from above), and quite independent of the teachers and pupils themselves. Hine gives many interesting examples of this process in school physics; he writes:

> 'Doing' heat includes such trivia as dropping hot objects into cool liquids, discussing hot water systems (but not as genuine technological problems), and the clinical thermometer . . . the calculation of the energy required to produce a hot bath . . . [though] the concept of a society dependent on particular energy slaves, for instance, is not included.[10]

This section has sketched aspects of the historical and contemporary character of school science that confronts teachers who consider strategies for change. The traditions of science teaching that have emerged in the last century are expressions of wider contexts and act on those contexts. It is to these features of science as a crucial force of production and determinant of the division of labour that I turn in the next section.

2

Science teaching, as my earlier discussion suggested, began and continues with its main purpose to maintain the supply of future scientists. This has two inter-related, and in effect self-justifying outcomes — the mass scientific and technological ignorance of a people in an increasingly technologically dominated society, who see themselves as dependent on experts in more and more aspects of their life, and a community of scientists who see the knowledge which they are responsible for producing and validating as *necessarily* not available to the community at large. Arguments about the inherent difficulties of science, the inherent limitations of science teaching,[11] or the innate inabilities of the majority can, of course, be refuted 'in theory'. The problem is more serious, because increasingly they are going to have to be disproved 'in practice'. I'd like to take two examples — the first of which draws on material from Clutterbuck's 'Death in a Plastics' Factory'.[12] Everyone is familiar with the PVC of cables, pipes and plastic macs. Evidence has recently appeared that over-exposure to the monomer vinyl chloride from which PVC is made can lead to a rare and fatal liver cancer; large sums have recently been invested in production plants which require too high a degree of exposure, and not surprisingly further large sums would be required to modify the plants to reduce it to a safe level. The health of PVC workers has in this case become a trade union issue — a political struggle between management and workers. However, the unions face certain problems which take us back to the failure of science education for all but the specialist few. Lacking knowledge of the physiological processes involved, of the technology of a plant they had no part in designing, and in particular, the technology of very accurate detectors no one had yet designed, they remained largely dependent on experts.

In this case, if it had not been for a BSSRS group, the workers involved would have had no reason to question that the existing level of risk was unalterable, which raises quite different notions of relevance to those espoused by, for example, the Schools Council.

As high technology industries find decreasing markets for their products, the familiar outcomes are for management to lay off workers who respond with factory sit-ins demanding the 'right to work'. In some cases, of which Lucas Aerospace is an early example, the shop stewards have broadened the basis of their demands to put forward a programme which includes alternative production priorities (solar cells, electric cars, medical equipment, etc.) as well as alternative modes of production.[13]   The significance of this, as with the industrial health example referred to above, is that the majority of the Lucas workers involved will have left school with only the minimum of education in science and technology. So long as production is hierarchically organized and some conceive the technology for others to operate, the problem is masked. Once, as in Lucas and other examples, there is pressure for participation of wide sections of the work force in production decisions, the training of specialized technologists and the unavailability of the basic principles underlying the technology to shop-floor workers become a constraint on the possibility of alternative modes of production, but also potentially a dynamic for change.

Both these examples point to the way traditions of science and technical education are being challenged, not just through the failure to recruit students but in the changing production contexts of which they were originally an expression. I want therefore to turn to a more detailed consideration of the practices by which prevailing traditions of school science are sustained — or, to put it another way, how science teaching expresses those wider features of the division of labour referred to in the examples which I have described.

3

It is inescapable that most of those who become 'successes' in school science are systematically denied the opportunity to grasp science as an integral and inseparable part of social life – as an expression of man's historical attempts to transform the natural world, rather than a mere body of knowledge about nature external to man. The 'failures', equally systematically, leave school to become part of the mass of scientific illiterates, who may in their work learn enough technology to supervise and repair complex machines but will never learn about the social relations of which the designing and manning of machines is a part.[14]

Except in the specific context of their work, and possibly in leisure pursuits such as car maintenance, our increasingly technologically dominated world remains for the majority as much a mystery as the theological mysteries of feudal times. How is this achieved in school science? To ask this question is not to suggest that science teachers are alone responsible or that an awareness of the assumptions underlying school science would lead to any sudden transformation – school science is far too embedded both in the way school knowledge has been institutionalized and in the wider context of the emergence of compulsory schooling. It is rather to point to some of the 'within school' processes that would need to be transformed if a very different model of science education to that established in the late nineteenth century were to develop.

The development of state schooling since the nineteenth century can be seen as an intervention into aspects of the everyday lives of the majority of the people in the interests of social control and economic productivity. This, as accounts such as Layton's and others show, was more visible in the nineteenth century, and was not a feature peculiar to school science.[15] The separation of science as a specialized activity is no less a feature of contemporary schooling. Aspects of this process in contemporary science teaching and the way it reproduces features of the social division of labour outside school will now be considered.

(*a*) School science separates science from pupils' everyday lives, and in particular their non-school knowledge of the natural world. It is learnt primarily as a *laboratory* activity, in a room full of special rules, many of which have no *real* necessity except in terms of the social organization of the school. An almost classic example of this process of alienation is illustrated in how the teacher in this transcript specifically sets science apart from everyday life and all other school work (this is the very first time a first-year class enters a secondary school science lab).

> It may well be the first time you've done science and there are a whole lot of different things about working in a lab than there are in all the other classrooms in the school . . . you have to work with certain kinds of rules which are different . . . later we'll give you a list of them which you can put in your folder . . . there are things that are potentially dangerous . . . we've got gas taps here . . . those of you who've been in a kitchen do not

need to be told this (so abstracted from the real world is the teacher that he can even imagine that *some* kids may never have been in a kitchen!).*

The rules the teacher recounts all present a view of the lab world as a closed one, which finishes at the end of the lesson period. Some kids, of course, don't take over this 'separation' and bring in things from home — something, no doubt, they've learnt to do in primary school.

Apparatus and diagrams often affirm this separation — one only has to think of the relation between the traditional textbook diagram of a domestic hot water system and a child actually trying to understand the particular one in the house he lives in. An instance of this separation, which dramatized the problem for me, was a physics teacher who had worked through a whole term on optics, including telescopes and microscopes, and later found that one of his pupils, who had achieved nothing in school physics, had actually designed and built a telescope at home, taken readings of stars, and photographed an eclipse of the moon.[16]

That this separation is expressed in the interaction between teachers and pupils is illustrated by an analysis of two transcripts drawn from a first-year lesson, in which I was particularly concerned to explore the variety of ways in which school science as a conception of 'knowledge to be transmitted' underpins the teacher's talk and his way of listening to pupils' questions and responses. There are a whole variety of other practices, from what I would call the 'subject habit' of sequence making from lesson to lesson and the reconstruction of 'how it was', to the way science teachers formulate for pupils what they are going to do that might have and need to be considered.

Any teacher (or pupil) response is embedded in a theory (of a lesson, learning, science, etc.), which alone can provide for the particular as opposed to the multitude of senses that might be given to any question, but which is never available to the pupils. Their responses, their way of making sense, cannot therefore be treated by the teacher as reasonable accounts, unless by habit, chance or tradition, pupils are able to guess the teacher's sense.[17] For the teacher, then, appropriate pupil knowledge is only produced if pupils pick up that which teachers do not make available. In other words, if he produces the reply that the teacher's theory, not his question, calls for. Likewise, the procedures of making sense that the pupil engages in in producing responses, whether or not appropriate, are not available to the teacher. This raises some problems for typical notions of 'education as cultural transmission'; though science teachers are widely concerned to improve their teaching, the ways in which pupils generate recognizably effective displays of competence bear little or no relation to the practices teachers recognize as 'efficient'.

I'd like to turn briefly to the transcript extracts, with the question in mind as to what kind of practical 'theories' the pupil and teacher responses might be embedded in. Teacher 'theories' are not treated as a topic by teachers, no more are pupil theories. Both, however, can be understood as being used as a resource through which sustaining talk about school science is not a problem for either

* In this and alternate lessons the formal 'roles' of teacher and researcher were reversed.

teacher or pupil.

A1 (Teacher): It will be what you call the pea shoot . . .

Comment: Teacher's account involves a theory of the classification of different parts of the pea.

A2 (Pupil): What kind of pea is it?

Comment: Teacher's theory not necessarily available; pupil's question involves another theory, concerned with the classification of different types of pea. (This possibility arose not from reading the transcript myself but in working through this bit of transcript with the teacher collaborating with me who explained the pupil's question in terms of pea classification — as, if you like, a pervasive feature of the folk biology of West Indian culture.)

A4 (Teacher): It's a dried pea, probably a dried pea that you buy in a shop.

Comment: Pupil theorizing (in A2) not recognized — so teacher, in terms of his resource (knowledge of the structure of the pea), closes rather than explores the pupil's question, displaying to the pupil 'that there are *no* kinds of dried peas', or that, if there are, they are not relevant to his concerns as 'knowledge transmitter', and therefore not part of school science.

B1 (Teacher): Have you ever seen examples of when (soil) is produced?

Comment: The teacher's question involves 'ecological' relevance criteria to enable him to treat earth inside the worm in the context of its normal habitat.

B4 (Boy): No, I just seen holes in the grass.

Comment: The pupil also has an 'ecological' theory, but with different relevance, he describes the holes or burrows worms make.

B5 (Teacher): Have you ever seen anything else that might tell you there was a worm on the grass?

Comment: The teacher listens, but in terms of his theory does not hear pupils saying 'holes' as appropriate.

B10 (Boy): Leaves.

Comment: The pupil displays further knowledge of 'worm life', which teacher through his relevance criteria does not appear to notice.

One problem raised for me by my interpretation of the transcript relates to the conventional wisdom that calls for relevance for the so-called less able child, where relevance is associated with assumed links to pupils' everyday life. The teacher, in this case, can be understood as invoking a theory of relevance which links worm casts to football fields. A quite different notion of relevance might involve the project of discovering pupil relevancies, their theories of the natural world, which are, even from these short transcripts, potentially available. This is

55

quite different from accepting pupils' 'theories' uncritically or assuming that all pupils are potential Einsteins, but it would involve transforming typical conceptions of a lesson and of teaching, and accepting an inbuilt unpredictability of outcomes through the following of pupil initiatives rather than attempting to guide pupils to fit in to the teacher's prior plan of the lesson. This would inevitably confront the teacher with problems not resolvable within the classroom or lab alone, and would raise very concretely questions about timetables and school organization.

I have attempted a partial analysis of how pupil and teacher talk in school science might be made sense of by invoking the 'theories' that each uses as resources in the interaction but which are not themselves made explicit. This is then one possibility of displaying these resources, assumed by participants, which sustain and thus become recognizable as school science. I have suggested that in terms of his conception of school knowledge, the teacher does not recognize the pupil as himself a theorist. This can be seen as an aspect of treating science as an objectively available body of knowledge, and how its selective recognition is unproblematic except in terms of 'getting it over'.

What constitutes school science would, I suggest, be very different if teachers were to see themselves *and* pupils as scientific theorists. It would be, if you like, an attempt to de-alienate scientific knowledge, to recognize that knowledge is inextricably linked to its production by people, in a political context, not only in the school, which is dominated by a 'culture of positivism' which locates knowing in methods, not persons.

(b) School science, reflecting the individualism that is often seen as an inescapable part of scientific discovery, separates pupils from each other and any sense of link with others who have engaged in similar problems. Newton's laws of motion, for example, are learnt as disembodied 'facts', separated from their relation to Newton as a man who like ourselves lived at a specific historical time with all its conflicts and troubles. This is not just a plea for adding the 'history of science' to school science but rather a questioning of the whole way in which a concept of scientific knowledge, as something for the individual to adapt to, is confirmed by science teaching practice.

(c) From its establishment, school science has sustained a separation of knowledge from its use. When the applications of some scientific understanding are referred to they are treated as a kind of appendix or set of properties; the density and reactivity of chlorine, for example, is followed by its use in bleaching and hygiene — as if uses did not embody in this case a whole history of public health regulations and state intervention into the contaminated water systems that were the by-products of Victorian capitalism. Even if a lesson starts with a concrete example of pupils' life experience — the way camping gas cookers work, for instance — the *real* problem is learning Boyle's Law and how volumes of gases change under pressure, not the practical problem of storing butane. It is difficult for pupils not to learn that it is deriving and doing calculations from Boyle's Law that is real science, whatever the teacher's intentions. In this way potentially exciting scientific discoveries, which provide ways of solving real problems and transforming aspects of our environment, become self-justifying and, for many, boring and difficult and pointless. Too often science educators see this difficulty as either intrinsic to the subject, a failure of his or her teaching, or a lack of ability of the pupils concerned. The abstract and mathematical character of physics is treated as an unchallengeable representation of scientific truth, widely expressed in the way the subject is examined and the status given to 'theoretical' physics. The possibility is hardly considered that this particular notion of 'truth', and its inhibiting social consequences for the divorce of science from technology, does not rest on any foundations of our understanding of nature, but on the emergence of a society in which mental and manual labour are increasingly separate. This is not to dismiss mathematics but to suggest that, in the schooling of science, the abstract certainties of mathematical models become more important than asking why we, whether scientists or others, might want such certainties and for what purpose.

It is perhaps not surprising that a science that is proud of its 'irrelevance' to human problems, and dismisses the technology which it informs and on which it depends, should have indirectly encouraged, among other things, an ultimately self-defeating anti-science, anti-technology counter-culture.

(*d*) School science separates pupils and teachers from themselves as people, by presenting it as the 'school subjects' – physics, chemistry and biology – forgetful not only of their history but of the physics, chemistry and biology of ourselves and how we relate to our environment. This is perhaps best illustrated in biological and medical education. School biology is increasingly characterized by a reductionism to molecular levels of explanation. This reductionism, a relatively recent phenomenon of school biology is a reflection of much current research practice. What is involved is not a viewing of man's consciousness as interrelated with his biology, but an essentially passive view of man increasingly subject to control by genetic and other experts.[18] Not so dissimilar is Laing's account of his medical education in which as a future doctor he learnt to dissect bodies as if he too were not a body.

(*e*) In the process of schooling science, it has progressively been separated, in assumptions, organization and promotional hierarchies of the school, not only from technology and pupils' and teachers' everyday lives but from the range of other inquiries and activities within the school – history, art, politics, music and Literature. It is as if the particular way in which science was established, which, as Layton's example of the exclusion of geology illustrates well, [19] was more concerned with the protection of a particular social order than opening up ways in which the natural world might be understood and transformed, had become accepted as a kind of inevitable reality, rather than the product of particular historical circumstances.

In developing this critique of science in schools I have wanted to emphasize the assumptions about knowledge that have been embedded in the process of its schooling and the links between this process and changing political and economic circumstances. Equally it would be inaccurate to deny the 'real' progress that has taken place. There are more opportunities for children to question, to *do* rather than *see* experiments, to test ideas, in at least an overtly more open way, with more emphasis on thinking for oneself and less on the reproduction of textbook answers. The possibilities as well as the limitations of these changes within the given school context are well illustrated by an example of the Nuffield A level Physical Science course in practice.[20] In the school where I spent some time observing, the sixth form students spent one double session a week on their project and the rest on normal teaching. This double session was unlike anything I'd seen in a school lab before — even a sixth form. Staff and students drifted in and started various activities — without prior knowledge it was difficult, unlike in a normal class, to tell who was teacher, pupil or lab technician. The pupils were engaged in various stages of a variety of projects from examining the degeneration of albumen during the shelf life of eggs, to a study of the various strength properties of resin bonded fibre glass which is used for splints for those with broken or deformed limbs — particularly in African countries where rickets is widespread. From time to time a pupil would go up to a teacher and they would discuss the problem. Though the teacher might be able to point to an alternative method or technique or a useful reference source, it was the pupil who took the initiative and who knew more about the particular project at hand. In a less rigidly authoritarian school structure, the teachers too would doubtless have been engaged in projects of their own. But then, to put it crudely, teachers are supposed to transmit the knowledge created elsewhere, not actually to *create* knowledge themselves. Later in the week I sat in on several of the same group's non-project classes. The girls all came in, and sat in a row in the front bench facing where the teacher would be when she arrived. Except for a few whispers, they sat in silence, waiting for the teacher to come. She was friendly, not much older than her pupils, and obviously got on well with them. 'We are going to start by revising the periodic table', she began, 'What can you tell me about group 1?' Silence — In the next forty-five minutes, by relying largely on two of the girls, she was able to extract from them an account of the patterns of periodicity of the elements. The point I want to make is *not* that this was bad teaching, or that the teacher and pupils did not have a good relationship — they did.

I want to emphasize the difference between the two situations the girls and teacher found themselves in. Comparing the project class, which took up about one sixth of their time, with the typical non-project class I described, the initiative and responsibility was almost completely shifted from learner to teacher. A group of intelligent and responsible students who coped with complicated theories and sophisticated apparatus in their projects were transformed, in the interests of covering the syllabus, into passive, ignorant receptacles, feeling that there was no way that they could assert their control over the situation, and retain their identity as senior members of the school. I give this example in some detail as I think it illustrates the limited character of what have been called innovations in school science — even within their own terms.

This is not to claim that projects are in any sense a crucial strategy for liberating school science, for no methods are free from the possibilities of being coopted within an existing order. It is rather to point to the kind of contradictions within the existing contexts of school science that might be the basis of wider strategies for change.

4

Conclusions

Science education was envisaged, as David Layton tells us, by some early nineteenth century radicals like Richard Carlile as undermining dogma and leading to social emancipation.[21] The process and practice of the schooling of science, for all its changes, has, as I have tried to show, become almost the opposite — 'necessarily dogmatic' according to Jevons and many others, and producing technological domination rather than emancipation. This paper has largely been limited to the processes within education — the ways they have been part of a wider process of economic and political domination have been little more than hinted at. Inevitably oversimplifying, I would summarize what I have tried to say by suggesting that the schooling of science has produced three kinds of people, whose interrelations have up till now led to opposition to any attempts to realize the emancipatory potential Carlile saw. They are :

(a) 'Pure scientists', whose relations with nature are at best those of abstracted understanding. This is not to deny the discoveries that have been made, but to state that the purposes that have given meaning to the scientists' pursuit of truth have been success in and the sustaining of the scientific establishment.

(b) The 'applied scientist' whose identity is fundamentally pragmatic — given something to be done, he will work out how to do it. Ends are given, but no one asks by or for whom. Just as the pure scientist, from his early training, absolves himself from the uses to which his discoveries are put, rather than seeing that the discoveries themselves are inescapably linked to an economy on which he depends for support, so the applied scientist accepts that others define the goals that he has to achieve rather than seeing that his own means or technology itself presupposes a social order, set of priorities or goals.

(c) The identifiable failures of school science — the anti-science antitechnologists who can see science *only* as domination rather than that science as domination is itself a historical product, and the mass of people whose schooling teaches them that science is a specialized activity over which they neither have nor could have any control.

These 'successes' and 'failures' of school science have emerged from a society in which people have been separated from their knowledge of the natural world, which is experienced as external to them. The schooling of science, therefore, has begun with the knowledge, not the people, who have been expected to adapt to it. If, however, we start with a concept of man as part of nature *and* acting on nature, and that this acting on or appropriating has historically been in terms of particular purposes, then the abstracted pure scientist, the technologist, applied scientist, the anti-science intellectual and the mass of the scientifically ignorant are not just products of the schooling of science. We can see them as identities that have emerged in context of the history and development of modern capitalism — a society in which men have become increasingly separated from the products of their labour, mental and manual. The analysis and transfor mation of school science, and the separations that characterize it, then becomes a part of a much wider struggle for the realization of a socialist society. A radically different school science may not be possible in our society as it is, but unless we develop a critique that involves strategies for transforming it, any wider change in the social relations of production is likely to replace one form of domination by another.

Notes

1 R. Schofield, 'Schools and Physics', *Physics Bulletin* (May 1975).

2 B. Woolnough, 'Happy facts about Physics', *Times Educational Supplement* (26 September 1975).

3 P. S. C. Matthews, 'Has Science Education a Future?', *School Science Review* (1975).

4 D. Layton, 'Science or Education?', *University of Leeds Review,* vol. 18 (1975). The quotations on the following pages are also taken from the same source.

5 D. Layton, *Science for the People* (London, George Allen & Unwin, 1973).

6 D. Layton, 'The Educational Work of the Parliamentary Committee of the British Association for the Advancement of Science', *History of Education*, vol. 5, No. 1 (1976).   1

7 M. F. D. Young, 'Curriculum Change: Limits and Possibilities', *Educational Studies*, vol. 1, No. 2 (1975). Reprinted in M. Young and G. Whitty (eds), *Society, State and Schooling* (Brighton, Falmer Press, 1976).

8 C. Green, Review of Layton (1973), *Radical Science Journal*, No. 2/3 (1975).

9 M. Shayer, 'Conceptual demands in the Nuffield O Level Physics Course', *School Science Review*, vol. 54 (1972), p. 186.

10 B. J. Hine, 'Political Bias in School Physics', *Hard Cheese*, No. 4/5 (1975).

11 J. Ravetz, (*Scientific Knowledge and its Social Problems*, London, Oxford University Press, 1971) writes: 'these inherent limitations of the school teaching situation . . . must be recognized' (p. 207). He nowhere attempts to explain why they should be 'inherent'.

12 This account is based on an earlier draft of Charlie Clutterbuck's 'Death in a Plastics Factory' which appears in *Radical Science Journal*, vol. 4 (1976).

13 A good account of the Lucas Aerospace Combine Shop Stewards Committee proposals and some of their political implications is given by Dave Elliott in Nos. 12 and 13 of *Undercurrents. The Corporate Plan* produced by the Shop Stewards Committee is available from E. F. Scarbrow, 86 Mellow Lane Street, Hayes, Middlesex.

14 H. Braverman, *Labour and Monopoly Capital: The Degradation of Work in the Twentieth Century* (Monthly Review Press, 1974), and A. Gorz, 'Technical Intelligence and the Capitalist Division of Labour', *Telos*, vol. 12 (1971). Reprinted in M. Young and G. Whitty (eds), op. cit.

15 P. Corrigan and S. Frith, 'The Politics of Youth Culture', *Cultural Studies* 7/8 (1975), and D. Steed, *History as School Knowledge* (MA dissertation, University of London Institute of Education, 1974).

16 I owe this example to Anthony Hoskyns, Sir William Collins School, London.

17 This idea is also developed in Rosalind Driver's 'The Name of the Game', *School Science Review* (1975). I am grateful for a number of perceptive comments by Rosalind Driver on an earlier version of part of this paper – particularly her references to the 'Commo-

dity knowledge' assumption of the 'Patterns' model of learning used by SCISP, and of the various independent learning schemes that have been developed claiming to 'solve' the problems of mixed ability classes.

18 This point is from a talk on 'Reductionism in Biology' by Jonathan Cooke of the Medical Research Council Unit, Mill Hill, though he is not responsible for extending its implications to school biology.

19 D. Layton (1975) quotes a witness to the Public School Commissioners as follows, 'the theory of geology could not be received by mere boys without violent disturbance to their religious beliefs'.

20 I am particularly grateful to Mr B. J. Hine for opportunities to see and discuss the teaching of the Nuffield Physical Science Course.

21 Richard Carlile, 'An Address to Men of Science' referred to by Layton (1976). See also Note 15 above.

Glossary

PVC   Polyvinylchloride
BSSRS   British Society for Social Responsibility in Science
SCISP   Schools Council Integrated Science Project

Part 2: The politics of the hidden curriculum

Phrases like the 'hidden curriculum', used by radical educationists such as Ivan Illich, point to characteristics of schooling which are normally taken for granted. They emphasize that what is important about what pupils learn in school is not primarily the 'overt' curriculum of subjects like French and Biology, but values and beliefs such as conformity, knowing one's place, waiting one's turn, competitiveness, individual worth, and deference to authority. The hidden curriculum teaches pupils 'the way life is', and that education is something that is done to them, rather than something which they do. The prevailing values of society are, it is argued, 'picked up' by pupils through the experience of participating or adapting to what Illich would call the invariant structures of school. The paradox of such analyses is that, while presented as a form of radical criticism, they remove what is central to their critique from the intervention of those most centrally involved — teachers and pupils. By conceiving of the constraints of schooling in terms of an invariant structure, they merely confirm for teachers a sense of their own impotence, rather than pointing to any possibilities for action. The papers in this part set out to show how some of the most commonplace teacher activities, marking, writing reports, using textbooks, etc., create and sustain these invariant structures, and thus form the social basis both of the hidden and the overt curriculum. They also indicate some of the ways in which it is in the most individual of teacher activities that the contradictions of the production relations of capitalist society are expressed.

In Chapters 5 and 6, Hextall and Winter describe how two of the teacher's most familiar and unquestioned practices, giving marks or grades and writing reports for student records, produce the authoritative facts on which decisions about students' educational identities and future careers are created. They argue that the 'factual' character of marks and reports masks the power relations involved within the interactional contexts in which marking and reportings get done. In considering the implications of abolishing these practices, they make clear their fundamentally political character and the way they are expressions of the social relations of capitalist society, not merely of the school.

Integral to concepts of 'what education is' are our conceptions of knowledge, and the way in which certain knowledge attains an almost 'natural' authority. Hardy's and Tulloch's papers are concerned with some of the concrete practices through which the factual character of educational knowledge is achieved. Hardy's paper compares textbook accounts of 'what actually happens' in a typical elementary science experiment, to the way pupils in discussion generate

63

their account of the same experiment. The relations of the teacher and pupils to the packaged textbook account, and the way in which the pupils modify their own accounts to the expectation that only knowledge separated from persons is objective and therefore authoritative, are indicative of the within-school process by which a conformity to knowledge as some 'thing', both external and given, is learnt. However, schools, as our contributors emphasize, do not exist in a social vacuum, and Tulloch's paper demonstrates how important for any politics of school knowledge is an awareness of other educational contexts, in this case television, which contribute to the schooling of knowledge and the legitimation of the *status quo*. By taking quiz shows as a case study, he shows that crucial categories which characterize the divisiveness of educational knowledge, such as 'academic' and 'relevant', 'intellectually demanding' and 'of immediate interest', are institutionalized in the programming policies of the television networks. He shows the presentation of school knowledge as 'factual' through textbooks to be paralleled in the production of radio and television quiz programmes, where knowledge is displayed as a response to questions for which there are only right and wrong answers. In both cases, the social relations of knowledge are effectively obscured.

The process by which teachers themselves are schooled clearly contributes to their capacity to perpetuate the schooling of society. Teachers are 'schooled', Bartholomew argues in his paper, to separate what they learn in 'practice' from what they learn in 'theory', and they are rewarded for achieving this separation with good grades on practice and high marks on theory. What his paper points to in the context of teacher training is the way this separation sustains the authority relations in the college, as the staff remain guardians of the 'theory' which has validity independent of the contexts of its 'transmission'. The processes by which teacher/pupil relations sustain a conception of 'knowledge', separate both from the context of teacher/pupil interaction and from others in the world outside school, are likewise features of the social division of labour that are not restricted to educational institutions alone.

Chapter 5

Marking work

Ian Hextall

In this paper I am attempting to present some problems and dilemmas which arise from the evaluation of the work of pupils and students.[1] My approach differs in some ways from the conventional treatment of assessment-evaluation in educational literature. This is because I find that much of the theoretical writing on the topic seems to miss important points. Detailed considerations of standardization procedures, objective testing, and criterion referencing fail to reflect for me what assessment and marking felt like (and feels like) as a teacher. Marking was a troublesome activity, and in my talks with other teachers this sense of trouble seems apparent in their attitudes and opinions about marking. So this can be seen as a position paper in the sense that it constitutes an endeavour to write of these troubles, and also tries to suggest relationships between such 'personal troubles' and broader 'public, social issues'.

An initially interesting feature of marking is that it is a very obvious activity. It is obvious in the sense that it is highly visible. It can be observed in almost any school at any time. Teachers do a great deal of marking on a regular basis, along with a great many other routine activities. These are relatively trivial observations, but they underscore the obvious character of marking as a commonplace activity. Presumably the fact that marking occupies an important position in teachers' activities indicates that it is considered a significant item in their repertoire of jobs. Certainly, as a young teacher, it was impressed upon me how important it was to 'keep up' with my marking, and its significance does not seem to have declined. Strangely, however, given the significance attributed to marking, it seems to have largely escaped the attention of researchers and educational writers. This dualism of centrality and neglect seems paradoxical.

If, as I have claimed, marking is seen as a very obvious and routine aspect of what goes on in schools, then why is it worth considering? If this is not to be seen as a pointless analysis or merely another case of a 'theorist' making something problematic, then I must at least present reasons for focusing on it. Marking is not for me an isolated activity which goes on in some world of its own. It is frequently viewed as a highly specific and individualistic labour — for example, when teachers worry about the amount of marking they have to do, or whether they are going to get the books of three classes all done over the weekend in time to hand back on Monday. When you have sixty books to carry home on the bus and to return by tomorrow, you certainly feel you have a specific and technical problem in hand. When we know that our marks are going to be compared with those of other members of the department, then issues of objectivity and standards are likely to feel significant. When we are in the early stages of teaching, we may experience severe qualms about the kinds of criteria with which we are working. As I hope will become apparent, these problems are all a part with the total argument, but they remain rooted firmly within the sense that marking is specifically a problem for teachers, the school or education in general. It is all of these things but also more. What I am trying to do is to begin to place marking within a political and social context, and yet do this in such a way that it doesn't lose its contact with concrete issues of the sort mentioned above. Such concrete problems may provide for the birth of critique but they themselves must be placed in context unless we are to view education, teaching, learning, etc., as processes somehow existing in a social and political vacuum. Briefly, it is necessary to move beyond questions relating to issues of, say, accuracy, reliability and validity of marking conventions, and to consider the whole question of evaluation, what it does, and the form of social relations in which it is embedded.

Let me trace in some of the background which informs my approach. When I was teaching in a secondary school pupils handed work in to me on a fairly regular basis. I would then take their offerings and give them some form of symbolic grading. Whatever particular evaluation I made of any one piece of work was then recorded against the pupil's name in a mark book. Thus, over time each pupil came to acquire a constellation of marks against her/his name. Towards the end of each term a general mark sheet came round to all subject teachers of a particular class. On this, all the subjects which the pupils in this particular class 'did' were recorded on one axis, and the pupils' names on the other. For the subject(s) which I 'took' I was required to place a percentage grade for the term's work against each pupil's name. This task was laborious, and in the case of certain pupils who had failed to complete many assignments involved not a little imagination and diplomacy. When finally completed by subject teachers, these mark sheets were returned to the form (class) teachers who added each child's marks, divided the total by the number of subjects taken and arrived at an overall percentage mark. These final percentages provided the basis for the rank ordering of all the pupils in the class. The significance of these mark sheets was that, taken in conjunction with the end-of-year examinations (forty minutes each subject for first and second years, and an hour for third years), they formed the basis on which stream and set allocation was done, as well as providing important grounds for the attribution of scholastic identity to pupils by themselves, their friends, their teachers and their parents.

This account is unlikely to be much of a surprise to anyone reading it. The details may differ in particular circumstances but the broad pattern of the activity remains familiar.[2] Yet what it reflects very starkly is the relationship between the evaluation of pupils' work and the hierarchic organization and structuring of schools. Streams, sets, bands, examination and non-examination groups, GCE and CSE forms, etc., do not come into existence of their own accord. The routine acts of evaluating and marking pupils' work provide an important basis for populating such hierarchic categories. Further to this, what we do in schools is not confined in its significance only to the educational sphere.

The differentiation and grading which we accomplish in school is articulated with the broader, more encompassing social division of labour. This is not to claim that there exists a direct one-to-one link between differentiation in education and, say, the occupational division of labour. Clearly, such an assumption would be mechanistic and facile. But by our grading activities we are helping to establish the general framework of the labour force which the market later refines into specific occupational categories. In this way the procedures that occur in schools are a part of the political-economic context within which the schools are located. The differentiations, evaluations and judgements of worth which are made in schools are tenaciously related to particular forms of the social division of labour. In short, as well as marking the work of pupils who will become doctors, lawyers, teachers, accountants, and so on, we are also dealing with those who will enter occupations with high unemployment risks, with low rates of pay, with severe risks of industrial disablement and disease. It is difficult to accept but naive to forget the part we play in sustaining such a division of labour.

One way of relating to issues raised by such an argument is to consider the nature of marking as an activity. Certainly an important feature of what happens in marking is that childrens' products are evaluated in relation to some sets of standards or criteria. Thus, for example, standards of volume, accuracy, effort, creativity, neatness, etc., may be invoked to enable the marker to place one piece of work in relation to another. This seems very mundane. It is so obvious that this is what happens that it seems pointless to mention it. It now becomes clear why little work has been done on marking – there is little to do! In come the exercise books, they get marked by teachers according to certain sets of criteria, and then they are returned to the pupils. But, of course, questions do present themselves. What are the variations between various subjects in terms of the standards that are applied? Do different schools possess variant conventions by means of which they evaluate work? Given that marking is a social activity what do teachers make use of to do it to their own and others' satisfaction, and how do pupils interpret the marks they receive? Such variations and differences constitute important areas for investigation. There now exists a developed body of material on the topic of teacher-pupil interaction and the workings of mechanisms such as the self-fulfilling prophecy. Marking is one facet of such an interactional complex. One significant means through which pupils come to have identities attributed to them, and come to be labelled, is through the evaluation of their work which teachers carry out. As a social activity the marking of work possesses features which can be analysed sociologically. Like many other routine activities, the fact that it goes on, apparently unquestioned, for long periods of time, conducted by large numbers of teachers, and having fateful consequences for large numbers of pupils, has somehow served to render it common-sensical, obvious, and unworthy of detailed investigation. Such an approach to marking could begin with an exploration of the ways in which it gets done, the meanings it has for pupils and teachers, how markers manage to distinguish between various qualities and how these distinctions are perceived by those whose work is evaluated. Just how is marking acquired as a 'skill' which can be used to show

67

one's professional competence, in what manner and according to what procedures are rules and rationalities invoked?

Even to begin to ask questions of this sort would require a stance towards evaluation which has been notably missing in literature on assessment. To take only one facet, there has been a marked neglect of questions of *how* evaluation gets done.[3] This neglect indicates the technical stance which is adopted towards the topic. Once marking procedures, instruments and measures are provided, gradings and their application may come to be seen as technical activities − technical and neutral rather than interpretative and expressive of forms of social relationship which are embodied within the idea of evaluation itself. Similarly, there has been little detailed consideration of the ways in which various schemes of evaluation and marking conventions have come to be established historically, culturally and institutionally. Such issues are apparently 'no problem'. The tools are there, available and to be worked with, in a way analogous to the manner in which legal codes and systems were there for deviance theory. 'The law provides the framework; let's find out who are the criminals and deviants'. Such a perspective ignores the social base and forms of relationship which ground the total concept of 'the law'. I would argue that similarly technical, politically conservative assumptions characterize, for example, the concept of 'standard' which undergirds our marking activities.

As we have already seen, some notion of standard provides the basis on which marking can be carried out. It is invoked in order to evaluate and grade various items of work on a comparative basis. But, as well as providing the procedural base for the activity of marking, the idea of standards also legitimates the products of the activity. It resides in the very notion of standard that the marking is being conducted objectively, according to common dimensions, and on a base which holds equally for all the pieces of work to which the standard applies. Again, there may be serious differences in our views of the extent to which actual marking corresponds to such a picture, but underpinning our responses and criticisms may well be a firm sense of the possibility of its achievement. One element in the hierarchic authority of the marker in relation to the marked lies precisely in the assumption that the former possesses access to 'the standards' which enable him to evaluate the work of the pupil. Clearly this contributes an important element in our conceptions of the division of labour. A characteristic feature of hierarchic relations of production stems precisely from the presumption of possession of specialist knowledge, which provides the basis for the social situation where some may interpret and grade others, and have their interpretations and gradings accepted by the graded. Thus, one of the abiding characteristics of marking is the limited extent to which it is ever questioned. In general, children, other teachers and parents accept the marks they are presented with, and one of the reasons for this lies in the assumption that they have been awarded 'according to certain standards', and that these standards are legitimate.

When we put it this way it becomes clear that the idea of standard carries with it connotations of a world of reality, about which there is no doubt (again, I think that there are parallels between such a version of standards, and those of justice, a fair wage, health, and so on). The standard operates as that which provides the measure or index of the approximation between a particular product or piece of work and some 'reality' against which it is ranged. The 'real' thus comes to possess a tangibility which enables it to provide the basis for comparison and grading. Furthermore, it is precisely by recourse to the presumed existence of such a real base for our standards that our evaluation is accorded legitimacy by both ourselves and others (in case I am misunderstood on this point, I should like to make it clear that I am not only referring to those subjects in which some recourse to a 'real' world is explicitly assumed, e.g. natural sciences, geography, history, etc.; the point relates also to notions such as creative writing, musical sensitivity, and dramatic insight). Clearly, when expressed as directly as this, few are likely to find this picture congenial. Nevertheless, it appears to me as an important element which informs our practices of marking, and one which has crucial social implications.

Perhaps the most obvious point is that it places man and his products in a subservient relationship to the world of 'reality'. Thus the pupil who has her/his maths work marked knows clearly that it is the demands of maths, as a real body of knowledge, which provide the basis on which the marking is done.[4] A wedge is driven between the knowledge and the knower whereby the knowledge is accorded an existence independent of the actions of knowers. It is literally the reality and constraints of knowledge itself to which the pupil must accommodate. By means of such a classic inversion the creation and development of knowledge and ways of knowing by man are subtly obscured. The kid who receives back his work with a mark inscribed on it grasps clearly his passive relationship to nature and reality. He is being kept informed as to the fact that his products must be submitted to the authority of certain standards before they can be given value, and that these standards themselves derive their legitimation from the reality of the world. This alienation through the holding apart of the relationship between man and his product should not be seen as being limited to kids. Teachers also are given a subordinate place in relationship to knowledge. They clearly have a hierarchically superior position in relation to pupils in that they actually make the judgements and evaluations of work. But, in so far as they have recourse to notions of standards and criteria in order to legitimate their work, they also place themselves in a subordinate relation to these very standards. Like pupils they remain imprisoned in the service of a reality from which creation and transformation have been removed. Such an orientation to knowledge mediated through the activity of marking has important implications in sustaining the conservative legitimacy of the *status quo*. It succeeds in mystifying the relationship between knowledge and the social interests it serves by sundering the link between the knower and the known. The pupil's relation to knowledge becomes that of reproducing the known, the teacher's that of evaluating the quality of that reproduction according to given standards. But standards do not reside in a cultural vacuum. They do not possess some universal, absolute quality which renders them unproblematic and above debate. It is precisely this taxing recognition which places the evaluation of children's work as a feature of the politics of school practice, and raises questions as to the political-economic location of all educational activity. What goes on in schools is not divorced from what goes on elsewhere. Schooling is part of what Miliband has called 'the legitimation process', which serves to sustain a particular economic structure and political order.[5] Thus, when we make use of conceptions of 'standards' in validating our marks or assessments we are implicitly accepting particular notions of standards and value. In this sense marking is not a technical activity but a political act.

Let me adopt a different approach to these issues. By making use of the idea of standard in order to evaluate work we are implicitly placing one child's work and another child's work in a comparative relation to that standard. Thus their offerings are given different values on the basis of a common criterion. What could be fairer than that! A fair day's pay for a fair day's work! Now we know that this standard is not unidimensional, and that we make various adjustments for the ways in which different children measure up. For example, at the most basic level we use different standards for children of different ages; it would be unthinkable to apply the same criteria to the writing of a six-year-old and a sixteen-year-old. And there are many other adjustments to be made. But these adjustments retain the status of manipulations in the calculations made in order to ensure that the comparisons are made fairly. It is an interpretative activity which is firmly rooted in the calculative aim of ensuring that the pupil receives a fair return for his work (other things being equal, as the economist would say). The pain and mystery of this for me is that such a fundamentally quantitative, calculative orientation to work is so embedded that an alternative version is literally inconceivable. But let me push it a little further. If, as I claim, this evaluation activity is based on the idea of returns for work done, then what constitutes those returns? The most obvious response is that the marks, grades, comments, etc., constitute the return. However, if we recall briefly the earlier argument as to the relational character of evaluation and, say, streaming, and further the occupational and social division of labour, then the political and economic impact of the calculative orientation becomes more striking. As with the industrial worker who comes to see his labour potential as a commodity to be disposed of in the market, so the pupil has represented to him that the value of his work resides in its exchange value. Does this provide a way of grasping why it is that some pupils will only, say, write when their work is going to be seen by a teacher, why some will only paint or draw when they know their work is to be graded? Also what about kids who complain that 'You haven't marked it!', or voice a parallel complaint when some teacher changes the currency by shifting from, say, number marking to letter grading.

In short, I am maintaining that in so far as pupils come to see their labour and its products as being commodities which can be given a price according to some kind of calculative procedure, they are in a relationship similar to the worker who has his rewards established according to the established 'laws of economics'. Rather than these laws, or the evaluative standards, being perceived as themselves humanly produced and reflecting in their constitution the work of interests, rather they come to stand for 'the reality' which makes their wages (or marks) just or natural. The situation is mystified in the classic sense that both those whose interests it represents, and those whom it oppresses, see it as a natural situation which expresses the reality of how things are, rather than as a historic moment which embodies particular forms of social relationships — relationships of hierarchy, control, authority, rights, conflict and cooperation. Between the participants and their social relationships are interposed apparently factual things — for example, economic principles, IQ tests, reading standards, army regulations, marking criteria. And by recourse to these 'facts' we render opaque the forms of social relationship which legitimate and sustain these very 'facts' themselves.

One of the characteristics of accounts such as the one I have provided is that it could be used as a point of departure for any number of discussions. We could use it to consider the question of the internal organization and structure of schools, as a base for looking at the linkages between division of labour and educational procedures, as another way into discussion of teacher-pupil interaction, as a case study in the political economy of education, and so on. This seems to me wholly characteristic. A given concrete circumstance contains within it the potentiality for many complex analyses. Any given analysis indicates what can be done with a concrete situation but never what could be done.

What then have I attempted to do with my account? Perhaps the most central point has been to express the impossibility of sundering the relationship between particular activities, which may be seen as routine or mundane, and their origination in and sustenance of more inclusive forms of social relationship in which they are located. This constitutes a teasing dialectic. On the one hand there exists the linkage between a given, particular, isolated act or constellation of actions (in this case my marking activities, and those of friends, colleagues and unknown others) and the part played by such activities in the generation and maintenance of social relationships such as academic hierarchies and the division of labour. But, as well as this, and juxtaposed with it, there is another dimension. What is it in our forms of social relationship that makes an activity such as marking so acceptable, so routine and so sensible a social act? If we can conceive of the part played by our evaluation activities in sustaining a social order, what is the form of social order that utilizes such evaluation as a feature of its sustenance? Directly, if marking contributes to populating our division of labour, what is the form of division of labour which entails such marking activities?

This discussion has endeavoured to provide a political, social context in which to consider marking and evaluation activities. Doing this points very starkly to the limitations in significance of papers such as this one. I see it as romantic and Utopian to assume that major social transformations are likely to be brought about through changes in the forms and processes of education. To assume this would be to isolate one particular part of the institutional structure and to lose its interrelationship with others. To grant to the educative process some particular salience or primacy in its capacity to instigate liberation and change is idealist and conveys the message that change resides in men's heads.

But if education has no independent, regenerative character, taken in context and viewed in relation with other political and economic action it plays a significant part in the formation of social relations. Any attempt to consider the present nature of social relations or changes in them must somehow comprehend and respect man's consciousness and its transformation. How do political and economic influences instigate particular forms of educational activities, what part do such particular procedures play in the forms of social relations, what do relations in education signify in terms of sexual, familial, occupational relations; what part do educational changes occupy in relation to overall patterns of change? These and many others are questions of the dialectic relation of educational processes and social transformation, and further address the issue of our own relating of practice and theory. Clearly no resolution is going to ensue from a consideration of the way we mark children's work. But I would want to claim that any serious socialist movement would wish to consider deeply how to convey a sense of human worth, what it saw as the quality of human labour, and the modes it possessed for enabling man to engage with man in joint, social activities of judgement and evaluation.

In what must be a brief conclusion it is not possible to do more than make reference to a number of problems which have stuck with me as I have written this article.

It would be possible to view what I have written as constituting an attack on standards and a drive for the abolition of evaluation. Rather, I would prefer it to be seen as an analysis of the specific and socially grounded concrete practices in which we are involved at the present. This presents us with the more demanding task of working out what would constitute a stance towards standards which could both help us to accomplish social change and which would be appropriate in transformed conditions. If our current practices may be seen as sustaining a social order which we wish to see replaced, and if they establish forms of social relationships which we view as alienative and oppressive, then at least a part of our activity lies in a sustained critique of such practices. It is in not going past criticism into the area of positive alternatives that most people will see the greatest weakness of this paper. 'What has it got to offer in terms of practical suggestions?' 'What does it put in the place of what it knocks down?' Quite rightly these are questions which people will ask, and to both questions the answer may well be: 'Not a lot!'

Without wishing to evade the issues raised by such questions I think that some general points are worth considering. I have been attempting to argue throughout this paper that it is not appropriate to isolate evaluation as an activity from the political economic relations of capitalism within which education and schooling is situated.[6] Given this as a framework, we must consider how valid it is to ask for practical suggestions when we need to place our analyses within a knowledge of concrete circumstances. We will need to work collectively with other teachers, with parents, with kids, with outsiders, to analyse and reformulate our activities. To look to expertise as a resolution to the issues is to retreat to a form of social and technical engineering which presumes that we can somehow 'get our marking right' in isolation. This doesn't mean that we don't have experiences we can share. We have ideas and projects we have worked on. We may have developed various insights into ways of working through our situations. These we must share.[7]

Evaluation is about man and our conception of him. It is about hierarchy and who has the power to denote one person or product as superior to another. It is about knowing and who has the right to know. It reflects the structure of our society and the forms of social relationships within it. In all these ways it is intensely political and we need to consider it in the light of such recognition.

Notes

1   From this point onwards I tend to use 'teachers', 'pupils', 'schools' and 'marking' as the main anchors for my argument. This is for the sake of convenience since I think that my position would change little if I substituted the terms 'lecturer', 'student' and 'college/ university'. Hopefully the points raised are of relevance in both contexts.

2   I don't mean to imply by this that it doesn't make any difference what form of assessment we use. Arguments about continuous assessment, objective tests, collaborative marking, project assessment, self-evaluation procedures, are important. But, I would suggest that the boundaries for debate need extending. We must move beyond constrained considerations of standardization, reliability, validity, criteria-referencing, which are issues internal to the assessment game. We must ask what our modes of assessment reflect about the relationship between pupils' work and, say, the hierarchic organization and structuring of schools. It is a big step to move from asking 'how we assess?' to asking 'what we assess for?' or 'to what purposes is our marking put?'

3   This is not the place to engage in a detailed critique of the literature on evaluation and assessment. A point made earlier bears repeating − namely, that such literature conducts its analysis within certain bounds and that these are largely boundaries of a 'technical' nature. Within such a framework issues about the social relationships which generate and legitimate our current modes of assessment are out of court, as also are questions regarding the social use which is made of these modes. Easily available examples of such literature are:
      D. Pidgeon and A. Yates, *An Introduction to Educational Measurement* (London, Routledge & Kegan Paul, 1969).
      E. Stones (ed.), *Readings in Educational Psychology* (London, Methuen, 1970), section 7.

4   It is clear that choosing 'maths' as an example here may raise problems. Generally maths is seen as the *par excellence* 'objective' subject. Marking Maths is seen as characteristically the most 'objective, standardized' form of all marking. But just a couple of points may be worth making. Firstly, maths itself as a school/university subject is not fixed in character and essence for all time. It has changed in form and will continue to do so. What counts as 'good maths' in one time or place is not the same for all times and places. Thus 'maths' changes (and these changes can be dramatic) but it does not change itself; it can only be changed by human activity. Secondly, and this relates to the first point, mathematization of his world was a capacity which man developed originally for his use; he did it because it was of relevance to him. Do the abstract computations which we ask pupils to do in school continue to reflect that sense of use-value or do we ask them rather to show us that they have the mental 'agility and competence' to handle calculations which are seen as ends in themselves rather than having direct relationship to their life-in-the-world.

5   For a beginning in exploring the general issues raised here it is worth looking at H. Gintis's article, 'Towards a Political Economy of Education', which is available in I. Lister's reader called *Deschooling* (Cambridge, Cambridge University Press, 1974). As a more specific look at the link between the economy and our processes of evaluating

people, Clarence Karier's 'Testing for Order and Control in the Corporate Liberal State' raises suggestive points, even though its focus is upon IQ tests. It is most readily available in C. Karier, P. Violas and J. Spring, *Roots of Crisis* (Chicago, Rand McNally, 1973).

6 A rather fuller development of this argument can be found in I. Hextall and M. Sarup, 'School Knowledge , Evaluation and Alienation', in M. Young and G. Whitty, *Society, State and Schooling* (Brighton, Falmer Press, 1976).

7 Should anyone reading this feel the need to respond, I can easily be contacted through Goldsmiths' College, London. Perhaps we could then begin to share our experiences, our proposals for change, and our sense of the strengths and shortcomings of current approaches (including mine).

Chapter 6

Keeping files : aspects of bureaucracy and education

Richard Winter

Introduction

I have never met anyone who said he actually enjoyed writing reports. Attempting to put down on paper a summary of 'how well' the individual pupils or students in our classes have done seems to provoke a sense of embarrassment rather than anything else. Perhaps one just feels bewildered: what is it that we want/ought to say, if anything? What constraints or notions of our role lead us, almost in spite of ourselves, to produce phrases like 'satisfactory progress' or other more elaborate constructions that seem as we write them to be mere question-begging evasions? Is it that we are engaged in being 'objective'? (If so, how, and for whom?) Are we exercising 'professional responsibility'? (Why then this sense of paralysis and absurdity?) Or are we copping out, betraying with our notes, grades and reports the students and pupils whose trust we have gained?

In the following pages I hope that tentative answers to some of these questions will emerge. Firstly, examples of reports and files are presented in order to bring out more precisely the sort of problems and worries hinted at so far. Then the staffroom/classroom reality is placed in a wider sociological context to try to link the problem of files and reports in educational institutions with ideas about bureaucracies, the division of labour, and the creation and control of information. Finally the practical question is faced: how might files be reformed?

1 The teaching situation: problems of objectivity and assessment

In this section I shall be drawing on my own experience as a creator of files on education course students, and on a detailed perusal of some (anonymous) files on primary school children. I hope that the extracts given and the comments made will remind you of problems you have encountered in your own file-creating activities.

The first issue I wish to raise is the method by which the reports we write seem to create a sense of authority and certainty. For example, when I write 'X has contributed well to class discussions', I am giving credit to the pupil. When I write 'Y has tended to opt out of class discussions', or '. . . has seemed somewhat shy in class discussions', I am quite clearly making a criticism of the pupil. In both cases my own activities as a teacher are kept out of the question, taken for granted, and thus, implicitly, assumed to be 'normal'. When I write that someone

I have taught is 'mature' ('X has shown great maturity in his approach to the course'), there is implicitly a claim being made that I also am mature, mature enough indeed to evaluate the maturity being displayed by students. Imagine that sixth-formers or students submitted reports on their teachers at the end of the year, and that instead of writing 'Mr X made the lessons very enjoyable' they wrote 'Mr X showed a mature approach to his work this year', I suggest that we (as staff) might experience the compliment itself as a put-down. 'Intelligent' is a word that works in the same way, I think. It is not possible to avoid this issue by careful choice of words or by exclusive concern with 'objective' data like examination or essay grades. Instructions on an LEA Primary School Confidential Record Card were that the reports (on transfer from infant to junior, and from junior to secondary school) should cover '. . . Personality, Capacity for Leadership, Sense of Responsibility, Self-Confidence, Sociability, Conscientiousness, Stability, and Attitude to Work'. Teachers' competence to judge such matters is taken for granted.

Quite simply, the point I am making is that if I am writing a report on someone else's response to my teaching, then I am reporting an interaction, and yet the conventional way in which reports are presented in educational establishments treats the teacher's side of the affair as irrelevant in order to present a direct evaluation of the pupil and to hold the pupil alone responsible for his performance. We are all aware of our specific limitations as teachers and as people (we get on better with some types than with others) and yet report writing seems to require the teacher to forget his doubts and imperfections, and to assume an authoritative stance. Report writing reminds us that we (teachers) have POWER over our classes.

Linked with the problem just outlined (that the report does not allow the teacher to notice the quality of his own activities) is the problem of objectivity. To what extent can it make sense to suppose that the documents in the file add up to an objective account of the subject of the file? Consider these statements made by Peter Rance about the nature of good record keeping:[1]

Records must still be informative when considered years later.

Records should be . . . based on knowledge which is common to all teachers.

Records should provide enough detail about a subject for a balanced judgement to be made by another teacher.

Records should enable additional facts to be constructed from them which will reveal any general trends in a child's . . . or a school's progress.

Rance is implying that a pupil's file can make that pupil available to a reader for scrutiny, rather as if we could summon him or her into our room for a brief interview, or as though the pupil himself had been conveniently bottled! He seems to think that the pupil is there in the file so that we can, by opening the file, inspect the pupil. Now clearly is unrealistic: records (as we have already seen) are 'based on' teachers' views of their own interactions with the pupil; they cannot possibly, therefore be based on knowledge which is 'common to all teachers'. Hence any subsequent judgements made by another teacher cannot be 'balanced' but must remain crucially ignorant (of the reality underlying the account in the record). Hence any construction, later, of 'additional facts' must be largely speculative.

We can see the nature and scope of the problem when we turn to an example. Here are the grades and reports which accompanied a nine-year-old girl transferring from one junior school to another. I will call her Elaine for ease of reference.

LEA Confidential Record Card

Educational Record	Infant	Junior (Yr 1)	(Yr 2)
Speech or Oral English	C	C	C
Reading	C	110	98
English, written	C	108	108
Number or Arithmetic	C/D	111	103
General Intelligence	C	107	102

Final Report on Transfer to Junior School

Reserved and self-contained, Elaine has been a quiet, but happy pupil. Her observation is good and in written work her attention to detail is interesting, similarly with drawing, etc. However, Elaine has not shown much keenness for number work, which has caused difficulty. This does not appear to concern her. In a large class she melts quietly into the background, adjusting happily to any group, or any new situation.

Junior School First Year Report

Attendance Good/Fair/Poor . . . . Good

	Ability level	Effort and progress	Remarks
Reading	C	C+	Elaine shows little interest in reading, yet can read well.*
Oral English	C	B	Sensible answers, but Elaine is often shy and hesitant.
Written Work	C+	A	Elaine obviously takes pleasure in writing stories.
Handwriting	–	A	Beautiful, even writing; well formed.
General Neatness	–	A	Elaine's work is a pleasure to see, it is so neat.
Mathematics	C+	B	Elaine's work has improved tremendously. A good year's work.

77

Creative Work		Carefully planned and executed work.
Conduct		Quiet and shy but very sensible.
Social Attitudes		Helpful at all times, Elaine shows great common sense. Always willing to join in class activities.

General Assessment Effort and enthusiasm   A   Ⓑ   C   D   E
Academic   A   B   Ⓒ   D   E

*Spends hours reading at home (signed: Elaine's father)

Junior School Second Year Report

Attendance: Good/Fair/Poor . . . . Good

	Ability level	Effort and progress	Remarks
Reading	C	C	Good.
Oral English	C+	C+	Good.
Written Work	C	C	Good, but disappointing in that I feel Elaine could produce better work.
Handwriting	–	B-	Very neat.
General Neatness	–	C+	Good.
Mathematics	C	C+	Elaine has some difficulty with this subject, but tries hard.
Creative Work		C+	Good.
Conduct			Very good. Elaine is always well behaved and polite.
Social Attitudes			Elaine is very quet, but seems to have a good circle of friends within the class.

General Assessment Effort and enthusiasm   A   B   Ⓒ   D   E
Academic   A   B   Ⓒ   D   E

(Elaine's file also contained briefer mid-year reports for the two junior years by the same teachers, record sheets indicating her attainments in number work and reading, and a variety of NFER tests which Elaine had completed, presumably the basis of the scores in the two junior columns on the 'Confidential Record Card'.

Clearly lots of problems are raised by these documents, but let us at this stage concentrate on the problem of objectivity. Firstly, what do these grades A, B, C, D, E mean? On the back of the LEA record card is an explanation:

Entries should be made in terms of a five point scale: A, B, C, D, E. Category A shall be interpreted as meaning that out of 100 representative pupils those classified as A would be found among the top 5 per cent, those assessed as B would correspond to the next 20 per cent, and so on as shown below:

A	B	C	D	E
5	20	50	20	5

But how on earth can we decide that we have in mind 100 'representative' pupils? If we take the idea seriously, it ought to mean that this grading system should not be used by primary teachers in their first two years, since they will not even have *met* 100 pupils except on a casual basis. But of course the LEA only says that A, B, C, D, E 'shall be interpreted' in that way, not that the teacher is really expected to do it like that. The letter grades are used to *look* more objective, but, as we all know, their meaning is totally locked into individuals' own usages and personalities (some teachers are notoriously enthusiastic, and flash A's and B's around, to their colleagues' consternation!). We may also wonder what C/D and all the pluses and minuses mean. Is it that the teacher is using a more finely graded and thus more *accurate* scale than the LEA require, so that we are being told that out of 100 pupils the teacher knows that Elaine's arithmetical ability would be ranked between 70th and 80th? Remembering my own feelings when asked to grade on an A-E scale, I am more inclined to think it is a resurgence of the subjective, emotionally loaded quality of the relationship between teacher and pupil: 'She hasn't really got the hang of number work at all yet, but she's a nice little kid — certainly not a D'. Similarly, we can note that C+ appears more often on the junior school reports than C. I am tempted to suggest that C looks rather like 'damning with faint praise': it is too neutral a response. It is difficult to teach someone all year, get to know him well, and then summarize your response to his work baldly as 'average'.

It is particularly interesting to note that the first year teacher gave Elaine consistently higher grades for Effort than for Ability, whereas in the second year this difference disappears. Does this mean that Elaine has stopped trying, or that the teachers have different ideas as to what degree of effort is creditable? If Elaine is trying less hard for her second year teacher, it is equally clear that the second year teacher's comments suggest a much cooler response to this particular girl. Nevertheless Elaine's 'Effort and enthusiasm' grade moves from B to C as though in an unambiguous way it is *her* performance alone which has changed. Thus A, B, C, D, E here are rhetorical devices to create an impression (for whom and why?) that objective assessments are being made, i.e. those that 'anyone' or 'most people' would agree with.

The test scores in the two columns for the junior school present different but related problems. The main one, again, is that the apparent precision of numbers is being used to present the pupils' qualities as fixed and certain. The columns of figures hovering around 100 evoke general memories of quotients and standard deviations; however, when we look closer we find that we are not told which test the Reading scores refer to; and the General Intelligence score is in one case a non-verbal test and in the other case (eighteen months later) a verbal test, so the two scores are in no way comparable: yet they can all too easily be read from left to right in their columns as indicating progress from year 1 to year 2 (The LEA instruction was that teachers should not use a test for General Intelligence but should make an estimate and present it on the A-E scale).

In general it seems misleading to sum up a pupil's overall attainment in an area of work with a single test score, and even more so to put the score on the card without a note of which test it refers to. Naturally, certain tests can be useful to a teacher as diagnostic techniques — as methods of deciding on particular forms of work with particular pupils. But this is quite different from creating out of one or two such tests an 'Educational Record' — a supposed summary of the pupil's intellectual attainment divorced from any immediate work context or purpose. So why is it, we may ask, that we are continually asked to create accounts of our work with pupils in such a spuriously objective style? Who is it for?

A similar point can be made about the Records of Work. Included in Elaine's file are sheets bearing lists of (a) reading books of different series and (b) maths topics. Some reading books and maths topics are ticked off and others are not. This looks at first sight like a form of objective mapping of a pupil's attainment, but notoriously it is not. Horror stories are rife: 'She was supposed to be up to book four, but she couldn't even . . .', etc. As a headmistress friend put it to me — it all depends on what the ticks mean. When the teacher ticks off 'Fractions' on thirty record sheets, the tick will have thirty different meanings and these are precisely what the next teacher will always have to find out about. Ticking off items of a check list implies a very oversimplified notion of the learning process, creating yet again the illusion of accuracy, objectivity and comparability, as though the extent of a pupil's understanding could be filed as a fact.

Finally, what about the teachers' remarks and reports. Who are they written for and why? It seems that the yearly reports are written with the parents in mind. The letter grades suggest that Elaine's work is mediocre, and the remarks seem to me to be aimed at reassuring and enlisting the support of the parents. They are to be persuaded not to worry: 'Good' (repeated), 'Tries hard', 'Has a good circle of friends', 'Beautiful writing', 'Has improved tremendously'. At one point the possibility is raised of the parents bringing pressure to bear to help the school: 'I feel Elaine could produce better work'. The remarks on the first year report about Elaine's reading seem designed to draw the parents' attention to a contradiction in her work, to which the father responds with a relevant piece of information which could be of use to her teacher. Perhaps her 'shyness' is raised as something the parents might do something to help. These year reports, then, seem to be communications situated within a fairly clear institutional relationship between parents and teacher, with the pupil as a shared concern. The message for the parents in year 1 is: 'Don't worry; she won't set the world alight, but she's a nice child'. In year 2 the message is (for some reason) rather more austere: 'She won't set the world alight but don't worry'. The unique style of school reports, then, which often seems so curiously stilted, can thus be seen *not* as an attempt to be *objective,* but as an attempt to be *diplomatic.*

This would suggest that reports can be understood as negotiations within the on-going partnership between parents and teachers. If so, it seems worth raising the point that the files relating to this partnership should at least contain documents from both sides (and, indeed, from the pupil as well). Clearly this hardly ever happens. And this suggests that, even if teachers write reports as moves in a diplomatic game with parents, this is not why they are filed. The filing of the report removes it from the situation in which it was originally useful (*that* particular teacher, after *that* discussion with the mother, about the child in *that* mood, at *that* particularly awkward time for the family, etc.) and instead turns the report into yet another supposedly objective source of data on the child's characteristics. From being (ideally perhaps) a sort of working document, by being filed it will almost certainly become an assessment.

When we turn to Elaine's 'Final Report on Transfer to Junior School' the problem of the relevance and purpose of the file becomes yet more acute. The LEA instruction is that these reports should be: 'as comprehensive as possible, covering Special Aptitudes (Art, Craft, Music, Sports); Personality; Capacity for Leadership; Sense of Responsibility; Self-Confidence, Sociability; Conscientiousness, Stability; and Attitude to Work'.

When the precise, limited list of Elaine's qualities is compared with the comprehensive list of the LEA's very general concerns, it is hard to resist the feeling that Elaine emerges in a rather negative light. Her 'Aptitude' for noting details is minimally creditable ('interesting'); the only 'Attitude to Work' noted is her lack of keenness in number work (what about other work?); and the main positive point about her seems to be that she does not create problems in the classroom situation: she is 'happy', so when she quietly 'melts into the background' we don't need to worry about her: she has 'friends'; she will always 'adjust'.

Can one imagine a general report describing a pupil in detail which could be genuinely necessary or even useful (*not* just 'of interest') to Elaine's future teachers? I am rather doubtful, because I suspect that most teachers have their own ways of finding out (from pupils and others) what they need to know in order to teach. In any case it is hard to think how this particular description of Elaine could be used by a teacher to help her. Instead I would interpret it as yet another assessment, addressed vaguely to the educational bureaucracy, of how far Elaine is likely to be successful and how much trouble she is likely to cause. Answer in both cases: negative. This interpretation of the report may seem somewhat melodramatic or jaundiced, but consider the following section from a slightly later version of the LEA 'Primary School Record': there is the heading 'Qualities of Temperament' (indicate very positive (+) or very negative (-) only) and then six columns (for six years of primary school) against each of the

81

following categories: Initiative, Reliability, Perseverance, Self-Confidence, Cooperation, Aggression. The list itself seems almost to conjure forth precise images of socially desirable and undesirable pupils.

Another category on the LEA Record Card is 'Home Circumstances and Parental Attitude', which introduces a further type of controversial information created for and by the pupil's file. Recently a student returned from a pre-teaching-practice visit to a school armed with details about the 'background' of every child in the class: whose parents were separated (and who left whom); whose background was 'poor', 'good', 'settled', 'normal'; whose parents were 'overanxious', 'rather aggressive', 'disinterested', 'German', 'Irish Catholics', who was an only child or from a 'large' family, and even whose elder brother or sister was on probation. Again, one is worried that once statements of this type concerning children have been created and filed, they may come to be treated first as facts, and then as explanations: when we have information readily to hand about someone we can always use it one way or another, depending on what it is we feel needs explaining.

The theme of most of these remarks on files is that they present a series of necessarily subjective accounts of a pupil or student in a remarkably authoritative style, as though to be read as factual statements or descriptions. It is important to realize how difficult it would be to remedy this. For example, the LEA I have referred to is just introducing a new format of pupil file, in which 'samples' of work will be kept in the main folder along with 'Attainment Record Cards'. But the questions will still arise: who will decide which work goes into the file, what is 'a sample', what is the 'average' or 'typical' work of the child, what was his best piece (and did his elder sister help with it anyway?), what interpretations will be made of the work, and by whom? Peter Rance presents a variety of ways in which pupils can fill in their own records of work and even allot themselves marks for the work they have done.[2] He seems to be suggesting that teachers and pupils should continuously create the records of their work by processes rather like clocking in, keeping minutes, or filling in job cards. Instead of formal reports he suggests 'personality records', to which staff contribute comments as and when they wish. Thus the classroom files are to be created by 'informal', 'democratic' processes; the pupil will be allowed to *participate* in the creation of his own file.

However, as when workers 'participate' by sending representatives along to management meetings, such reforms are unlikely to change the nature of the work experience within the institution. The problem is not that particular forms of reporting are used, or that certain teachers' reports are either inadequate or unfair. Rather the problem is the relationship between institutional hierarchies, the types of information they create, and the way they use it. Notes, grades and reports on pupils are assembled by us (staff, or even staff, parents *and* pupils themselves) in our everyday work. We do this responsibly and, of course, reasonably, but (inevitably) for our own purposes and hence with our own slant, our own notions of relevance built in. But then the institutional structure we work within recreates these documents as authoritative incontrovertible *files,* which are used as part of the institutional, bureaucratic reality to which we and our pupils or students are subjected. It is the nature of this phenomenon I now wish to consider in order to place the foregoing discussion of files in a broader theoretical and political framework.

2 Bureaucratic information: sociological perspectives

We can begin by thinking of bureaucratic organizations, as Weber did, as ones in which authority is rigidly hierarchical.[3] And one of the ways in which they are enabled to be so is that management decisions can be based on documentary evidence (the files) which (as we have seen) are presented as objective and factual; thus the decisions which emerge when the appropriate official consults the appropriate file are assumed to be as rational as possible and thus fully competent. However, this rationality and objectivity (as we have also seen) is in many ways spurious: the files are used to *justify* management decisions, of course, but clearly they can never *guarantee* that those decisions will be wise or humane, let alone the best ones under the circumstances. Bureaucratic files, then, can be considered sociologically as ways of *legitimating* the exercise of power.

Consider, for example, the simple matter of information flow within an institution. Rules concerning the confidentiality of files mean that superiors have access to files on inferiors, but not vice versa. LEA officials have access to files on teachers; teachers have access to files on pupils. Imagine how we would react if it became known that our pupils or students had for the last five years been keeping a file on each member of staff, keeping it up to date by selecting and collating material as it was fed in from different sources (our neighbours, our children, local shop assistants, pupils from our different classes) and passing it on to succeeding generations of incoming pupils. Knowledge is power, they say: so the distribution of knowledge is a clue to the distribution of power.

A file is an attempt to create a version of the client of an institution in terms of the purposes of that institution. It is by means of his file that the client can be manipulated, processed (an instructive example to remember here would be Winston Smith's activities in Orwell's *1984,* which included making sure that filed accounts of historical personages were in accordance with current relevancies, even to the extent of inventing them or obliterating them!). How, then, are these bureaucratized, abstract versions of clients created by staff? Firstly by consulting their expertise. We all bring to a new situation expectations (based on previous experience) of what the situation will probably turn out to be like. In areas of experience where we consider ourselves expert (e.g. our *professional* areas) our expectations are likely to become firmly established, and routine notions of 'typical cases' will emerge.[4] When confronted with an individual case to be professionally handled, we will inevitably draw on these routine ideas. Thus compilers of files can be thought of as 'on the watch' for certain types of behaviour. Files are not the result of *observing* passively 'what happened'; they are answers to questions posed, the result of testing to see which of a limited range of professionally expected possibilities best fits the case.

But files reflect not only the perspective of the individual member of the institutional staff, but in some way the purposes of the institution itself. How, then, does staff consciousness become translated into institutional purposes, and vice versa? Garfinkel suggests that staff are aware that they are working within the terms of an informal ('unformulated') contract.[5] When institutions offer a service or a process to people, they implicitly enter into a specialized contract with each client to provide plausible diagnosis and treatment. In the course of offering the service (education, medicine, the renewal of road licences) members of staff know that one of a certain range of possibilities will arise, that they will have to take certain decisions, and thereby shoulder certain responsibilities. In order to do this smoothly the institution will have to have a justification up its sleeve for whatever is chosen to be the appropriate outcome. Thus the file is a *potential* justification for an anticipated range of future actions (e.g. to 'give a good reference', to promote/demote to a different set, to pass, to fail, to warn parents, to recommend a particular curriculum course, etc.). Within this perspective the school may be thought of as contracting to educate pupils in so far as they display 'ability'. That there will be a correspondence between the pupil's ability and his educational career is the substance of the implicit contract between schools and (on the one hand) the pupil and (on the other hand) the employer. It is to this end that the pupil's abilities, achievements, and 'relevant' background factors (personality, home, health, etc.) need to be filed. The contents of pupils' files can thus be seen as a build-up to the justification of an estimate of the market value of the pupil. The school contracts with the employer and the pupil to 'get it right'. Hence my suggestion earlier that one could interpret Elaine's Final Report on Transfer to Junior School as measuring her against the relevancies of the education system: will she be worth sponsoring for educational and social success, or will she perhaps need watching as a source of institutional trouble? [6]

At this point we are clearly already talking about politics. Educational institutions are inextricably bound up with the division of labour in society. As the scale of operations has become larger, institutional decision making has come to depend more and more on information which is further and further away from the experience to which it relates, and which has been prepackaged in the light of administrative purposes. Thus one can suggest that in contrast to an original sociable reality created between people who are interacting face to face, modern institutions have created an administrative reality based on files of documents assembled with the specific purpose that when the time comes an administrator will be able, without moving from his office, to take a decision concerning people who are 'under his jurisdiction'. Thus the files make possible the removal of decisions from the contexts in which their origins and results are experienced (this, of course, has been the long-standing complaint against bureaucracy, from Tolstoy to Illich). Thus, it is partly by means of the fact that the social world has been abstracted into the bureaucrat's files that the social world is brought under the control of the bureaucrat; and so the division of labour becomes a hierarchical pattern of rulers and ruled. 'The social organization preserves conceptions and means of description which represent the world as it is for those who rule it, rather than as it is for those who are ruled' (Dorothy Smith).[7]

Applying this to the use of files in educational institutions, one can see general analogies with Marx's theory of alienation. In a capitalist economic system alienating relationships of production transform the industrial worker and his product into commodities for the commercial market; in a capitalist education system alienating relationships of perception and communication (e.g. (amongst other things) the creation by staff of files on pupils) transform the pupil and his school work into commodities for the employment market.[8] Files, one might sum up, make available the pupil's 'exchange value'.

Conclusion

I am grateful to the student who responded to the above argument by saying: 'So what do you propose we should do about it?' Clearly, having argued the crucial social and political importance of educational files, it would be Quixotic to propose that we teachers should suddenly attempt to do without them (for example, one problem is that it is the existence of these apparently objective educational assessments which I have criticized that enables working class individuals to claim positions where previously they would have been excluded by crude forms of nepotism and discrimination). Thus it is important to distinguish between a radical critique of social forms based on theories of a possible transformed reality, and an exploration of strategies and possibilities in the present for immediate action. But actions and critiques are of course always linked. I hope that, in the light of the general critique I have presented, the following limited suggestions for action will seem both politically relevant and feasible.

1 A file should always be open to the subject of the file (or, in the case of a younger child, to parents). If a matter is to be officially filed it must be possible to justify its inclusion. If I cannot justify my comments to the satisfaction of the person about whom I am making them, then an adjudication is needed. So appeals machinery must be available (this degree of honesty and administrative openness should be non-controversial – it isn't, of course!).

2 We should attempt to limit our contributions to students' and pupils' files to materials which we are convinced would be of *direct* use to the next teacher, and we should phrase our comments as suggestions, theories, and possibilities, rather than as descriptions of pupils' characteristics. Also it might be worth agreeing to file copies of what we take to be the pupils' best work, if it means one can avoid presenting general assessments of pupils on an A-E scale.

3 In a more general way we need to try to influence the procedures by which people are allocated to jobs. For example, at present bureaucratic and especially educational documentation is made to seem to *qualify* people for particular types of employment, and therefore the decision to employ or not to employ can be at all levels a 'management' decision (from above) ('He will come to work with you'), rather than a 'worker' decision ('Let's have him to come and work with us'). As teachers, therefore, we should encourage and cooperate with people in

the work contexts to which we send our pupils and students in considering ways in which appointments in those contexts could be made more democratically. In that way we would be taking some of the pressure away from our own file-creating activities. Thus we are reminded that, although we can best work for change in the situations where we are involved and responsible, the reform of schools cannot be separated from the reform of other institutions.

Notes

1 P. Rance, *Record-Keeping in the Progressive Primary School* (London, Ward Lock, 1972), p. 16.

2 Ibid., see especially pp. 36, 49, 59, 64.

3 M. Weber, 'Some Characteristics of Bureaucracy' in L. A. Coser and B. Rosenberg (eds), *Sociological Theory: A Book of Readings* (London, Collier-Macmillan, 1964, 2nd ed.), pp. 465-73.

4 See A. Cicourel, *The Social Organization of Juvenile Justice* (New York, John Wiley, 1968).

5 See H. Garfinkel, 'Good Organizational Reasons for Bad Clinic Records' in R. Turner, *Ethnomethodology* (Harmondsworth, Penguin, 1974).

6 Of course I am not suggesting that the teacher who wrote those few tentative lines about seven-year-old Elaine would have explained the report in these terms!

7 D. Smith, 'The Social Construction of Documentary Reality' *Sociological Inquiry*, vol. 44 (1974). Clearly the social organization of the communications industries also exemplifies how 'means of description which represent the world' are linked with the distribution of power.

8 See I. Hextall and M. Sarup, 'School Knowledge, Evaluation, and Alienation', paper presented to the BSA Conference (1975), and published in M. Young and G. Whitty (eds), *Society, State and Schooling* (Brighton, Falmer Press, 1976). See also I. Hextall's Chapter 5 in this volume.

Chapter 7

Textbooks and classroom knowledge : the politics of explanation and description

Jan Hardy

> . . . it was soft and blubbery and long and rubbery. God, he'd havε a fit.
> Not God, you know, Einstein . . .
> (Student, North London High School, Spring 1974).

Textbooks provide an important means of students acquiring knowledge within the context of learning at school. In the past, the content of school textbooks largely came into question when either the scope of the examination curriculum changed, or when the book reached such an age that, even at school level, its validity came into question. More recently, it is the form of textbooks, the way in which content is presented and transmitted, which has attracted critical attention. This concern has mirrored a change in the general objectives involved in both teaching and learning. While previously it was the factual content of a 'body of knowledge' which was to be taught, the emphasis has moved towards the teaching of concepts and the development of understanding. Learning is seen somewhat less as a passive mastery of fact. Rather, it is the discovery of underlying patterns and an appreciation of form which is encouraged. This change in direction has already led to a considerable rethink, both in the nature of school textbooks, and in the way in which books are used. Two forms of text have emerged. Firstly, those which either provide instructions for students, or for teachers on behalf of students, on suitable tasks and projects for discovery learning. Secondly, 'back up', or supplementary material, similar to the more 'traditional' textbooks, but designed to add both breadth and depth to students' own productions.

I shall argue here that this particular 'solution' has been largely unsatisfactory to both teachers and their students. The 'bridge' between discovery and the mastery of a 'body of knowledge' remains a wide one. Teachers have generally found discovery and experimentation no substitutes for reading and 'chalk and talk'. A great deal of direction has been required to make discovery methods worthwhile, and even then they form an addition to, rather than a substitute for, direct teaching. Given the constraints on time in following an examination syllabus, such an addition understandably becomes somewhat of a luxury. This phenomenon is clearly important to examine, for it seems to suggest that there is something in the nature of our teaching methods or something about our students, which prevents them from taking part in 'authentic' knowledge production.

In this article I shall be examining the form which 'textbook' knowledge takes. Science textbooks will be used as an example, but I would suggest strongly that my analysis applies more widely than to the field of science. I shall suggest that the form which textbooks take involves a particular view of knowledge, which, taken over by its readers, irrevocably separates them both from its (the textbook's) and from their own knowledge production. It is not the epistemological status of established 'bodies of knowledge' that I am examining or questioning here, but rather the social relations involved both in their production and acquisition.

Below are three extracts from textbooks, concerning the conversion of liquid sulphur to plastic sulphur. All three describe and explain this physical phenomenon in a factual way. By 'factual' I mean that each extract is not only a description and explanation of what happens when liquid sulphur is added to cold water, but also that it is written in such a way that it can be read as 'what actually happens' when liquid sulphur is added to cold water. That the three 'texts' are different is a feature of scientific knowledge which is frequently neglected. Scientific knowledge stands not only to describe and explain phenomena as facts, but also to describe and explain them in particular contexts; that is, with a 'particular audience' and 'purpose' in mind. In the case of the three texts below, some indication of the particular audiences and purposes may be found in the prefacing (as shown).

Text 1

Preface: The object of this book is to provide a complete introduction to chemistry, and it therefore contains a subject matter for four years' work . . .

If liquid sulphur at, or near, its boiling point is poured into cold water (quenched), plastic sulphur, a gummy substance, is formed. X-ray examinations show that the atoms in it are arranged in chains, and this suggests the same arrangement in the liquid from which it is formed. This arrangement resembles that of the atoms in plastics, but it is unstable, and the atoms rearrange themselves into a hard mass, consisting partly of S_8 molecules, and partly of the complex arrangement of atoms in amorphous sulphur.[1]

Text 2

Preface: The object of this book is to present inorganic chemistry in this way (. . . a mature science founded on clear powerful principles which bind the facts . . .) to students beginning their advanced study of the subject in schools and universities.

Plastic sulphur is made by melting roll sulphur, heating the liquid to a temperature near to its boiling point, then pouring it into cold water. The resulting solid, plastic sulphur, is transparent, and of a colour varying from amber to rich brown. The solid has little elasticity, but can be kneaded like putty, and pulled into very long thin fibres, in a way similar to glass softened by strong heating. Also, like glass, it is a highly viscous super-cooled liquid, which has been shown to consist of long chains , each containing thousands of sulphur atoms arranged in spirals, with eight atoms per turn. Insoluble in all liquids including carbon disulphide, it reverts gradually to orthorhombic sulphur.[2]

Text 3

Preface: . . . the content of this book . . . provides a reasonable achievement for students at the BSc Honours level in British Universities, and at the senior year of first year graduate level in American Universities . . .

Plastic or amorphous sulfur is obtained by quenching liquid sulfur heated to $160^{o}C$ or more, for example by pouring it into water. This material can be drawn into fibres of considerable tensile strength, and X-ray studies have shown that the fibres contain helical chains of sulfur atoms with eight sulfur atoms per cycle of that helix. Amorphous sulfur can be made in other ways, but in all cases it is insoluble in organic solvents, and slowly reverts to the crystalline form.[3]

A scientist's production of knowledge, of which the above texts might be seen as examples, reflects his sense of what is appropriate in terms of his audience. How do such concerns enter the productions? Since each extract can be read factually, these concerns are not found directly. If this were the case, the texts would read 'What I think you need to know, and what I think you can understand about this particular phenomenon, for the following reasons', rather than 'What there is to know about this particular phenomenon'. The prefacing appears simply to restrict who it is there are to be facts for, without telling us how such concerns enter the text itself. Instead, one might look at the choice of what is excluded or included in each text, and at the concepts and categories used in describing and explaining. Such choices will be made not only in relating to the phenomenon in question, but also to relate to the intended audience.

Let us take one or two examples from the texts

(a) *Appearance and physical properties of plastic sulphur.*

Text 1:   ' . . . a gummy substance . . . but it is unstable, and the atoms rearrange themselves into a hard mass . . .'

Text 2:   ' . . . transparent, and of a colour varying from amber to rich brown. The solid has little elasticity, but can be kneaded like putty, and pulled into very long thin fibres. . . . Insoluble in all liquids, including carbon disulphide, it reverts gradually to orthorhombic sulphur'.

Text 3:   'This material can be drawn into fibres of considerable tensile strength . . . in all cases it is insoluble in organic solvents, and slowly reverts to the crystalline form'.

What is clear is that, out of all the possible aspects of appearance and physical properties, each author has selected certain aspects as being important. These particular aspects are then conceptualized in a way

89

which is considered suitable, not only to describe them, but also to describe them to the intended audience.

(b) *Structures of plastic sulphur*

> *Text 1:* 'X-ray examinations show that the atoms in it are arranged in chains. . . .'
>
> *Text 2:* 'has been shown to consist of long chains, each containing thousands of sulphur atoms arranged in spirals, with eight atoms per turn.'
>
> *Text 3:* 'X-ray studies have shown that the fibres contain helical chains of sulfur atoms, with eight sulfur atoms per cycle of that helix.'

Here, a clear 'hierarchy' of 'sophistication' appears in the way the texts are organized.

As author, or teller, the scientist's subjectivity enters into the organization of his 'knowing a phenomenon', into 'knowledge of a phenomenon'. Although such an analysis may be available here, in that we can suspend judgement over the factual nature of any particular scientific statement, be it verbal or written, it is not available in relating to scientific statements on a purely factual basis. When this is done, the reader or hearer enters into a social relationship between himself, the author or teller, and other knowers, as a consequence of the social organization of the fact. This is not available to him, but appears as facts about the phenomenon. For example, to know that the structure of plastic sulphur is 'chains of atoms' (see Text 1), as a fact about sulphur, is also to enter into a social relationship with other knowers who may know the structure of sulphur to be 'spiral chains' (see Text 2), or 'helical chains' (see Text 3). Such a relationship is recognized and produced in the way in which facts are organized with respect to their intended audiences, but is not available to the knowers in relating to them as facts. Hence, though social relations are necessarily implicated in the organization of knowledge, they disappear in a factual product.

What are the consequences of this analysis to the teaching of science? In so far as school science is taught factually, that is, in so far as students can relate to school science as a series of facts about the world, it suggests that they enter into hierarchical and structural relationships of an unquestioned kind, where the way in which they know the world is in fact determined by others for them. Such a position, with its undertones of dogmatism and indoctrination, is clearly one which science teachers would wish to avoid. Indeed, in science education today, there has been a trend towards discovery learning and student participation in experiment and fact finding, which would appear to invite students to 'make their own knowledge': 'We think that, however chemistry is taught, it is learned in an individual way, and that every student makes his own individual pattern of knowledge' Text 1.

The following transcript is of some pupils discussing, on their own, an experiment in which they prepared the allotropes of sulphur. I am presenting an extract in which they discuss the preparation of plastic sulphur, so that it can be compared to the extracts on the same topics provided in the texts above. The

students were given only cookbook instructions on what to do. No indication was given of what to expect, or of how to explain it. The discussion group consists of students from separate experimental groups. They are in the fourth year of a secondary school, and have completed two terms only of chemistry.

A: Now, Experiment 2. Which one are you going to do as 2 then?   1

C: The ... no ... in the water.

A: First you. What happened to your one?

C: Well...

A: What did you do?   5

(It seems important to note here that A is not in fact a teacher, though his responses at times are interestingly teacher-like.)

C: It changed colour.

A: This is the method.

C: It changed colour as you were heating it, like the first one, and as you poured it in, it cooled and went all rubbery in long streaks.

D: Like rubber solution glue.   10

C: Yeah.

A: Didn't you notice that it was already treacle when you were pouring it in?

C: Yes it was. It was very hard.

A: Like treacle, right, very thick treacle. Now. Oh, you've got some-   15
thing. You'd better keep that, because I don't know, I don't
think ... (Laughter.)

B: It's all hard.

C: How did you get yours like that?

B: Uh!   20

A: No, because, look, only some of it went. You see, it's brown there. It's yellow there.

B: I know.

A: You (untranscribable) twice.

D: We found that. Listen, when you ... when you ...   25

B: First one's all right, my one.

D: Put the sulphur in water. You got a brown outside, you know, (Yeah.) round with the water.

F: It oxidizes. I should imagine, you know, then, hyd. H_2Os (Yeah.)
and inside where the water and oxygen had an effect on it, you got   30
a yellow.

C: Ah, but we didn't have that.

A: Anybody.

C: It was brown all the way through.

A: Yeah. Same with ours.   35

B: It went straight down.

A: Could anyone give an ex.?

B: Kind of brown.

A: Can anyone . . .? On our one, what we did, we put the sulphur in
the crucible and we heated it. Now, after we heated it, we found that   40
er, when we put the lid on it, when we left it there, you know, for a
little while, as in the other one, it began to evaporate. I don't know. . .

C: What began to evaporate?

A: It began to go down. Now, I don't know if it's (untranscribable). . . .

D: Do you think it could have been boiling, you know, and . . .?   45

C: Yeah, some of it.

D: The atoms in it were excited, and therefore. . .

C: Exciting, huh?

D: And, therefore, were coming out of the cruc . . ., like when you boil
water.   50

?   Experiment 2 not boil right. You don't have to.

D: You know, like when you boil water right, you know it, all the
atoms shoots out as steam. (Yeah.) You see it bubbled up.

A: Didn't you notice that crystals formed on top, as well, with the
magnifying glass, (C: Yeah.) crystals right now. (Crystals.) What   55
could that be?

C: Could some . . . could be some impurities in the bowl.

A: This is before we poured it. The first experiment, the crystals
formed on top, and it was a thin coating too. (Yeah.) Can anyone
give an explanation for that? Could it be, um, (untranscribable) like   60
in the, you know, when we did copper, we got crystals with it. We
mixed the copper with, er, an acid, (Sulphur, we done.) and we got
crystals.

?   You mean copper sulphate?

F: Oh, you mean copper and hydrochloric acid?   65

A: Now we had sulphur, then could it combine with oxygen, for
crystals? Well, you know, we don't know about that for sure.

F: No, we don't know about that. We can only assume.

A: Assume that. Well, going on to the second one, what can anybody
give me an explanation for why it went?   70

C: (Untranscribable) . . . talking.

A: Yeah, why it went rubbery.

?   It didn't go rubbery. It went hard in water.

A: Why was it? Why didn't it go rubbery? Why didn't it go hard, the one, when it was in the water?   75

D: Could it be a force quenching it, you know. It didn't have time to solidify.

C: It went straight.

D: It went straight, and cooled so fast. (?: So fast, yeah.)

A: When we tossed ours in, and it was hot in the, er, crucible. (Yeah.)   80

C: Ours isn't hard, didn't go hard.

A: No, nor did ours. That's what I mean.

C: What it's ours didn't go hard at all. It stayed, you know. . .

A: When we took it out, it went . . . (untranscribable).

C: Ours was rubbery.   85

?   Yeah, our was completely rubber.

C: . . . (untranscribable) gone hard.

B: Ours looked rubbery, but . . . (untranscribable) did too.

C: No, but ours is still rubbery.

B: Our one . . .   90

A: Does anyone see similarities? Does anyone see the, er . . .? In the first one, we got a brown dark top, and in the second one, the whole thing went brown . . . (untranscribable). We let it solidify.

B: Yeah . . . (untranscribable) went brown.

F: Yeah, but I'm saying you got a yellow inside.   95

?   Yet, when you poured it in water. . .

B: When you poured it in water . . . (untranscribable) break up.

F: Well, that's what I said. You know, maybe it oxidizes water, and thing, and only the outside oxidized. It's still got its oxide coating.

C: Wouldn't you get an acid, as it hits the water, because you've got   100 hydrogen, haven't you?

A: Hydrogen, yes. (Sulphur.) Sulphuric acid.

F: Will do, yes.

A: Yeah. Did anyone see bubbles forming on the side of the beaker? (No. No.) On mine, I don't know why that is. . . .   105

D: Well, that could well have been, you know, er, like even if you drop, um, you know, er. . . . Say you dropped a cherry in water, the air what on the cherry bubbles out . . . .

In the first part of this transcript, particularly lines 1 to 28, the students are concerned with describing what happened to each other. To do so, they elicit features of their everyday world (which they may assume they hold in common). That is, they extend their experiences of the everyday world to the experiment. We can notice how certain everyday descriptive categories are invoked to describe the experiment. Everyday experiences of shape, colour, texture, physical state; everyday actions and time, for example, allow them to organize their experience of sulphur into a description, in the same way as they might be used to describe their experience of any other feature of their worlds.

Shape:	'Long streaks' (line 9), 'crystals' (line 55 and others), 'thin coating' (line 59 and others).
Colour:	'Changed colour (line 6), 'brown . . . yellow' (line 21-2), 'brown dark top' (line 92), 'yellow inside' (line 95).
Texture:	'Rubbery' (line 9), 'like rubber solution glue' (line 10), 'it's all hard' (line 18).
Physical state:	Like 'treacle' (line 15), 'like rubber solution glue' (line 10).
Everyday actions:	'Pouring' (line 13), 'it went straight down' (line 36).
Time:	'It changed colour as you were heating it, like the first one, and as you poured it in, it cooled and went all rubbery in long streaks' (lines 8-9).

The description here also orders the observations. This order is made available through students' everyday understanding of how time enters into descriptions.

Some things which are seen are excluded as observations, by common agreement. For example, the laboratory in which they perform the experiment, and the bunsen burner used for heating, are never mentioned. Other observations are discussed, and rejected afterwards. See, for example, at the end of the transcript (lines 104-8), where a student notices that 'bubbles' appear on the side of the beaker when the liquid sulphur is poured into the beaker. Here, the observation is rejected on the grounds that this is a common happening when anything is dropped into water (a cherry is used as an example), and therefore does not count as an observation.

In the second part of the transcript (line 29), there is a move towards attempts at explanation. Here, they use various 'scientific' concepts to relate the phenomena. Oxidation (line 29), evaporation (line 42), 'atomic theory' (line 47), crystallization (line 55), and force (line 76), for example, are used to explain aspects of the phenomenon. Such positions, taken from previous knowledge of science, cannot express the students' everyday experience of the phenomena, but are taken from science as ways of describing and explaining the phenomena. They are selected in a context of explaining these phenomena, where certain aspects are experienced as similar, in varying ways, to other phenomena whose explanations have been given in these terms. For example, the formation of crystals leads to postulating the involvement of an acid. Such an explanation makes sense in a context where students' previous experience of crystal formation is limited to making salts from acids (see lines 55-68 and 100-3).

Let us now re-examine aspects of the three factual 'texts' on this phenomenon, and compare them to the students' productions.

1 'If liquid sulphur at or near the boiling point is poured into cold water. . . .' (Text 1)

It is clear from the transcript that students want to address the liquid formed when sulphur is heated in more detail than this.

C: It changed colour as you were heating it (8).

A: It was already treacle when you were pouring it in (12, 13). Like treacle, right, very thick treacle now (15).

If we refer to the second textbook, we find, under a heading 'Dynamic Equilibrium in Liquid Sulphur', the following: 'Sulphur melts . . . to form an amber coloured mobile liquid. On further heating, the colour darkens, and viscosity increases, until at about $190^{O}C$ the liquid is dark red brown, then quite suddenly becomes so viscous that it will not pour.' So we find that these observations by students are quite sound. That these observations do not appear in Texts 1, 2 or 3 about the formation of plastic sulphur is a function of the way the scientists have organized their knowledge. Such observations must be available every time the experiment is performed, but, as a consequence of organizing the observations into 'properties of liquid sulphur' and 'formation of plastic sulphur' (the rules for which are not available to the pupils), they are left out from statements concerning the formation of plastic sulphur. That these rules are undisclosed means that the students might be seen or see themselves as making irrelevant or inappropriate observations.

2 'Plastic sulphur, a gummy substance, is formed. . . .' (Text 2) 'The resulting solid, plastic sulphur, is transparent, and of a colour varying from amber to rich brown. The solid has little elasticity, but can be kneaded like putty, and pulled into very long fibres.' (Text 2)

'. . . plastic sulfur. This material can be drawn into fibres of considerable tensile strength.' (Text 3)

In the students' transcript, they too experience the solid formed, and describe their experience of it:

C: . . . rubbery, in long streaks. . . .(9)

D: Like rubber solution glue.(10)

What they 'fail' to discover, however, is that this 'rubbery' substance is sulphur. Now, it is quite clear, it seems to me, that, simply from this one experiment, the knowledge that the 'gummy' substance formed is sulphur is not directly available to the students. Indeed, for it to be available to them would either presuppose a knowledge that this is so, or a number of other experiments which enable them to produce that knowledge. However, the 'other experiments' which make plastic sulphur a reasonable knowledge production are not available to students as direct experiences, *nor,* and this is more important, as referred to experiences of the authors of the texts. They

can then only relate to such a conclusion factually, and to their own conclusions, as wrong.

3 The 'unknowable' nature of the solid formed also has important consequences
   for their attempts at explanation. They attempt to explain by trying to
   'connect' their observations, starting from the liquid formed from melting
   sulphur and water. They cannot presuppose the solid to be sulphur.

F: It oxidizes. . . . I should imagine you know, then, hyd, H_2Os, (Yeah.) and
    inside where the water and oxygen had an effect on it, you got a yellow.
    (29-31).

Here, the changes in appearance and colour are connected to similar experiences in a previous experiment, in which he has been told that oxidation
takes place.

A: Now, we had sulphur. Then could it combine with oxygen . . . form
    crystals? Well, you know, we don't know about that for sure.

F: No, we don't know about that. We can only assume.

A: Assume that. Well, going on to the second one, can anyone give me an
    explanation for why it went?

C: . . . talking.

D: Yeah, why it remains rubbery.

?: Didn't . . . rubbery, it went hard . . . in water.

A: Why was it? Why did it go rubbery? Why didn't it go hard, the one, when
    it was in water?

D; Could it have been a force quenching it, you know, it didn't have time to
    solidify?

C: It went straight.

D: It went straight, and cooled so fast. (66-79).

Here the explanation is an inability to crystallize, because it 'cooled so fast'.
From an observation that crystals were formed when the liquid was allowed
to cool, they suggest an incomplete crystallization for this particular phenomenon. If we compare this to Textbook 2, again in the section in which
liquid sulphur is considered, we find: 'When this liquid is cooled suddenly,
the equilibrium is fixed, and plastic sulphur is formed.' The similarity
between this explanation and the pupil's is, I would argue, quite startling.

In the text extracts, however, we find an absence of any explicit explanation.
The reason for this, it seems to me, is that, since the texts presuppose that the
liquid is 'liquid sulphur' and the solid is 'plastic sulphur', the explanation is
implicit (i.e. that the atoms and molecules arrange themselves in a certain way
on cooling).

In my analysis so far I have tried to show how students describing and
explaining a phenomenon may be seen to be acting within the limits of their
everyday and scientific experience. I have also tried to point out how the kind of
descriptions and explanations we provide as teachers, or which are provided in

textbooks, while standing for 'what actually happens', are in fact not only scientific, but also social organizations of 'what is experienced as happening', into 'what is to count as knowledge of what happens'. When we regard disparagingly the possibilities of students learning scientific knowledge through experiment, we disregard, it seems to me, the nature of the scientific knowledge which we expect them to acquire. That is, we ourselves treat scientific knowledge as 'what actually happens', rather than recognizing the way in which it is organized.

The advent of discovery learning marks the opening of a context in which we ask pupils to participate in knowledge production. At the same time, its beginnings have created certain problems for teachers and their students, in displaying an apparent dichotomy between their own productions and those more formal accounts found in textbooks. It is to these sources that students go for further information and detail. As I have tried to show, the appearance of these texts is such that students are confronted by a 'body of knowledge', which denies its own production. As a consequence, they may only relate to the text in a factual way, and their own productions may appear pathological. The transcript below is extracted from a group of pupils discussing the previous transcript (involving the discussion of the formation of plastic sulphur). The students have been provided with a 'formal' explanation of the formation of plastic sulphur.

A: Oh no, it was a bit vague, right? It was vague, and if you got Einstein in here, he probably wouldn't be able to work out what we were on about. (Shut up.)

C: . . . Columbo.

A: It was. It was soft and blubbery, and long and rubbery. God, he'd have a fit. Not God, you know, Einstein.

G: Yeah, now look, you see, now. Oh, where was it, um: 'you know when we did copper with, er, an acid, sulphur we done, and we got crystals'. (Laughter.) This . . . doesn't mean 'copper sulphate crystals', if you say crystals.

A: And we . . . say . . . we didn't go.

G: What colour they are, what?

A: We didn't go on about them, or anything.

G: You took that copper sulphate. That's got nothing to do with it. I don't know what copper sulphate. . . .

It would not be surprising to find that these students have gained little from their practical experience, regardless of the intrinsic worth, that they might prefer to reproduce a textbook account, than to reflect upon their own theorizing.

It is often regarded as incumbent on a critic to display solutions. In the field of education, such a practice seems loaded with pitfalls. While an article such as this locates its problem within the school and classroom context, its solution may be of a very different order. For example, I have suggested that the way in which school knowledge is organized reflects social relationships. Such relationships are part of wider structures than those involved in school. I have argued that, while school knowledge is indeed produced and socially organized, it appears to be fixed and asocial. The social consequences and functions of such an appearance need to be examined and explained, rather than treated as an epistemological or educational necessity. These kinds of problems are not dealt with in this article, and it may be that they cannot be raised in the context of purely educational research. To articulate educational problems, while recognizing the limited nature of the context in which they are raised, may nevertheless be useful as part of the struggle to understand them.

References

1   J. W. Davis and J. Zussman, *Introduction to Chemistry* (London, John Murray, 1968).

2   J. G. Wilson and A. B. Newall, *General and Inorganic Chemistry* (Cambridge, Cambridge University Press, 1971).

3   F. A. Cotton and G. Wilkinson, *Advanced Inorganic Chemistry: A Comprehensive Text* (Chichester, Interscience, 1972).

Chapter 8

Gradgrind's heirs: the quiz and the presentation of `knowledge´ by British television

John Tulloch

> The spectator's need nowadays to be distracted from his daily warfare is continually reproduced by that daily warfare, but just as continually in conflict with his need to be able to control his own fate. (Brecht).

Television is no more a 'window on the world' than a Shakespeare play is a 'mirror held up to Nature' but the worn image has an instructive edge. Windows occur in buildings, the concrete expression of social modes of production. Television — in its dominant form of organization in Western bourgeois society — involves a mosaic of technical devices pointed at people by people in the context of large organizations with close, problematic ties to the apparatus of the state, working through what are assumed to be shared symbolic systems — versions of the society — and subject to the formal and informal structures of power of the broadcasting organization and the containing society which it continuously interprets.

Undeniably the British 'window' does present a 'world', a dominant version of 'reality' which in practice runs across the broadcasters' self-ascribed categories of (for example) 'information', 'education' and 'entertainment' programmes. Indeed, to press a somewhat unfashionable cliché further, that version of 'reality' is implicit in the 'window' image, with its relationship between 'viewer' and 'world' outside the 'window' — *passive* viewer, *objective* world and *transparent* medium.

In other words, British television presents, with few exceptions, a view of knowledge that can be termed 'objectivistic', 'which disguises as given a world which has to be continually interpreted'.[1] It is a presentation which characteristically pretends not to be a presentation, not a version of events but those events themselves. Consider, for instance, the implications of the statement, 'Here is the Nine O'Clock News', and the opening caption of the world seen from a space capsule — a total, composed, peaceful image, a serene *overview*. Or the mating of ITN's *News at Ten* headlines with the strokes of that most naturalized, unquestionable timeteller, Big Ben.

Inescapably this is the concrete expression of an ideology. But the *illusion* of 'objectivity', of 'truth to events', means that its ideological function is masked or, in Stuart Hall's terms, 'neutralized'.[2] The realist myth that the world is 'out there' waiting to be recorded by the cameras is a version of a familiar contradiction.

This 'ideology of objectivity' derives from one of the most profound myths in the liberal ideology: the absolute distinction between fact and value, the distinction which appears as a *commonsense 'rule'* in newspaper practice as 'the distinction between facts and interpretation': the empiricist illusion, the Utopia of naturalism.[3] (my italics)

British television has evolved a repertoire of practice to sustain such illusions, involving the elaborate pretence that studio, cameras and expensive industrial operation are not there at all — that Richard Baker is, in truth, in your living room.[4] This practice is systematized by what pass for commonsense 'rules' of television production. Desmond Davis's *Grammar of Television Production* (by far the best known of a number of practice handbooks described in its blurb as 'the standard textbook on the subject') says, for example: 'Do not pan across a static scene merely to get the camera from one point of interest to another. Only pan with a moving person or object.'[5] The reason given for this rule is that: 'As soon as the camera moves independently in this way it *draws attention to itself and the technique* and distracts the mind of the audience from the subject and the content matter' (my italics). The distinction between 'facts' and 'interpretation' here is indeed 'absolute'.

British television's presentation of knowledge is part of a continuous, ongoing process of cultural reproduction. And in this sense at least it does act as a 'mirror', reflecting and affirming 'commonsense' notions of what knowledge is and what it is to be knowledgeable, taking part in the general meaning maintenance of 'commonsense' liberal positions. Political life, for example, is defined by parliamentary institutions. Official pronouncements of policy by both the BBC and IBA make such commonsense positions unreflectively explicit. Here is an extract from the *BBC Television Handbook:*

> Over a period of time the news tends to be self-balancing. Thus there may be a day when the Prime Minister makes an important political speech, which is fully reported in the news, but when there is nothing newsworthy to report from the Opposition side; a day or two later the reverse may well be the case.[6]

Later in the same passage the concept of news is more fully developed:

> The content of bulletins is manifestly dependent on the uncontrolled events which make the news, from hour to hour and from day to day. To attempt to balance it artificially would be no distort it. . . .

Thus the news is 'made' by external, unmediated events. No problem is perceived in the *selection* of these events — they are, indeed, 'uncontrolled'. And the resonance of 'manifestly' is deeply confident, asserting that 'this is the only way things *could* be' — a commonsense reflex. 'News' itself is presented as an external thing, an agglomeration of objective facts. To use Berger and Luckmann's terms, it is 'apprehended as a non-human facticity'.[7] Ultimately the argument reveals itself as circular — news is news, news is that which is newsworthy. Human activity is seen as if it were something else than a human product and in the process pragmatism transforms itself into its opposite.

Mechanical materialism, whose strength lies in its insistence upon the concept of the reflection of objective reality and in its maintenance of this view in aesthetics, is transformed into idealism as a result of its incapacity to comprehend motion, history . . . .[8]

In a sense, the genres of news and documentary production are those in which this objectivistic view of knowledge is most clear cut, though embedded and formidably difficult not to 'take for granted'. But I have contended that the objectivistic view is a general characteristic of British television.

In what ways does this view manifest itself? One programming form that explicitly concerns itself with knowledge whilst claiming the status of 'entertainment' is the television quiz. The current television quizzes – such as *University Challenge, Top of the Form, Ask the Family, Sale of the Century* and *Mastermind* – command vast audiences. The genre provides some of the most durable television programmes and – apart from occasional allegations of rigging – among the least problematic for the broadcasting agencies. If it is accepted that television plays *some* role (of unestablished magnitude) in the reproduction of an objectivistic view of knowledge it is at least reasonable to enquire what part such a popular genre has in the process.

There are several strands in the development of the quiz genre. One root perhaps lies in the 'display of knowledge in a casual form'[9] that started with *The Brains Trust* during the last war. Another root for the form lies in the long-established parlour games of the middle classes. By the end of the war a radio genre had been created (in the form of programmes like *Round Britain Quiz*) that I shall describe as the 'intellectual' quiz.

But in addition the demands of the war – the urgent need to maintain a consensus and therefore to reach a mass, working class audience – helped to create a second distinctive strand in the genre which I will call the 'populist' form of the quiz. The first example was the hugely successful *Have a Go* series.

Although *Have a Go* was as concerned with the *performance* of its contestants as an intellectual quiz, the whole point of the questions and of the performance they elicited was different. Wilfred Pickles, the master of ceremonies, used the questions as a means of getting the participants to talk as 'ordinary folks'. Rather than admiring or learning from their performance, the audience was expected to sympathetically identify with them. In a sense the contestant was Everyman. And this made the situation posed by the show accessible to a wide working class audience in a way that has never been true of the intellectual quiz. Broadcast from a different location each week – factories, working men's clubs, public halls – the show excelled at orchestrating that peculiarly British and Northern mixture of jocular good humour and sentimental sense of solidarity caught in such national catchphrases as 'Have a go, Joe' and 'Give 'im the money, Mabel.'

However, the creation of commercial television, the translation of the quiz into television terms and the influence of American formats have contributed to transform both the style and the objectives of the populist quiz. But there are two strands still to be discerned. The intellectual and populist quiz offer what seem to be radically different forms of entertainment. But, whilst the values

101

they affirm appear to be contradictory, I shall argue that they function in such a way as to complement each other, each as much a part of the liberal ideology of British television as news programming. The analysis which follows is an attempt to articulate this argument in a concrete way by examining a representative show from each strand of the genre.

The two strands compared: Mastermind v. Sale of the Century

. . . dominant in the culture . . . is the demand to be able to think and act quickly, a demand most clearly revealed (and success rewarded) in the exam system.[10]

'How did it all begin?' asks the executive producer of *Mastermind* in a recently published collection of questions from the show.

It began in the quiz unit offices of the Entertainment Department of Outside Broadcasts — a unit that has been responsible for *Television Top of the Form, Quiz Ball* and *Transworld Top Team.* We produced a television version of the *Brain of Britain* some years ago, but I had always thought that television ought to be able to produce an intellectual quiz that was entirely original.[11]

It may be unfair to ascribe too much weight to Wright's use of the term 'intellectual' in a passage from what clearly sets out to be a light-hearted introduction. But the usage is significant. The dominant sense is that given in the OED of 'appealing to or engaging the intellect'. But it has other resonances in British culture. The chief of them is concerned with the holders of intellectual powers — what the OED drily defines as 'an intellectual being; a person possessing or supposed to possess superior powers of intellect'. The carefully expressed ambiguity of 'possessing or supposed to possess' points to what Raymond Williams has recently described as a 'social tension around the word':

. . . ranging from an old kind of opposition to a group of people who use theory or even organized knowledge to make judgements on general matters, to a different but sometimes related opposition to elites who claim not only specialized but directing kinds of knowledge . . . [12]

Wright's statement is a claim for cultural legitimacy for a form relatively low in status. In a sense it is a gesture at what are felt to be 'serious', 'legitimate' intellectual fields. Pierre Bourdieu suggests that this concern is a characteristic of Western culture:

. . . in a given society at a given moment in time not all cultural signs — theatrical performances, sporting spectacles, recitals of songs, poetry or chamber music, operettas or operas — are equal in dignity and value, nor do they call forth the same approach with the same degree of insistence . . . the various systems of expression from the theatre to television are objectively organized *according to a hierarchy independent of individual opinions that defines cultural legitimacy* and its degrees.[13] (my italics)

Mr Wright's statement is also useful in revealing something of the pressures on producers to create an 'original' form of the same formula. This form, he says, 'gradually took shape from the basic concept of a single contestant with an interrogator firing questions'. Entertainment and education uneasily nudge elbows here. The basic concept is a dramatic one — the formula, for instance, of innumerable war films, courtroom dramas, etc. Clearly the formula has obvious advantages for television — supplying that element of visual drama presumably lacking in quiz shows directly translated to television from radio.

But the concept also carries resonances of a particular type of educational relationship — one not apparent to Wright but undeniably there. A good embodiment of this relationship is located in the novel to which my title refers:

Girl number twenty ... Give me your definition of a horse ...

In M'Choakumchild's classroom there is only one 'right' answer to that question:

Quadruped. Graminivorous. Forty teeth, namely twenty-four grinders, four eye teeth, and twelve incisive. Sheds coat in the spring; in marshy countries sheds hoofs too ....

What are the implications of this kind of educational relationship? John Holt illuminates the link between 'right answers' and the formation of attitudes:

Practically everything we do in school tends to make children answer-centred. In the first place, right answers pay off. Schools are a kind of temple of worship for 'right answers' and *the only way to get ahead is to lay plenty of them on the altar.* The chances are good that teachers themselves are answer-centred ... One ironic consequence is that children are too busy to think.[14] (my italics)

Later in his introduction Wright defines the necessary qualifications for a contestant on *Mastermind:*

To qualify as *Mastermind* material you have to know your chosen subject thoroughly to stand any chance at all. Couple the degree of excellence in a given subject with a *sharp, decisive and concise mind* and you have the qualifications required to enter for the title 'Mastermind of the United Kingdom'. (my italics)

The reification of the participant — '*Mastermind* material' — goes hand in hand with the reification of knowledge in this statement. Commonsense notions of what constitutes intellectual ability — 'sharp, decisive and concise mind' — are linked to the notion of a delimited 'given subject' in which 'excellence' can be displayed.

The gesture at 'intellectual' status is a characteristic of *Mastermind.* It is always prerecorded at a university — a location emphasized in preprogramme trailers and during the show itself. The programme adheres to a rigid ritual. Left of frame on the establishing long shot sits chairman Magnus Magnusson, at a desk facing an empty chair right of frame. The four contenders — Magnusson so describes them — sit together in the front row of the audience.

Contenders are called individually to the chair facing Magnusson. The same introduction is made for each contender each week in the form of an interrogation — 'Your name? Your occupation?' On the night I took detailed notes the contenders described themselves as: a systems analyst, a law student, a chartered surveyor, and a coal miner. Such a range of contestants is untypical for the programme on at least two counts. The great majority of programmes include contenders from the educational professions — university or college lecturers and teachers. And contenders from working class occupations are in a tiny minority — indeed the programme that night rather stressed its coal miner in the way the Open University in the past has stressed the 'steelmaker from Scunthorpe' among its students.

Contenders might first answer questions on a 'special subject' of their own choice. In the second part of the show they answer 'general knowledge' questions. Contenders answer as many questions as they can in two minutes. They can 'pass' a question — in which case Magnusson gives the 'right' answer at the end of their time. But if they get the answer 'wrong' they are given the 'right' answer at once, losing time in the process.

The systems analyst opts for 'The Life and Works of Isambard Kingdom Brunel'. Questions range from 'Why was he turned upside down?' to 'At what age did he master Euclid?' and 'How many cigars did his cigar box hold?' Having opted for 'The City of Rome' the law student is asked a series of 'historical' and 'topographical' questions such as 'What happened to the bronze panels in the Pantheon?'

During the interrogation the auditorium lights are dimmed whilst a spotlight illuminates the contender. The principal shot during question and answer sessions is a medium close up of the contender, with the score superimposed left of frame. The dominant imagery therefore is that of an isolated individual under pressure, performing 'well' or 'badly' according to the rules of the game, competing with others in the same situation.

One intriguing aspect of the show's design is the way that it directly penalizes thinking — in the sense of hesitation or pauses for thought, consideration of possible alternatives, etc. The main pressure contenders face is time — those who pause to think lose time and points. As a winning tactic it is better to 'pass' than risk a 'wrong' answer and a time-consuming correction from Magnusson. To paraphrase John Holt, one ironic consequence is that contenders appear to be too busy to think. As Trevor Pateman observes, 'To speak without thinking implies unselfconsciousness of what one is saying, its status and even the very fact of speaking'.[15] In the same way the quiz also penalizes long description, in line with Wright's prescription for ideal *Mastermind* material 'sharp, decisive and concise'.

Both producer and programme make certain implicit claims about the nature of knowledge. In *Mastermind*'s terms, knowledge is a *thing* which can be *possessed*. Possession is demonstrated by skill and agility in the use of 'facts'. The overview of knowledge implied is that of a constellation of rigidly defined 'subjects' with a content of 'facts'. With few exceptions the bulk of these facts fit easily into a traditional, received, liberal definition of the 'Humanities' — principally History and Literature.[16] Subjects in a recent collection of *Mastermind* questions range from French Literature to Scandinavian Mythology, Tudor

History to Assassination and Murders, the Sea and Ships and the History of Aeronautics. The components in fact are those of a 'middlebrow' culture, with the popular forms of the biography, the novel and the colour supplement article. Science is present in Chemistry, Mammals and Astronomy but is much less frequent as a category — I suspect that this is a result of preprogramme planning on the programme makers assumption that only a relatively small proportion of the audience will have much acquaintance with Science at all.

Within the restrictions of the programme's format it is difficult to see how questions could be cast in anything but a fixed 'How? When? Where?' format of 'convergent' questions. Expecting 'Why?' questions is like demanding conversational answers to a crossword puzzle. It is true that 'Why?' questions do appear, but in a particular, restricted form — that is, 'Why (for what one reason did)?' etc. Thus: 'Why was he [Brunel] turned upside down?'

Such a view of 'knowledge' abolishes explanation. Inside such a definition of intellectual competence there *can* be no explanation, rather as though the historical continuum was defined as the Chronicle of Events in Pears Cyclopaedia. The type of verbal exchanges that go on in *Mastermind* are akin to what Postman and Weingartner call 'Guess what I'm thinking questions'. In the teaching situation they outline 'what students mostly do . . . is guess what the teacher wants them to say. Constantly, they must supply the Right Answer.'[17] They attempt to define certain 'messages' that come out of such situations:

> Recall is the highest form of intellectual achievement, and the collection of unrelated 'facts' is the goal of education. The voice of authority is to be trusted and valued more than independent judgement.
> There is always a single, unambiguous Right Answer to a question.
> *English is not history and history is not science and science is not art and art is not music* . . . (my italics)

Within the format of *Mastermind* both questions and answers are curiously devoid of meaning in themselves. What is the meaning of the 'fact' that Isambard Kingdom Brunel's cigar case held a certain number of cigars? The answer can only be that its meaning resides in its context — that is, it is the answer to a crossword puzzle, the occasion for a certain kind of performance that stands for the notion of knowledge and what it is to be knowledgeable which the programme presents.

This view of knowledge presents itself in an institutional context. It derives its legitimacy from an educational system that broadly promulgates the same view of knowledge. If this is not the case, how else can the fact be explained that *Television Top of the Form* employs real schools — with presumably enthusiastic support from the relevant authorities — or that *University Challenge* pits real universities against each other?

In the same way *Mastermind* roots itself on actual university campuses (including the Open University!) and in 'subjects' with questions supplied by 'authorities' (for example, questions for the subject 'British Politics since 1900' were set by Dr David Butler).[18] The view of intellectual competence that the programme presents grows from and is buttressed by a dominant social notion of

105

what constitutes the 'intellectual'.

Sale of the Century represents the second, populist, strand in the genre. Occupying a time slot early on Independent Television's Saturday evening (*Mastermind* is broadcast on BBC2 for a weekday evening) its audience is roughly three times that for *Mastermind*.

There appear to be few similarities in format between the two programmes. In *Sale of the Century* the three contestants sit in a row behind desks adorned with score panels facing the question master. But the 'score' is numbered in pounds rather than points. Contestants compete in answering questions posed by the quizmaster, Nicholas Parsons. The first contestant to press his buzzer in response to each question gets the chance to answer.

Questions are linked to sums of money and are arranged in the widely used 'starter' and 'bonus' system. At certain points during the show the flow of questions ceases and a curtain goes up to reveal a particular prize item 'on offer' at a 'price' that is a fraction of its market value — a feature emphasized in the description given of each item. Contestants use their buzzers to 'buy' the revealed object in competition with each other. Thus they amass cash and consumer goods in exchange for cash. But there are advantages in 'saving' money not 'buying' goods, for at the end of the show the contestant with the highest cash total 'wins' and is given the chance to buy the star bargain which is worth several hundred pounds. As the title suggests, the claims that the show makes for 'intellectual' status are minimal. Instead of competing for a title such as 'Mastermind of the United Kingdom' — a prize in a sense external to the show — contestants in *Sale of the Century* compete for the visible cash and goods presented forcefully within the show. Any status element involved is implicit in the cash and — more strongly — the consumer goods available, with their associations of an affluent life style. *Sale of the Century* is *about* people winning things, acquiring goods. It seems a long way from *Have a Go*.

However, underlying the features that might be characterized as Transatlantic — the big prizes (taking around £1000 of the programme's weekly budget), the give away aspect (no one goes on the show without winning something) and the emphasis on the quizmaster as 'showman' — there are recognizable links relating it directly to the home-grown populist version of the quiz. If *Mastermind* makes large claims for 'intellectual' status, *Sale of the Century* is concerned to underplay any 'intellectual' pretensions that the quiz might have. Instead it aims to excite what the programme's devisers assume to be two conflicting impulses in their large, predominantly working class audience — the desire to 'snatch up' an outrageous bargain and the countervailing impulse to ignore blandishments in the hope of amassing some savings or acquiring an even more substantial bargain. [19] To this end the show presents a fantasy that could be called the apotheosis of 'consumer sovereignty' — the individual spending his cash in a series of seemingly open choices, the Bargain Hunter of commercial mythology writ large.

Nicholas Parsons acts the reverse of an inquisitorial figure, indulging in non-stop patter, contriving to be 'jolly' and implicitly condescending at the same time. His first words are 'Hello and welcome.' [20] He uses the first names of the contestants. On one night I watched, Eileen was a secretary with a design centre, Frank a clerk with the Customs and Excise. Crudely speaking, *Mastermind* and *Sale of the Century* tend to draw their contestants from different social groups. *Mastermind* contenders tend to come from the 'professions' with a very large proportion of teachers and lecturers. *Sale of the Century* contestants are chiefly drawn from the lower middle class.

The form that questions take in *Sale of the Century* is best illustrated by a typical example:

What happened to Rembrandt's painting *The Night Watch?*
It was slashed.
Yes, and what a sad and tragic event that was.

The viewing audience is constantly apostrophized with statements by the quizmaster such as 'What will they do? Will they take the money or spend it?' Much time is devoted to descriptions of the goods that can be 'bought'. Such decisions also act as occasions for patter. At one juncture Frank opts for the bicycles and Parsons comments 'You've got two children so the bikes will come in useful.' It is a performance of considerable — if nauseating — skill. At the commercial break there is a surprising lack of hiatus between advertisements and programme. I suspect that this is because both are concerned to sell life styles in the shape of consumer artefacts — selling, that is, the prospect of a more comfortable life transformed by the goods and the status that goes with them.

At the end of the show Frank has amassed £127 answering questions such as 'Where is the tomb of Napoleon?' and 'With what do you associate Thomas Sheraton?' Parsons comments that 'It could have been anyone's game.' The show reaches its finale. 'Now, Frank, take your £127 and spend it with me in the Sale of the Century.' Frank faces a royal blue car for £125, a dishwashing machine, a stereo and a full length palamino mink coat. The items are lovingly described. 'Will you buy a lovely mink coat for your wife, the stereo or the washing machine? Or will you buy the car? Frank, you've got ten seconds to decide.' Frank takes three seconds to opt for the car. Attendant girls put their arms around Frank and lead him to the car. They all get in. Closing shots show smiling Frank in the driver's seat.

Although the questions posed in *Sale of the Century* take a similar form to those in *Mastermind,* they serve different purposes and are embedded in a radically different context. The comparative 'easiness' of the questions (to a middle class viewer with fifteen years of state education) can be presumed to be a spur to the identification of the majority of viewers with the contestant. The questions tend to be generally available to a working class audience in a way that *Mastermind* questions are not. For the programme is not concerned with *displays* of knowledge. This becomes clear in those isolated instances when the implicit rules of the programme are transgressed. One programme provided some particularly clear examples. On that occasion a contestant answered correctly something like 90 per cent of the questions. Both the other contestants achieved very low scores. To make matters worse, the dominant contestant bought up every item revealed *before* the curtain was fully raised. It was a very instructive situation. Predictably the quizmaster took to mocking him on the few occasions when he answered wrongly with comments such as 'Ah, you were a bit too fast there.' A feeling of considerable hostility was generated, with the studio audience appearing to support the quizmaster's line.

What the unfortunate (though well rewarded) contestant was infringing was that sense of solidarity — of no contestant being exceptional or 'too clever' or 'too greedy' — that the populist show has to cultivate if it is to succeed. For if Everyman is too fast in his replies, or too clever, he comes perilously close to being Mastermind instead. So by mocking the contestant I believe that the quizmaster was trying (perhaps intuitively) to rescue the situation, sponsoring what he may have suspected to be the reaction of the viewers.

If *Have a Go* was concerned with 'getting people to talk' and in a sense celebrating their individuality in a context of the familiar (thus enhancing a sense of solidarity), *Sale of the Century* celebrates the individuality of its contestants *as consumers* — that is, people making 'consumer choices' — and therefore their basic 'ordinariness' in fulfilling a role that the programme assumes its audience would like to play as well. To this considerable extent the populist genre has changed with the development of (what until recently was presumed to be) mass consumption capitalism and an 'affluent' working class.

What happens in *Sale of the Century* might be described in Marcuse's terms as 'the transplantation of social into individual needs'.[21] When the viewer is asked 'What will they do?' he is not being invited to regard the contestants as 'experts' or 'intellectuals' or even as people with whom to compete. He is not being asked to admire their knowledge. Instead the show makes a simple (but cleverly calculated) appeal to the viewer to identify with the contestant — 'if I was him I'd keep the money' is one way the looked-for response could be described. Placing contestants in a situation where goods that represent hard saving, HP debts or wistful dreams to a large part of the audience are available at 'give away' prices is a superb stroke of gimmickry. In a sense it is a delivery of the promises that advertisers make.

Richard Dyer in his BFI Television Monograph on light entertainment [22] locates three features he regards as definitive in the entertainment version of the world — abundance, energy and community. To use his terms, *Sale of the Century* and other quizzes of a populist stamp aim to create a 'dream of abundance'. This imagery of the individual winning and choosing 'freely' is beamed into a society which has ample resources to ensure equal life chances for all but distributes its resources in an irrational and unequal way.

Marcuse regards this conversion of social into individual needs as one of the principal forms of social control under late capitalism. Describing what he calls the rational character of the system's irrationality, he says:

> Its productivity and efficiency, its capacity to increase and spread comforts, to turn waste into need, and destruction into construction, the extent to which this civilization transforms the object world into an extension of man's mind and body makes the very notion of alienation questionable. The people recognize themselves in their commodities; they find their soul

in their automobile, hi-fi set, split-level home, kitchen equipment. *The very mechanism which ties the individual to his society has changed, and social control is anchored in the new needs it has produced.*[23] (my italics)

Some tentative conclusions

I find I know more than I thought.
I feel I have improved myself.
I feel respect for the people on the programme.
I think over some of the questions afterwards.
Educational . . . .
(Extract from a cluster analysis of statements relating to TV quiz programmes from McQuail, Blumler & Brown, 'The Television Audience: A Revised Perspective'.)

McQuail, Blumler and Brown are concerned in their essay to demolish the 'escapist' theory of television viewing — that is, the tradition of research and writing about television which assumes a fundamental division in broadcast output between 'reality seeking' genres such as 'news, documentaries, interviews, public affairs programmes and educational television' and genres such as the 'soap opera', the serial and the quiz show that are presented by the tradition as serving an escapist and fantasizing function for the audience.

The effect is to exclude from serious consideration (of television materials in the domain of reality) a wide range of television content which could have an important bearing on the individual's perception and understanding of the real world without appearing in an explicitly cognitive form.[24]

Basing their tests on *University Challenge, TV Brain of Britain* and *Ask the Family* (which they describe as quizzes 'involving genuine tests of knowledge rather than . . . parlour games with big prizes, gimmicks and a prominent element of chance') they analyse what they see as four basic types of gratification afforded by the television quiz: a 'self-rating appeal', a 'basis for social interaction', an 'excitement' appeal, and an 'educational' appeal.

One of their conclusions is that 'working class fans' are more concerned to 'rate themselves' through quiz programmes than middle class viewers. Their analysis also rates highly what they term the 'educational appeal' of the quiz programmes which they say is 'strongest for those individuals with the most limited school experience'. They interpret the cluster of statements that I have placed at the head of this section as 'expressive of the function of quiz programmes in projecting and enforcing educational values.'

One of the many valuable aspects of this analysis is the attempt to articulate the 'cognitive' features of the quiz show, which usefully shifts the focus of discussion away from the unhelpful categories of 'information, education and entertainment' — the categories by which the broadcasting agencies tend to describe their output. But this attempt is a *refocusing* rather than a fundamental rethinking of the social categories of description. Marcuse poses the question 'Can one really distinguish between the mass media as instruments of infor-

109

mation and entertainment, and as agents of manipulation and indoctrination?' [25] – that is, of social control. McQuail, Blumler and Brown adopt in their analysis, with some misgivings, the dominant notion of 'educational values' which quizzes as a broadcast form support and affirm. Consider, for instance, the notion of a *'genuine* test of knowledge' and the hierarchical idea of the quiz genre implied in their distinction between 'tests' – what I have termed the 'intellectual', middle class strand of the genre – and 'parlour games' (the question of the celebrity television parlour game is, I think, a separate issue).

What are these 'educational values'? Questions may serve a different function in the intellectual and populist quiz but both forms are based on the assumption that 'facts' are in a 'neutral' domain, that they are significant. The intellectual quiz affirms its intellectual status by making these 'facts' stand as the content of a 'subject'. In the quiz facts stand 'in themselves', immutable, unquestionable objects rent from the social and historical process.

A related assumption common to both forms is that all questions have unambiguous 'right' answers. As Postman and Weingartner observe, society conditions us to suspect that an instant, fluent response to a question denotes status:

> One does not 'blame' men, especially if they are politicians, for providing instant answers to all questions. The public requires that they do, *since the public has learned that instant answer giving is the most important sign of an educated man.* [26] (my italics)

Educational values of a particular type are also 'enforced' by the form of relationship between quizmaster and contestant presented by shows in each strand of the genre. These relationships are suggestive of that wider system of communication situations through which knowledge is mediated in British society. The supply of 'Right' answers must come from a 'Right' – that is, a legitimate – source. The trappings of Academe with which *Mastermind* clothes itself *serve to legitimate the relationship between quizmaster and quizzed.* The quizmaster's immediate position as 'the man with all the answers' in *Mastermind* and the intellectual quiz depends on certain implicit assumptions about *where* the answers are coming from. Answers are supplied in *Mastermind* and the intellectual quiz generally by recognized 'authorities' – the academic, the media exposed 'expert' and (in many cases) the Encylopedia Britannica.

The populist quiz tends to adopt different strategies to legitimate its supply of right answers. Here the quizmaster is a different type of 'authority' figure – he is, in fact, invested with the authority of the showman, the performer, the 'professional'. Typically this involves the presentation of a seemingly 'classless' type of deference relationship between the (amateur) contestant and the (professional) quizmaster – the man who is fluent, who has 'all the answers'. Thus the status of a quizmaster like Hughie Green in a populist quiz show has very little to do with corpuses of knowledge and a lot to do with the way in which he 'orchestrates' the situation. This is in strong contrast to the quizmaster in the intellectual quiz, buttressed by 'authorities' and in his way as much an authority figure as the teacher – in commonsense terms the person who 'controls' (rather than 'orchestrates') the situation, who possesses the right answers, who defines the rate at which questions are put, who 'interrogates'.[27]

If the intellectual quiz weds 'knowledge' to the man who controls the situation it also creates the occasion for a performance by contestants of varying degrees of 'skill'. Contestants on *Mastermind* and on intellectual quizzes generally are predominantly middle class, professional people. Many of them can provide the 'right' answers in an appropriately 'sharp, decisive and concise' way. So the relationship of the working class viewer to the intellectual quiz may indeed involve the deference expressed in the statement 'I feel respect for the people on the programme', which, rephrased, might read 'They know more than me'. Indeed, the assumption that 'knowledge' is a possession which confers status (such as the title 'Mastermind of the United Kingdom') underpins the intellectual quiz. '*Mastermind* . . . is the contestant's chance to pit his knowledge against a leading professional in his particular subject', runs the blurb on the back of the first selection of questions from the show published by the BBC.

Whilst the objective of competing on *Mastermind* is, for the individual contestant, purely status, the objective of competing on a populist show like *Sale of the Century* must be the things that can be won. Thus in the populist show what you know is directly translated into things – and in a sense cash and consumer goods legitimate the operations of the populist quiz by its 'intellectual' pretensions. It could be argued that the populist quiz is an exercise in curriculum relevance, providing tangible benefits and advantages from the use of 'knowledge'. Up to a point this line can be sustained, but it encounters what is, perhaps, the major underlying assumption in the strand – this is that 'knowledge' is essentially trivial, not the key feature of the show, not what it is 'about'. To be available to Everyman, the curriculum of the populist quiz show must be resolutely non-academic. To appear in the guise of celebrating solidaristic values it must place a low value on competition, whilst having prizes, reassure its contestants with a showman/quizmaster who can control and sustain a seemingly 'classless' type of relationship with each contestant, which maintains a due deference on their part to facilitate the smooth running of the programme and 'package' each individual. 'Now, Frank, take your £127 and spend it with me . . . .'

Yet the 'knowledge' contained in the intellectual quiz can be regarded as equally 'trivial'. If questions such as 'What happened to Rembrandt's painting "The Night Watch"?' are placed alongside 'How many cigars did Brunel's cigar case hold?', it is clear that the only significant difference lies in the size of audience to which the questions can be presumed to be available – popular newspapers have larger readerships than biographies of great Victorian engineers. The difference lies in the context in which the questions are put.

A further feature links both forms of the quiz, linked to the notion that facts stand in themselves as an index of 'knowledge'. For to the extent to which this reflects the dominant ideology of contemporary scholarship and the mass media – the tenacious Namierite position that 'facts speak', the interview that promises the 'real facts' about the subject, the picture that 'says it all' – it can be expected that questions will focus on what this scholarship and media foreground – a view of the social process that concentrates on individuals rather than groups, events rather than processes, leaders rather than classes, professionals, 'experts', politicians, journalists, trade union leaders, etc., rather than people.

I have attempted to draw out of the quiz genre certain assumptions and practices stemming from a notion of 'knowledge' that seem to me part of an ideology which is common both to our educational system and the media — attempted, that is, to indicate how that ideology is produced in concrete practice. My argument depends on an assertion of the representative character of what many may take to be a trivial form of entertainment. My main assumption is that even seemingly trivial broadcast forms — forms that invite and depend on us taking them 'for granted' — play an important role in structuring consciousness and thereby ensuring the continued reproduction of social contradictions. For the media, 'the starting point and the goal are always, *if not always consciously,* an apologia for the existing order of things, or at least a proof of their immutability' [28] (my italics).

Notes

1 Geoffrey M. Esland, 'Teaching and Learning' in Michael F. D. Young, *Knowledge and Control* (London, Collier-Macmillan, 1971).

2 Stuart Hall, 'The Determination of News Photographs' in S. Cohen and J. Young, *The Manufacture of News* (London, Constable, 1973).

3 Ibid.

4 The comparatively recent use of certain devices to point up the mediatedness of television news — such as the brief shot of the studio at the start of the BBC's *Nine O'Clock News,* the use of a date caption and name captions for news readers — are framed within this basic ideology, with a certain unease. In the case of the *Nine O'Clock News,* they have now been abandoned. The new editor, Andrew Todd, was quoted in the *Evening Standard* (18 February 1976) as wishing 'to return to a less cluttered and *more direct style* of presentation':

> The 'fisheye' view of the news studio, the astronaut view of the world and the present titles are all to go. As widely expected Mr Todd has also gone back to the old system of using just one news reader on the main 9 o'clock news. [He] said, 'I feel two readers tend to fragment the news. I want to reestablish the news reader's role as the prime link between the news room and the public.' . . . He plans to make the news warmer by changing the colour of the studio . . . . He added, 'I am changing the present titles as I don't like them . . . I am removing some of the information given behind the news reader such as the date. When specialist correspondents appear we will just give their subject. We will also dispense with the panel in front of the reader with his or her name because this looks to me like an obstacle between the reader and the viewer . . . .

5 Desmond Davis, *The Grammar of Television Production* (London, Barrie & Jenkins, 1972, 3rd ed.).

6 *BBC Television Handbook* (London, BBC, 1974), pp. 280-1.

7 See Peter L. Berger and Thomas Luckmann, *The Social Construction of Reality* (Harmondsworth Penguin, 1971), pp. 106-7.

8 George Lukacs, 'Art and Objective Truth' in *Writer and Critic and Other Essays* (London, Merlin, 1971).

9 Peter Black, *The Biggest Aspidistra in the World* (London, BBC, 1972), pp. 99-109.

10 Trevor Pateman, *Language, Truth and Politics* (Sidmouth, Jean Stroud & Trevor Pateman, 1975).

11 BBC, *Mastermind* (London, BBC, 1974).

12 Raymond Williams, *Keywords* (London, Fontana, 1976).

13 Pierre Bourdieu, 'Systems of Education and Systems of Thought' in Michael F. D. Young, op. cit.

14 John Holt, *How Children Fail* (Harmondsworth, Penguin, 1964).

15 Trevor Pateman, op. cit.

16 The 'General Knowledge' category might seem an exception but the vast majority of questions set fall into these categories. Questions are chiefly to do with (for example) giving the name of a 'famous artist', a 'historical figure', etc. (e.g. 'His first play was *The Room* in 1957 and his other works include *The Servant*. What is his name?'), a 'date', a definition or a 'place'.

17 Neil Postman and Charles Weingartner, *Teaching as a Subversive Activity* (Harmondsworth, Penguin, 1971).

18 BBC, *Mastermind*.

19 Quizzes such as *Sale of the Century* are, from the programme-maker's viewpoint, very cheap shows to mount – unscripted, relatively low on labour and performance costs but very popular – despite the 'no expenses spared' aura of conspicuous consumption that prize-giving involves.

20 Although Parsons has been criticized in the popular press (e.g. the *News of the World*) for condenscension and patronage towards contestants.

21 Herbert Marcuse, *One Dimensional Man* (London, Routledge & Kegan Paul, 1964).

22 Richard Dyer, *Light Entertainment,* BFI Television Monograph No. 2 (London, British Film Institute, 1973).

23 Herbert Marcuse, op. cit. Marx's discussion of the nature of a commodity in Capital is relevant here. 'A commodity is therefore a mysterious thing, simply because in it the social character of men's labour appears to them as an objective character stamped upon the product of that labour.' In a recent paper Dorothy Smith rewrites Marx's account, substituting 'fact' for 'commodity' and points out that Marx draws a similar analogy with religion later in the same passage. Thus, 'a fact . . . is a mysterious thing, simply because in it the social character of man's consciousness appears to them as an objective character stamped upon the product of that consciousness.' (From Dorothy E. Smith, *The Social Construction of Documentary Reality*. A paper presented at the meetings of the Canadian Sociological and Anthropological Association, Queens University, Kingston, Ontario 1973. See *Sociological Inquiry*, vol. 44 (1974).

24 Denis McQuail, Jay Blumler and Roger Brown, 'The Television Audience, A Revised Perspective', in Denis McQuail (ed.), *The Sociology of Mass Communication* (Harmondsworth, Penguin, 1972).

25 Herbert Marcuse, op. cit.

26 Neil Postman and Charles Weingartner, op. cit.

27 I am using 'orchestrates' in something of a similar sense to the *O.E.D.*'s 'to combine harmoniously, like instruments in an orchestra' to point up this key aspect of the quizmaster's role as a *performer* in the populist quiz.

28 George Lukacs, *History and Class Consciousness* (London, Merlin, 1971).

Chapter 9

Schooling teachers: the myth of the liberal college

John Bartholomew

Introduction[1]

> I know that when you start teaching you lose a lot of your ideals because I
> have seen it happen with other teachers and I am wondering if I can stop it
> happening to me, but I am not sure how. (Fourth-year student)

There is no doubt that many students, when they become teachers, find that
they change their minds radically as to the practical possibility of carrying out
ideas that they had when they were students. Indeed, many students, as part of
their awareness of the inadequacy of their training, have an uneasiness, even
before they start teaching, about the possibility for the practical realization of
ideas they have developed as students. When they do become teachers they
adopt the widespread view of teachers on the inadequacy or irrelevance of
teacher education. This gap between theory and practice where ideas believed in
one set of institutions have minimal practical outcomes in another has also been
the topic of much research which has focused on effects of teacher education.
This paper is an attempt to explain the contribution of the college to a state of
affairs where thoughts and ideas developed in one institution have apparently
minimal practical realization in another. I hope to show that part of the way of
understanding the theory and practice gap between the college and the school is
through an understanding of the gap between theory and practice as it exists
within the college. This analysis will provide the largely liberal theory of the
college with a significance not normally attributed to it − that it hides from view
the fundamentally conservative practices of the college and through this the
conservative influence of the college. The thesis is that liberal theory is in fact
conservative in that it mystifies conservative practices.

Theory and practice

It may seem surprising to even suggest that the college has conservative influences
on schools. More usually, the colleges' influences are seen as minimal; you learn
to teach when you start teaching and not within the confines of an initial training institution. All the theory of college is, in this view, inappropriate, inappli-
cable and better forgotten. No doubt those in colleges see their theory as in
advance of school practices. Taylor expresses this view (with a caution).[2] He
says, 'School practice provides the principal setting in which the schools and the

114

colleges meet face to face. In so far as the colleges are innovatory and the schools conservative institutions — and the balance is not always this way round — the acquisition and trial of new ideas and techniques by students during the college course may be hampered by the slower pace of change in the schools where teaching practice is undertaken.' In opposition to this kind of view, which sees the college as having little influence on the everyday practices of its future teachers, I shall put the contrary view which sees the college as having a conservative influence. This derives not from the theory which is largely liberal, but from the teaching and learning practices through which such theory is transmitted.

We are endlessly being told that there is a serious gap between theory and practice in teacher education. Students not only see discontinuities between what they do on courses and what they do in schools as teachers, but also are quick to point out that their tutors endlessly fail to do themselves what they recommend for others.

> In their relationship with us they didn't seem to realize that they were the teachers and we were the pupils. Like feedback; they always say you must give children feedback but you have to wait months to get an essay back. (Fourth-year student)

Established teachers frequently comment on the inadequacy of the irrelevance of teacher education. The number of statements on the gap between theory and practice from those in teacher education is again an index of a widespread consciousness of this problem by those who might have thought were in the best position to do something about it.

To provide a more adequate understanding we need to conceive of the relations of theory and practice in further ways. We need to understand not just the outcomes of courses for practice, the relations of the theory in the college to the practices in the schools, but also the relationship of theory to practice *within* the college both for students and tutors. Practices in college may frequently be in contradiction with the theory.

The myth of the liberal college

There have been a large number of studies which compare attitudes during training with attitudes which develop in the first year of teaching. What these studies predictably and with great consistency show is an increase in 'radical', 'liberal' or 'progressive' attitudes by students during their course, which attitudes when they start teaching become more 'toughminded' and 'conservative'.

The research on attitudes shows the student moving from liberal to conservative attitudes as he moves from training to teaching. This makes the college look liberal relative to the schools which are made in this research to look conservative. The kind of explanation given for the change in attitudes supports the commonsense view that the college is in fact more liberal. Morrison and MacIntyre are typical in 'explaining' the increase in liberalism during training thus: 'The attitudes of individuals tend to change in the direction of those held by the majority in groups of which they are members, and also towards the attitudes held by groups to whose membership they aspire.'[3] The decline in liberalism of attitudes is then explained in terms of impracticability of such attitudes in the actual teaching situation. Taylor's explanation is similar to this.[4] He says, 'Any gap between what the college tutors seem to recommend and the teachers and the schools to value may produce a conflict in identification for the student. This is likely to be resolved in favour of the schools, which constitute a reference group of greater long-term import than the college, where the student spends only a limited period.'

This explanation, paralleling as it does the kind of commonsense explanation that a teacher might give, underpins the one-sided view of the college as a place of theory and not practice and of the school as a place of practice and not theory. It makes what happens in the college seem irrelevant to what happens in the school because the theory is seen as having no outcome within the context of the· school. The formulation which sees what happens in one institution (theory) as having minimal relevance to what happens in the other (practice) is very much related to the idea that one institution is theoretical and the other practical. Nothing could be further from the reality; both institutions are practical in their different ways. They are also both in their different ways theoretical in the sense that no human practice is mindless, without consciousness, as the notion of practice as opposed to theory might suggest. To see the college in terms of the attitudes or theory of its members, or in terms of the liberalism of its curriculum, is to avoid seeing that all these things have a basis on the human arrangements and practices of the college. The theorist may not practice what he preaches and the existence of these attitudes does not itself indicate the existence of liberal educational practice.

That practices in the college are a largely ignored but possibly relevant area of study has been indicated by Taylor: 'A problem that as yet remains untouched by research is the relationship between the teaching methods that the student experiences in college and those he uses in schools.'[5] Rather than seeing only theory, Taylor is suggesting that we look at practice. I shall understand teacher education in terms of the relationship between theory and practice, not just in terms of one or the other. It is through an understanding of these relations within the training institutions that we may begin to understand the relation of these institutions to school.

The explanation given for the development of liberal attitudes on the part of students has the following key features. Firstly, it takes as its starting point the prior existence of liberal attitudes. It does not attempt to explain what brought them into existence or keeps them in existence. Secondly, it sees anyone entering the colle₤e as either already having the attitudes which predominate there or, if not, then they will tend to change their attitudes to those prevailing because of the tendency people generally have to conform to group pressure. Clearly those whose starting point for the explanation of liberal attitudes is the prior existence of liberal group attitudes to which the student to varying degrees conforms are patently not even trying to provide an explanation for the existence of these attitudes in the first place. From the point of view of this analysis it is necessary to do so.

Paradoxically, the liberalism of the college in attitudes is an expression of its fundamental conservatism, basically because it is a liberalism that exists in theory only. That a greater liberalism is expressed in students in training is more an expression of the physical separation of those institutions from their objects – schools – and so from the real-life problems of actual teachers. In general the college's liberalism exists only in the context of thinking where there are no possibilities for having practical involvement in the objects of thought in real direct first-hand experience. This separation of thought and action exists in two spheres already mentioned. The first was between college theory and school practice and the second between college theory and college practice. This second sphere of separation applies to both students and staff, although to each in a different manner.

The research, in producing the more liberal view of the college, is not comparing like with like. What it does is to take the attitudes of students to events in schools, events which they are not experiencing at that time, and then it compares these with their attitudes towards those same classes of events when they become teachers and are experiencing them at first hand – in fact, practising them. It is in effect comparing college attitudes with school practices rather than college practices with school practices.

The liberal view of the college, then, is produced by comparing attitudes in the college with practices in the school. If we compare attitude or theory found in the college with practice in the college we find the same gap between liberal theory and conservative practice that can be found between the college and the school. Because the college is only seen in terms of its theory or attitudes, and not its practices, it is made to appear liberal, but the appearance masks a different reality. In this way research legitimates the college by mystifying the conservative practical basis of its liberal ideology.

The separation of thought and action

Students are presented with a curriculum which they learn, to varying extents. If they can demonstrate their learning by gaining the appropriate marks in essays, examinations, or whatever, they are able to survive – i.e. pass the course. The relevance of what they learn for their practices and strategies as learners is minimal. It is, of course, officially not meant to have any relevance at all anyway. Also the relevance of what students have to learn for their work as future teachers can easily be made problematic. Certainly, we have nothing approaching adequate documentation of the 'effects' of teacher education. Such documentation has been limited almost entirely to the very narrow conceptualization provided by attitude research. More importantly, it is not just what students learn that has minimal relevance to their official practices as learners but rather that success as a student in that situation depends on his learning the rules for keeping his life experiences, problems and practices as a student separated from what he officially has to learn. Keddie has shown a similar process occuring in schools.[6] In her study of an integrated curriculum in a comprehensive school she saw some children succeeding in official terms because they were able to keep their commonsense everyday knowledge separated from what they were being asked to learn. Those who were unable to, or for some reason didn't do this and questioned what teachers presented to them, were seen as asking inappropriate questions. In theory, the ideology was to start from the child's experiences; in practice this did not happen.

The report by Makins on Countesthorpe College must be extremely rare.[7] She quotes a teacher: 'The children just won't accept what sociologists take for granted. They give endless counter-examples, and the whole accepted notion of social class explodes. The more you try to defend it the more difficulty you get into.'

Because few studies look at the practical operation of curriculum we can only guess at the prevalence of the kind of situation indicated by Keddie. The two contrasting cases (Keddie and Makins) are used here to suggest that what Keddie describes is more typical. Any fundamental questioning on the part of pupils leads to the breakdown of what is generally taken to be normal teaching and learning because the resources for fundamental questioning do not arise from within the curriculum but from what the questioner brings from outside the paradigm of the particular curriculum. Education as we know it requires the separation of curriculum from the lives of learners.

Generally, then, it is part of the practical circumstances of the student as it may also be for the pupil in the school that he must treat what he learns as something separated from himself.

> She was saying you must be far more detached. You mustn't be so involved because it isn't actually what you think that they are interested in ... (First-year student, discussing a tutor's comments on an essay)

The student, for success, in official terms must start the process of a separation for himself as a student from himself in other spheres of his life. For example, a very typical comment in relation to essay writing from a second-year student: 'I work out what they want and give it to them, but I keep what I really believe to myself.' The form in which the student as a living subject is finally transformed into an object in which the form of grades and marks is achieved by others than himself (see Chapters 5 and 6 in this volume, by Hextall and Winter).

The same separation of thought and action that applies to the student also applies to staff. In their case, and I speak more specifically of the educational theorist, the relevance of what is purveyed is justified (if at all) in relation to events beyond the situation in which his theories and ideas have a public existence, never to any immediate situation to hand.

The relationship between the ideas propagated and the circumstances of their propogation is in a practical sense not raised. Theory or any kind of mental activity is never understood in relation to its practical context. The student for his practical purposes of staying the course carries out those actions that will enable others to objectify him and deliver him up in the form of marks and assessment. In doing these things he puts himself in a certain relation to curriculum knowledge as something outside himself to be learned. Likewise, staff must divorce what they know (or treat as knowledge) from their activities in propagating that knowledge. Such categories as curriculum and pedagogy give expression to underlying processes through which knowledge and mind make their appearance as separated from learners' and teachers' activities. These activities are the practical social basis which give the possibility for the appearance of thought and knowledge as separated from the practices of teachers and learners. But the two are connected. Without the practices, the knowledge would not have an existence and the practices and the knowledge have determined relations on each other.

Pupils and students achieve objective status in education through marks and assessments, which is a separation of them as mind (as intellectual products) from them as living individuals. The research on attitudes already mentioned also produces a split between the mental and the practical. It is a central problem of attitude research that we know almost nothing about the relationship of measures of attitude to how people act in their everyday lives. Such research, being only capable of conceiving of people statically and cognitively as attitudes and not as living processes, sustains this dualism and has no way of resolving it. These renderings of a thinker's circumstances as separable from his thoughts are crucial to the continuance of the practices and sets of social relations found in the division of labour between teacher and taught and between those who define the world as it is and those who get defined. That is the division of labour between those who theorize and those who practice. I have elaborated on this elsewhere.[8] The point here is that these ways of seeing people as only 'minds' (the examples given have been attitudes, curricula, and assessments) mystify their real-life circumstances and so are able to mystify the way in which liberal theory masks conservative practice.

College practices

It is reasonable to assume that practices in the college and the school are essentially similar. Gay *et al.* have indicated how features of the relations of kids in schools and their teachers are also found in the relations of students and tutors in colleges.[9] In both types of institutions there are students who truant (it is called something different in the college), who show no interest, work 'instrumentally', and generally fail to participate actively in lessons (or their equivalent). Yet the same students who cope with their course like this criticize schoolchildren for producing the same kinds of learning practices that they use. They also suggest that staff have parallel contradictions. For staff, an ideal student is one who engages seriously and critically in the educational enterprise. Yet, when a student behaves in this ideal manner staff find it uncomfortable. Students who show greater intellectual curiosity sometimes ask basic and uncomfortable questions, and in doing so break what staff would normally otherwise take for granted. In some cases staff disallow such questioning. 'On the topic of streaming the notion that ability may be socially defined was treated as an irrelevant area of knowledge.'[10] Not only are students expected to accept the assumptions or starting points of staff, but when areas of interest to students do get addressed, it is only 'within an institutional framework that effectively guillotines the debate'.[11] Of course, staff label such criticism from students, in some cases, as varieties of immaturity or idealism in the same way that their students will label kids when they become teachers, and so avoid confronting the problems that learners are raising.

There are further ways in which student practices in college may parallel those of pupils in schools. In both kinds of institutions the main form in which curriculum knowledge appears is as a corpus, as predefined 'worthwhile activities' existing in theory separately from teachers and learners. A transmission relationship in which supposedly what is in the teacher's mind becomes what is in the pupil's mind is the only possible relationship that can exist between teacher and taught with such a conception of knowledge. An important focus for student liberalism, and indeed of much educational theorizing, is the relationship between teacher and taught. This relationship is often seen as capable of becoming more cooperative, of starting from where the learner is, from his interests or life circumstances, and so on. Two possible requirements for such changes to occur are, firstly, that students gain experience of such relationships whilst on their courses, and, secondly, that in a deeper sense such changes can only occur if they involve changed conceptions of knowledge. Given that our dominant conceptions of knowledge necessitate a transmission relationship — that is, an authoritarian relationship of teacher as knower to pupil as non-knower — then it may be that liberalized conceptions of teacher/pupil relations are a theoretical possibility, but no more. This is because such notions must ultimately, in practice, be subjugated to the demands of transmitting what counts as proper knowledge.

Of course, the social relations of teaching and learning common to both schools and colleges operate to sustain this separated and 'out there' conception of knowledge. The 'reality' of this conception of knowledge, as I have suggested previously, is provided in existing and historically given sets of social relations of teacher and learner.

Liberal theory and conservative practice

The social organization of teaching and learning provides ample opportunity to the student to maintain and generate liberal attitudes. They have no practice in which to test them and they have to keep their own beliefs separated from the beliefs they must, if they are to pass the course, reproduce in essays or examinations. For many students it is an important strategy for survival to keep this separation between the official educational theory and their own. When students do attempt to theorize about their own circumstances they can be discouraged from doing so; the idea is alien to normal conceptions of education, as the following comment from a first-year student indicates:

> . . . a friend of mine was saying about democracy — she's very interested in it, you know — the democracy of schoolchildren and democracy of students. We asked if we could have a group where we could just sit around and talk about democracy, and Mrs B. said, well, not really, because once you've got a group you've got a tutor or lecturer and once you've got a lecturer he would want to prepare something which would

embody his views and so then the lecturer would take over the whole scene. What you would be saying wouldn't be valuable at all because he would say, 'Look I found you these references so if you'd like to go home and read them, then you could come back and discuss them'. It's a bit bad really because that wasn't the point she was making. She was just suggesting a very informal group sitting around discussing various kinds of democracy.

In her article on her educational psychology course Deena Jefferys puts it more succinctly: 'Not encouraged to take theories and elaborate upon them by discussion of our practical, actual experiences of situations of interactions between ourselves and kids'.[12]

A key, then, to understanding the liberal mind in the college is that colleges are organized in such a way that the thinking of staff and students is divorced from practice. When practice is considered, it is only considered in theory. For example, in essays some tutors seem to believe that if they ask the student to consider some issue, not only for its own sake but also for its 'implications for classroom practice', that they have somehow brought theory and practice together. In many courses there is a subject called theory and practice of education where predictably practice is nothing more than yet another 'theoretic category' and where once again theory is kept well clear of confronting practice practically. In moving from the college to the school, the student moves from one side of the educational fence to the other, in his becoming a teacher (transmitter) from being a student (receiver). His practices in both cases are from different sides of a fence but preserve the same transmission relationships.

Attitudes are liberal, then, not just because of 'group influence' but more fundamentally because they have been prevented from coming into contact with practice. Meanwhile, the conservative practical experiences gained in college, unlike the liberal attitudes which are documented as disappearing, may be highly relevant to the practices of teaching. Teacher education, then, far from being ineffectually liberal, is perhaps in its real effects conservative.

An example

The following example illustrates the not untypical situation where a student believes one thing in theory but describes 'problems' that arise out of the practical reality of having to teach in a way which contradicts his theoretical position. Within a social studies programme a first-year student had been teaching a lesson on 'Education and the Working Class' to a group of children who were themselves working class. In the lesson he had gone through the more traditional view which in effect and in various ways blames the working class child and his home background for his failure in education relative to the middle class child. He had been highly critical of these explanations primarily on the grounds of the derogatory and inferiority view that they entail of the working class child, who is seen in terms of a deprivation or deficit model. This model conceives of the working class child in terms of properties he does not possess, such as lack of motivation, lack of appropriate attitudes, or values, inability to use language adequately or to defer gratification and so on. He put forward a critique of this theory which shifted the focus for the explanation of the relative failure of the working class child on to the school (e.g. labelling or streaming) and agencies that control or influence the school. In one part of the lesson he had explained that one of the factors operating against children from working class backgrounds was that schools in the areas where they lived were inferior in many respects to those found in more middle class areas. Commenting on 'problems' that the children had had in understanding this particular point in the lesson, he said: ' . . . the problem in teaching these children is their limited experience in that this is the only school they know and so can't imagine what others are like.' During the lesson he had made it clear that he held to the 'blame the system' theory and had used ideas from this perspective to criticize the 'blame the child and his background' type theory. Yet here the student contradicts this theoretical position by blaming the child.

How is it possible for someone to have a critique of education and then himself become an example of that critique. The social context in which the critique of cultural deprivation theories is convincing is the college. The college is removed from the context of the events being described. Critiques of cultural deprivation theories can rapidly convince most students that working class culture cannot be considered as inferior to any other, yet the account of the problem as he had experienced it, within the practical context of teaching, was in contradiction to what he believed in theory. Like the theory he had criticized, he saw the problem as residing entirely within the child.

We cannot explain this in terms of norms prevailing in the schools which operate on the student to produce conformity via group pressure because there was no such pressure. Rather, the example shows the contextual nature of 'attitudes' which can result in apparent contradictions. It is important to note here that by context is meant a structure of social relations. In the college context the structure of social relations, because it separates mind from reality, makes possible liberal attitudes. The practice of teaching involves a different set of social relations out of which may arise a 'blame the child' consciousness. The contradictions, then, are not so much locatable in the individual but in the world inhabited by the individual, and they express his relations with that world. The 'blame the child' consciousness has its validity within the transmission view of education. As a teacher he is faced with the objects of his liberalized consciousness and his relationship to them is now mediated by the fact that he has to actually teach them something. Different problems arise out of this new relation; the child's incomprehension becomes a problem residing in the learners and not in the set-up in terms of which he was created as deficit.

How then could such a theory have come to be accepted in the colleges in the first place? Although the theories are generated within historical contexts, well beyond the confines of any college (where they enter into wider political debate), their adoption in the college is possible because they do not disturb the existing order. They do not disturb the existing order because they come to exist within a set of social relations within which what goes on in people's minds has parted company from what they do. A further reason why the theory does not disturb is that the concept of class used in the deficit difference debate rids it of the notion of class conflict, exploitation or domination. The radical flavour and truth status of the critique of cultural deprivation is achieved away from the context of teacher's practices. With the above individual case, in the context of practice, the theory was forgotten, not apparently because of group pressure inducing conformity, but because of the nature of educational production relations. These relations are the practical basis which make possible only certain theories, but the theories mystify their practical basis.

Conclusion

The social relations of teacher and taught entail the student in separating what goes on in his mind from his everyday practices of being a student. In as much as the separation of the mind also exists for staff, then, the student only experiences a world where theory is largely unproblematically separated from practice. On this thesis it is not, as some suppose, a question of the realism of the school that changes the students' attitudes; the college itself has its realisms, and they are both educational institutions in which similar processes occur. Rather, it is as a learner in the college negotiating life as a student that requires the production of a public consciousness (e.g. in an essay) which is removed from and does not address the realism of the college. The college official demands also make his practical experiences as a learner irrelevant so that his liberal attitudes achieve an appearance of independence from the conservative world through which they were produced. This split in the individual between theory and practice is a central key to understanding the shift to conservative attitudes when he becomes a teacher. The key is that as a student he never experiences in practice the liberalism which he is so freely allowed to express in theory. The change to conservative attitudes merely expresses what was the position in practice all the time.

Acknowledgements

I should like to thank Michael Young, Geoff Whitty, Colin Parfitt and Philip Stone for their very valuable comments on earlier versions of this paper.

Notes

1 The theoretical basis for this study (not made explicit within it) has been drawn from Marx's materialist theory of consciousness, especially as developed in the theory of alienation as a way of understanding production relations. This is to be found in the German Ideology and throughout his work – see, for example, Norman Geras, 'Marx and Critique of Political Economy' in Robin Blackburn (ed.), *Ideology in Social Science* (London, Fontana, 1972). Therefore, although I only discuss colleges of education and aspects of their relations to schools, this is not because I think that these institutions can be understood in some sort of historical isolation, but rather because a contribution to the understanding of the overall reproduction of this society may be had through an appreciation of the way in which its ideologies are sustained in education.

2 W. Taylor, *Society and the Education of Teachers* (London, Faber & Faber, 1969).

3   A. Morrison and D. McIntyre, *Teachers and Teaching* (Harmondsworth, Penguin, 1969), p. 71.

4   W. Taylor, op. cit., p. 145.

5   W. Taylor, 'Recent Research on the Education of Teachers: An Overview', *Colston Papers No. 20* (London, Butterworth, 1969), p. 239.

6   N. Keddie, 'Classroom Knowledge' in M. F. D. Young (ed.), *Knowledge and Control* (London, Collier-Macmillan, 1971).

7   V. Makins, 'Dividends of Change', *Times Educational Supplement* (25 May 1975), p. 18.

8   J. C. Bartholomew, 'Theory and Practice: An as yet Unaddressed Issue', *Education for Teaching*, No. 97 (Summer 1975).

9   J. Gay *et al.*, 'Behaving Like Kids', *Hard Cheese*, No. 4/5 (1975).

10 Ibid.

11 Ibid.

12 D. Jefferys, 'How Psychology Fails the Teacher', *British Journal of Teacher Education*, vol. I. No. 1 (1975), p. 65.

Part 3 : Developing alternatives

The argument developed in Parts 1 and 2 has been critical of current educational practice, and has, in varying degrees, recognized the limited character of any alternatives conceived of within educational contexts alone. It is therefore somewhat paradoxical that, in this part, the first three chapters are suggestions and case studies of such 'alternatives within', and these are followed by an admittedly qualified account of the radical possibilities of building television practice into the school context and by a description by the White Lion School of an alternative educational institution that in no way confronts the capitalist economic order, of which it cannot avoid being a part. We do not see these accounts as yet other attempts to perpetuate the illusion that educational liberation is ultimately possible from within (if only we had more radical teachers), nor are they a sop to those who ask critics to provide alternatives to what they knock down, for that is to perpetuate the separation of theory from practice, which it is part of the political concern of this book to overcome. What these accounts illustrate well, and what is often neglected, is that there is no straightforward relation between theory and practice. Just as critiques do not offer precise prescriptions for alternatives, so, often, as in several of the cases we include in this part, they are initiated independently of any explicit theory and may in fact sustain some of the very categories that sociologists have called into question. These accounts are exploratory in a rather different sense from those in the other parts of the book, and they indicate how the relations between sociology and educational practice must be both ongoing and dialectical if they are to make a real contribution to change.

In our view the positive value of these alternatives derives from a recognition that, if radical change is to be other than a mechanistic slogan, then the overcoming of capitalism involves the transformation of all aspects of everyday life, and the form and content of possible socialist alternatives (not only in education) must also be prefigured in the ongoing struggle. The political significance of 'developing alternatives' in education is therefore that, while every context expresses within it the dynamics and possibilities of change, such possibilities as those we have included, as any others, are doomed to cooptation, or toleration as irrelevant idiosyncrasies, if isolated from the wider political struggle.

Chapter 10 by Goodson develops from a critique of the 'transmission' model of teaching, and suggests an alternative based on involving students and teachers in what he calls reconstructing knowledge. While many primary school teachers, faced with forty children, will probably question his over-idealized view of their

125

work situation, and even though, in its present form, his alternative pedagogy is a somewhat individualistic one, it remains inescapable that a practical alternative to the prevailing 'transmission' model, based as it is on a positivistic conception of knowledge, is crucial if the rhetoric of educational transformation is to become a reality. Webb's highly personal and concrete account in Chapter 11 of the practical and personal difficulties he had in an ordinary secondary school, in trying to enable students to take control of their own learning, extends Goodson's suggestions; at its crudest, Webb is bringing home very starkly to teachers that pupils may not want to take the initiative in school, and that the problem is real, because there is nothing in the experience of school, particularly for so-called 'less able' kids, that would suggest that they should. Hoskyns, though working within a traditional school subject, physics, is concerned with essentially the same problem in Chapter 12. If you recognize that the majority of children reject school knowledge because, as in physics, they rightly see it as a pointless routine of rigged experiments and dreary calculations; what do you do? Hoskyns's chapter is an account of how he came to see the problem of students' understanding as the central issue for him as a teacher, and how this influenced the way in which his work as a Physics teacher developed. The work of both Webb and Hoskyns arose not as the application of theories generated within the academy but as responses to very particular concrete situations. They are thus bounded by and to that extent legitimate the separation of school knowledge (in the case of Hoskyns) and the hierarchical division between academic and non-academic pupils (in the case of Webb). It is, however, through such examples that we can begin to explore *practically* the limits of educational alternatives.

On a less concrete level, Collins examines in Chapter 13 the radical potential of enabling students to use video equipment in the production of their own television programmes. He points to the difficulties within the confines of any educational context of that kind of practical alternative becoming, in any significant sense, critical, let alone oppositional, to the cultural domination of the mass media. Yet it does suggest that activities within school can have some impact upon the effectiveness of those institutions of ideological control which are so often presented as frustrating the radical potential of education. Taken in conjunction with Chapter 8, it illustrates the way in which the prevailing ideologies of schooling and the mass media mutually reinforce each other and, in doing so, points to the real, if limited, possibilities for subverting that process.

Finally, we include, in Chapter 14, an account from the White Lion Free School of its 'curriculum'. The writers admit that their alternative is not, in any wider sense, politically radical; it is condoned and even partially funded by public authorities. Furthermore, in being unwilling to confront the ways in which external agencies such as examination boards impinge on their practice, they limit the extent to which those in other situations can learn from what they are trying to do. However, the Free School represents, albeit in a limited context, an attempt to involve parents and pupils, not just in a course, but in planning all their daily activities, when no constraint to participate has been imposed on them. In the broader context of politically radical changes, which would involve a shift of power to the mass of the working people, it is strategies of the type that teachers, parents and pupils are trying to develop at White Lion Street, that could form the basis of liberating educational practices.

Chapter 10

Towards an alternative pedagogy

Ivor Goodson

Current classroom practice is largely derived from the belief that the teacher's basic task is the 'transmission of knowledge'. At one level this statement is obviously true — any pedagogy is concerned with the transmission of values and ways of knowing — but at the level of rhetoric 'transmission' has come to characterize a particular view of practice and an associated view of knowledge as a commodity. The distinction between transmission as an aspect of pedagogy and transmission *as* pedagogy is in this sense crucial. What may seem a superficial confusion in educationists' language might mark a deeper confusion of considerable importance. Implicit in the notion of transmission is a one-way communication; it is to 'pass on, hand on'[1] knowledge *from* the teacher *to* the pupil. In this paper I take 'transmission' as characterizing any educational incident which sets the learning of knowledge *previously* planned or defined by the teacher as the basic objective. In thus characterizing transmission I am echoing practice derived from this model in that curricula and lessons centre on the prior definition of knowledge *for* transmission. The transmission pedagogue works to defend this prior definition against interactive redefinition.

By this definition a broad spectrum of teaching styles — 'chalk and talk', 'question and answer', 'discovery projects', 'discussion', 'individualized worksheets' — might be seen as following the transmission model. Hence in 'chalk and talk' the teacher will have decided beforehand what content, concepts or skills he wants to get across: in the 'question and answer' he will have decided what answers are the right ones that he is after: in 'discovery' he will know what he is aiming to help the child discover. In all cases the style of the encounter and the outcome are previously prescribed.

This paper will argue that if the intention of teaching is to involve *all* pupils in learning then transmission, with its dependence on the viability of preplanned educational incidents and outcomes, is particularly ill suited. In arguing this way I am not wishing to imply that pupil/teacher interaction should go on without using previously defined ideas, materials and conceptual structures, or that at no stage should ideas and content be transmitted from teacher to pupil. I am, however, arguing that it is misguided to set transmission as the basic role of the classroom teacher.

The substantial forces maintaining transmission as the dominant pedagogy only partly explain why the development of radical alternatives has largely gone in default. In spite of the enormous validity of its critique of transmission teaching, child-centred progressivism remains for most a negative creed: sure that

128

to transmit to an unwilling child is pointless, but unsure what to do instead. As a result, the 'failure' of the transmission classroom often becomes the 'problem' of the progressive teacher. By only reacting negatively to transmission pedagogy, progressivisim is in danger of becoming an extension of it.

It is time to move on from the negativity of progressivism to the definition of a positive alternative pedagogy. To do so might transform educational debate from the present 'no contest' between ideologies which both faithfully reproduce the social system into a dialectic concerned with educational priorities. Much is to be gained by teachers exploring the possibilities of changing their classroom practice, but to do so they need to move beyond the potent but frustrated plea: 'OK, but what's the alternative?' This article pursues a tentative search for an answer.

Classroom learning

The assumption which underpins transmission pedagogy is that what is decided in the preactive context can be made to work in the interactive context.[2] I want to question this assumption and argue that what is decided at the preactive stage of curriculum planning is commonly contradicted and subverted at the interactive stage.

The assumption that preactive decisions can and should be made to work in the interactive context is inevitably allied to the belief that learning consists of the child coming to accept and understand the teacher's expositions and definitions. In arguing that preactive decisions seldom stand up in the interactive context I am by implication arguing for a new model of classroom learning. Modern studies of learning show how information is idiosyncratically processed by each learner. Recognition of the uniqueness of individual processing and of the variability of individual interests is the prerequisite of any understanding of classroom life and of any move to describe a new pedagogy. The new pedagogy would seek to define a strategy which sensitized the teacher to individual processes and interests and positioned his response to these at the centre of his teaching: broad collective plans and decisions would be ancillary to this central response.

In many ways the new pedagogy would be seeking to formalize at the theoretical (preactive) level what already sometimes goes on at classroom (interactive) level: as we have argued, transmission is commonly subverted in the classroom. Studies of classroom interaction offer boundless evidence of such recurrent subversion. Philip Jackson's studies of 'Life in Classrooms' are widely regarded for their authentic flavour:

> As typically conducted, teaching is an opportunistic process. That is to say, neither the teacher nor his students can predict with any certainty exactly what will happen next. Plans are forever going awry and unexpected opportunities for the attainment of educational goals are constantly emerging. The seasoned teacher seizes upon these opportunities and uses them to his and his students' advantage ... in the classroom as elsewhere, the best laid schemes suffer their usual fate.[3]

The unpredictability of classroom life described by Jackson explains the most common classroom phenomena: one group of children working along the lines the teacher has laid down (e.g. listening, answering or filling in the worksheet); some just going through the motions by copying out bits or doodling, and another group thoroughly alienated, talking among themselves, staring out of the window, thinking of last night at the disco.

This range of responses is what most teachers will readily recognize as the 'reality' of their classrooms. The myth of transmission has it that it is only the teacher's inadequacy that explains why more children are not working along pre-determined lines. I am arguing that the recurrent failure to involve so many children in classroom learning can be most convincingly explained by fundamental flaws in the transmission model. A pedagogy so firmly situated in the preactive vacuum can only expect partial success, given the variabilities of interactive reality; no pedagogy so all-dependent on prediction could hope to encompass the diversity of the classroom.

Even more disturbingly, the fatal flaws of transmission pedagogy mean that teachers' expectations inevitably come to fit the partial successes which are transmission's inevitable achievement:

> The most wasteful and destructive aspect of our present educational system is the set of expectations about student learning each teacher brings to the beginning of a new course or term. The instructor expects a third of his pupils to learn what is taught, a third to learn less well, and a third to fail or just 'get by'. These expectations are transmitted to the pupils through school grading policies and practices and through the methods and materials of instruction. Students quickly learn to act in accordance with them, and the final sorting through the grading process approximates the teacher's original expectations. A pernicious self-fulfilling prophecy has been created.[4]

If the involvement of all students is to be our aim, and this article takes that view, then a pedagogy firmly situated in the interactive reality of the classroom is required: a pedagogy that accepts and works with the individual interests and processes which are at the centre of classroom learning.

Alternative theories and practice

In discussing an alternative pedagogy I am conscious that I am merely presenting a pedagogy in embryo, yet it is an embryo with a long history.

Central to an alternative theory is the focus of investigation upon the *individual* process of learning. Each individual pupil exhibits the most positive response in the learning process when the information being dealt with somehow 'meshes' with what he is interested in. 'A child's education (as opposed to schooling) can only proceed through the pursuit of his interests since it is only these which are of intrinsic value', and, further, 'Whatever enables him to appreciate and understand his interest more fully and to pursue it more actively and effectively is education'.[5] Over half a century ago Dewey was similarly disposed to focus on the individual experiences of the pupil. He saw:

the need of reinstating into experience the subject matter of the studies, or branches of learning. It must be restored to the experience from which it has been abstracted. It needs to be psychologized, turned over, translated into the immediate and individual experiencing within which it has its origin and significance. . . . [6] If the subject matter of the lessons be such as to have an appropriate place within the expanding consciousness of the child, if it grows out of his own past doing, thinkings, and sufferings and grows into application in further achievements and receptivities, then no device or trick or method has to be restored to in order to enlist 'interest'. The psychologized is of interest − that is, it is placed in the whole of conscious life so that it shares the work of that life. But the externally presented material, conceived and generated in standpoints and attitudes remote from the child, and developed in motives alien to him, has no such place of its own. Hence the recourse to adventitious leverage to push it in, to factitious drill to drive it in, to artificial bribe to lure it in.[7]

Acknowledgement of the crucial role of each individual pupil's interests and experience in the learning process is only a starting point for exploring a possible new pedagogy. Certainly such acknowledgement could be, and often is, used in amplifying transmission method pedagogies. 'This regard for children's interests in teaching has more relevance to the method of teaching than to its content . . . Children's existing interests can be used as a starting point from which they can be led on to take an interest in realms of whose existence they never dreamt.'[8] By this argument the child's interest can be used as a method but has little relevance to content: the teacher defines the content and uses the child's interest to transmit it to him.

Acknowledgement of the importance of the child's experience and interests *and* acceptance of these as valid knowledge content in classroom learning can lead to two distinctive alternative pedagogies. The first pedagogy, child-centred progressivism, would centre on the child's interests, *and* in doing so conclude that the pedagogy should aim to allow him to personally direct his own learning. W. H. Kilpatrick's views are closest to advocating this pedagogy; for him education starts where the child is so as to capitalize on the child's personally directed activity springing from his real interest.

> It is what pupils do of themselves that brings the best learning results, both in direct learning and in concomitant learnings. We can thus say, paradoxically, that the teacher's aim is to give as little help as possible, that is, to give the least degree of direct help consistent with the best personal work on the part of the pupils.[9]

A similar style of pedagogy is described by Charity James:

> . . . at its most elementary, if a group of students is engaged on Interdisciplinary Enquiry, within the area of investigation (say, some aspect of life in a technological society, or of human growth and development in childhood and adolescence) students formulate the questions they want to answer, identify the problems which they want to solve, create hypotheses

for their solutions, test them and revise the hypotheses.[10]

For James, as for Kilpatrick, the teacher is seen 'as a consultant to students in their self-directed enterprise'.[11]

Whilst sympathetic to the emphasis of Kilpatrick and James, I think the pedagogy they recommend is over-dependent (one might say solely dependent) on 'what pupils do themselves'.[12] Such an emphasis seems to be ill suited to the interactive character of classroom learning in two ways:

(a) A major part of the rationale for classroom learning must surely turn on those aspects the pupil learns in interaction with his peers and his teacher. This interactive dimension in learning can aid the development of the pupil's interests and ideas into other areas from those he might independently explore. Learning associated with the kind of pedagogy Kilpatrick and James advocate seems to miss most of the potential present in classroom interaction.

(b) A further aspect of classroom interaction is that the pupil's independent studies may well be subject to a good deal of interruption. The Kilpatrick model never seems to come to grips with the question of 'control' within the classroom. Any pedagogy that fails to address this question is surely doomed. This is not because the classroom teacher is an irremediable authoritarian by nature but because part of her/his job must be to ensure that pupil's work can go on uninterrupted. This means that he must be more than a consultant in his classroom. A viable pedagogy must acknowledge that in the classroom 'the crowds remain' to pull at the student's attention and divert the teacher's energy.[13]

A second pedagogy based on the child's individual interests and experiences addresses itself to the interactive potential and reality of the classroom. Acknowledgement of the paramount role of individual process in learning does not in this pedagogy lead on to the conclusion that individual process is self-sufficient. The paramountcy of individual process in learning does not preclude the role of external challenge and collaboration in that process; rather, it argues for such a role to be at the centre of the teacher's actions.

Towards an alternative pedagogy

A number of accounts of the introduction of innovative teaching courses, besides underlining the pervasive flaws of transmission, also indicate how an alternative pedagogy could remedy such flaws. The following quotation refers to a fourth-year Humanities course in a comprehensive school:

A theme is chosen, strategies worked out to relate it to the pupil's experience and interest, materials prepared, resources mobilized. The process is intensely exciting, above all, I think, because it incites us to pursue ourselves the course of study we are preparing to advocate to our pupils. Ironically, by the time the programme is ready to be presented to the pupils for whom it is intended, our own enthusiasm as teachers is often half-spent, or else has become so self-absorbing that we cannot appreciate that it will not be shared by everyone else. We have become our own curriculum's ideal pupils; our resources are beautifully designed to satisfy not our pupils' intellectual demands, but our own! [14]

An account of a first-year undergraduate course in economics makes the same points:

One puzzling factor in the situation was that, whilst students appeared to get very little out of the Demand Theory Package, the members of faculty who prepared it felt that they had learnt a lot. In preparing the Factor Pricing Package, therefore, our attention began to shift towards the problem of getting the students to share the experience which the faculty had had. It became clear that it was the process of 'sorting it all out', so important and necessary in developing self-instructional materials, which was the key to this problem. In presenting the students with a completed analysis we were concentrating their attention on predetermined solutions at the expense of focusing it on either the nature of the problem or the analytic process itself. [15]

From these two accounts it becomes apparent that what is needed is to involve the student in the process of 'sorting it all out' — what Dewey called 'the need of reinstating into experience the subject matter'. The need is to move the pedagogic focus from the preactive situation where it is divorced from the pupils to the interactive situation where the pupils are involved. By so changing the focus learning becomes less a matter of mastering externally presented material — more a case of actively reconstructing knowledge.

We have stated before that moving the pedagogic focus from implementing the preactive to interpreting the interactive does not imply an absence of planning (or for that matter, evaluation). As before, the teacher will be concerned to plan for his lessons but in the new situation will seek to ensure that the predictive does not become the prescriptive. E. W. Eisner comes near to the spirit of such a plan in describing expressive objectives: 'An expressive objective describes an educational encounter: it identifies a situation in which children are to work, a problem with which they are to cope, a task in which they are to engage; but it does not specify what from that encounter situation, problem or task they are to learn.' [16] In short, planning is concerned with the process of learning and does not prescribe what is going to be produced.

A number of examples of work based on this kind of pedagogic ideal are already in operation. An important minority of 'progressive' teachers in British primary schools and a growing body in middle schools already work an alternative pedagogy:

At her best the primary school teacher working in a more or less progressive English primary school is perhaps the only contemporary polymath, even if to herself she seems more like a jack of all trades. She is something of an expert in the psychology of learning and the nature of childhood, passionately committed to intellectual exploration within the most widely ranging areas of experience, rarely afraid to tackle, at the invitation of her pupils, new disciplines, and often the master of some particular part of experience which she teaches — art or nature or language. Doubtless to put it so badly is to idealize, but it is an idealization drawn from life.[17]

The guiding principle of this primary school tradition is 'intellectual exploration' — a working plan of principles of procedure will be needed to facilitate such exploration together with predictions as to worthwhile activities and useful resources.

The American Social Science curriculum, *Man: A Course of Study*, on which Bruner acted as consultant goes some way towards defining principles of procedure for an alternative pedagogy:

1. To initiate and develop in youngsters a process of question-posing (the inquiry method).

2 To teach a research methodology where children can look for information to answer questions they have raised and used the framework developed in the course (e.g. the concept of the life cycle) and apply it to new areas.

3 To help youngsters develop the ability to use a variety of first-hand sources as evidence from which to develop hypotheses and draw conclusions.

4 To conduct classroom discussions in which youngsters learn to listen to others as well as express their own view.

5 To legitimate the search: that is, to give sanction and support to open-ended discussions where definitive answers to many questions are not found.

6 To encourage children to reflect on their own experiences.[18]

Whilst not wishing to recommend the whole of Bruner's curriculum package as exemplifying an alternative pedagogy, this definition of principle does offer useful guidelines of a broad plan of interaction.

As well as broad principles of procedure it is also useful for teachers to have a working list of likely criteria for judging classroom activities. Raths recently attempted to produce such a list which included, for example, 'All other things being equal, one activity is more worthwhile than another if it permits children to make informed choices in carrying out the activity and to reflect on the consequences of their choices.'[19] But clearly lists of procedural principles and worthwhile activities might fall into the trap whereby preactive definition prescribes interactive interpretation. To avoid this it is important to try to 'catch the spirit' in which such lists should be used. 'The problem is to produce a specification to which teachers can work in the classroom, and thus to provide the basis for a new tradition. That specification needs to catch the implication of ideas for practice.'[20]

What might fulfil this need is a description of the kind of encounter which best characterizes the new tradition: an exemplar of the pedagogy in interaction. Peter Medway and I recently attempted to define an exemplar of what, for want of a better phrase, we called cooperative learning:

Imagine this situation in a secondary school. A teacher with a group in his classroom. He spends two mornings and two afternoons with them each week. He has set up a room that reflects many of his own interests and his predictions of what might grab his kids. There are charts and paintings on the wall, a trolley of assorted materials in the corner, some records, film-strips, paint and brushes and so on. It's a deliberately set up environment for learning.

It's noticeable that the teacher is relating very differently to different groups and individuals. Some he leaves alone; with others he sits down and looks at what they've done and makes vague situation-maintaining remarks – 'Yes, that's good, go on'; with others he's engaged in specific and animated point-by-point argument, explanation, planning, disagreement.

What is going on can be thought of as cooperative learning – cooperative, that is, between teacher and student. There may well also be cooperation between students, but we want to single out for attention here the type of relationship obtaining between the teacher and either individual students or small groups of friends. It's cooperative in that teacher and student look together at a topic, each presenting to the other his own perception of it, both feeling their way through dialogue towards a common perception. Cooperation is not a euphemism, a gentler way of doing the same old thing – by persuasion rather than imposition. The implied equality is meant to be taken seriously, and the learning relationship, starting on the teacher's side with a commitment to the principle of reciprocity, progresses to the point where reciprocity is experienced as a reality.

A cooperative learning enterprise that reaches the crucial learning thres-hold might pass through three stages:

First stage: The student says 'I want to do something on the second world war' and gets the reply, 'OK – get started. Here's some books and magazines, there's a filmstrip you can look at.' There follows a period during which the teacher can feel quite anxious about what's going on: there may be a lot of copying out of books, drawing pictures, unrelated bits and pieces of knowledge being collected – useless know-ledge it may seem, and so indeed it may sometimes turn out to be. But what *may* be going on is a process of exploration in which the student, often unconsciously, feels around the topic to locate the real source of its attraction for him – some problem or worry or preoccupation or powerful feeling related to it.

Second stage: The teacher, after watching all this and trying to detect underlying themes and concerns in the student's busy activity, while very gently maintaining it and restraining himself from criticism, and the student, who is beginning to get clearer about what it is in the topic that is really keeping him on it, get together to bring it into focus. 'So what you're really on about is the casual pointless way people could get killed, in ways that couldn't make any sense to them – you live your whole life, have an education, a family, fillings in your teeth, and end up in a ditch after some minor skirmish with an unimportant enemy outpost that was going to withdraw one minute later anyway.' The teacher goes on to suggest further ways of exploring the central interest. *Third stage:* The student is now experiencing the satisfaction of successfully getting into a topic for himself and bringing it under control. He has developed tenacity and perseverance, is making statements he can back up, is suggesting hypotheses with confidence and is able to improvise from knowledge. The project is out of the intensive care unit and the teacher can speak his mind about it without fear of killing it stone dead or putting the student down. The relationship has become robust, and stimulating to both sides. The student enjoys the teacher's company and challenges him. The teacher has got interested in the student *and* in the topic — about which he now knows a lot more than he did. He takes the student's challenges and suggestions seriously. He now experiences the cooperation which started off as abstract ideal.

This is the stage of synthesis. The student has a perspective on the whole topic which may be expressed in a piece of writing that integrates generalizations, facts, attitudes and his whole view of the world. The final writing or presentation will express the dynamic vigour of the reconstruction of knowledge that has gone on.[21]

If, as I intend, this description is taken as characterizing a new pedagogy at work, a number of important implications need to be clearly enunciated. Firstly, learning will often involve *individual* negotiation between pupil and teacher: the teacher learns alongside his pupils, an adult learner among young learners, though with additional responsibilities to those of his charges. The teacher helps the child isolate a problem which is puzzling him (the example given related to the second world war), together they devise a plan for investigating the problems, the investigation promotes a number of hypotheses, these are worked through and reformulated, and together the teacher and child discuss and define a mutually acceptable solution. In this case the teacher's energy, resource preparation and stock of commonsense and specialist knowledge is used in facilitating the child's inquiry into something he has become interested in. (In transmission the teacher puts much of his energy and resources into preparation *before* confronting the variety of children's interest — a fatiguing gamble which too seldom pays off.)

Secondly, the pedagogy implies a radical re-ordering of the way in which knowledge is defined. The rhetoric of tranmission schools maintains that the child gets a balanced 'diet' of 'subjects' which cover the main disciplines of knowledge. But this must be recognized as rhetoric: the knowledge which teachers transmit has *never* been 'received' by most children. That is why there are 2 million acknowledged adult illiterates, why I can do no mathematics and speak no foreign languages (not even Latin), why in many schools only the minority are even *offered* subject transmission while the rest do 'Parentcraft', 'Personal Development' and 'Motor Cycle Maintenance'. Knowledge as transmitted in schools has been described by Barnes: 'School knowledge is the knowledge which someone else presents to us. We partly grasp it, enough to answer examination questions, but it remains someone else's knowledge, not ours. If we never use this knowledge we probably forget it.'[22]

Although optimistic (how many pupils even sit exams, let alone answer the questions successfully?), this description catches the essence of school knowledge and Barnes goes on to argue for a new view of knowledge known as 'action knowledge':

> In so far as we use knowledge for our own purposes . . . we begin to incorporate it into our view of the world, and to use parts of it to cope with the exigencies of living. Once the knowledge becomes incorporated into our view of the world on which our actions are based, I would say it has become 'action knowledge'.[23]

Only if the teacher gives the child access to 'action knowledge' can learning take place. An alternative pedagogy would seek to offer the child such an opportunity whilst transmission pedagogy pre-empts it. In placing the individual pupil in such a central position in defining the approach to knowledge there is not only a psychological rationale (which some traditionalists concede) but a logical rationale too. All subject matter begins with an original attempt to solve problems and it is this unitary process of knowledge creation that should be the focus of pedagogy, not the transmission of its differentiated products. Only by involvement in this process can the pupil begin exploration of the wider fields and forms of knowledge: that successive broadening and deepening of knowledge which is the only route to a 'balanced curriculum' for each child.

Some constraints and problems

The most obvious constraint to centring a pedagogy around the pupil's inquiry in cooperation with the teacher is that pupils have to attend school and the teacher is responsible for such attendance. Yet this is the constraint within which any style of classroom learning has to operate; it is not a constraint which I see as advocating a transmission model, rather that an alternative pedagogy would better accommodate this fact of classroom life.

A more specific problem relates to the nature of classroom life, for 'the crowds remain to pull at the student's attention and to divert the teacher's energy'. There are two problems associated with an alternative pedagogy. (a) Is 'individual negotiation' possible in the hurly-burly of the classroom? (b) Does a role as an equal learner interfere with the teacher's control capacity? Undoubtedly most people would answer 'yes' at this stage and move on to conclude that only transmission can cope with classroom realities. A number of facts indicate that this could be an outdated perception. In a number of primary school classrooms with forty or forty-five pupils, of often noisy and mobile inclination, an alternative pedagogy has been made to work quite successfully. Exceptional teachers, perhaps, but what of the average teacher? In the upper secondary school the average teacher works in an organization which maximizes his opportunity for short, specialized sessions of transmission. As widely reported, it is at this level that 'control' is most difficult: where transmission is maximized 'control' problems are greatest. Even as a 'survival technique' it would appear that transmission is outmoded: the pedagogy and associated organizational structure work against the establishment of those individual and personal relationships which as well as alleviating 'control' problems might serve to increase the educative potential of the teacher.

The contradictions in transmission pedagogy have already encouraged new developments in our classrooms. Clearly the development of an alternative pedagogy can only be part of a much larger scheme of transformation, but acknowledgement of the enormity of the task should not inhibit developments, for this would seem one important place to begin. By exploring an alternative pedagogy in their classrooms teachers can clarify what is possible in schools, what purposes schools serve in our society, and perhaps bring new understandings of the rhetoric of transmission. That is a long way from accepting that transmission *is* teaching.

For 'progressive' models of education the development of an alternative pedagogy would provide that coherent and positive view of the teacher's involvement that has so far seemed lacking. Active challenging of and collaboration with the child might then have been seen as criteria for a successful pedagogy, rather than an outmoded pattern of teacher domination. Further, an alternative pedagogy should move beyond the individual negotiations that this paper has concentrated on; collective and group aspects need to be developed. From an individual knowledge of and relationship with each student the teacher can then, and only then, broaden his curriculum and group involvement. And from a clear definition of pedagogy new definitions of school and classroom might begin.

Notes

1 *Concise Oxford Dictionary.*

2 P. W. Jackson, *Life in Classrooms* (New York, Holt, Rinehart & Winston, 1968), p. 152. Using Jackson's distinction, what the teacher does before the lesson in the empty classroom is preactive; when the children enter the classroom it is interactive. Nell Keddie has drawn attention to a similar dichotomy between the 'educationist context' and the 'teacher context' (N. Keddie, 'Classroom Knowledge' in M. F. D. Young, (ed.), *Knowledge and Control* (London, Collier-Macmillan, 1971).

3 Jackson, op. cit., p. 166.

4 B. S. Bloom, 'Mastery Learning' in J. H. Block (ed.), *Mastering Learning: Theory and Practice* (New York, Holt, Rinehart & Winston, 1971), p. 47.

5 P. S. Wilson, *Interest and Discipline in Education* (London, Routledge & Kegan Paul, 1971), p. 67.

6 J. Dewey, *The Child and the Curriculum* (Chicago, University of Chicago Press, 1902, reprinted 1971), p. 22. I share the severe reservations about Dewey expressed most recently in the work of Clarence Karier.

7 Ibid. p. 27.

8 R. Peters and P. Hirst, *The Logic of Education* (London, Routledge & Kegan Paul, 1970), pp. 37, 38,

9　W. H. Kilpatrick, *Philosophy of Education* (New York, Macmillan, 1951), p. 307.

10　C. James, *Young Lives at Stake* (London, Collins, 1968), pp. 65-6.

11　Ibid., p. 65.

12　Kilpatrick, op. cit., p.307.

13　Jackson, op. cit., p.111.

14　M. Armstrong, 'The Role of the Teacher' in P. Buckman (ed.), *Education Without Schools* (London, Souvenir Press, 1974), p. 51.

15　M. Eraut, N. Mackenzie and I. Papps, 'The Mythology of Educational Development', *British Journal of Educational Technology,* vol. 6, No. 3 (October 1975).

16　W. J. Popham, E. W. Eisner, H. J. Sullivan and L. L. Tyler, *Instructional Objectives* (Chicago, Rand McNally, 1969), pp. 15-16.

17　Armstrong, op. cit., p. 56.

18　J. P. Hanley, D. K. Whitla, E. W. Moo and A. S. Walter, *Curiosity, Competence and Community. Man: a Course of Study* (Cambridge, Mass., Education Development Center, 1970), p. 5.

19　J. D. Raths, 'Teaching without Specific Objectives', *Educational Leadership,* (April 1971), pp. 714-20.

20　L. Stenhouse, 'Defining the Curriculum Problem', *Cambridge Journal of Education,* vol. 5, No. 2 (Easter 1975).

21　I. Goodson and P. Medway, 'The Feeling is Mutual', *Times Educational Supplement* (20 June 1975), p. 17.

22　D. Barnes, *From Communication to Curriculum* (Harmondsworth, Penguin, 1976), p. 81.

23　Ibid.

Chapter 11

An attempt at collaborative learning

Chris Webb

To be a reasonably good teacher in a large London comprehensive school is a seductive business. One can develop a style which is friendly, energetic, and caring, to the point at which this in itself can seem sufficient. The students will often accept and reinforce this kind of image, as it can offer a stability and an accessibility, rare commodities in the flux of large schools today. In terms of one's colleagues, often it will be sufficient that you can cope. In this way, you do not impinge on people's time, nor add fuel to the 'ever impending social crisis' by the example of your failure. Control metaphors are never far from the lips of staff or students, the latter often feeding the arguments of the teachers by their actions, and at the same time vindicating the professional's reaction in his own eyes, by their assertion of preference for order. One can become rather like the caricature of the benevolent town marshal, striding the corridors, dispensing rough justice, but underneath it all being on the side of the underdog. In this role, which comes in many guises, from the quiet intensity of supposed *rapport,* through to the torchbearing revolutionary, there is the possibility of complete corruption. That popular phrase 'for the kids' can begin to look as empty as most school corridors after four in the afternoon, particularly if an effort is not made to extricate oneself, the 'friendly, energetic, caring teacher', from the plots of one's own design.

After three years of teaching, these plots were beginning to thicken, and the action in them to develop a momentum all of its own. In many ways, it was a successful three years, in which I had covered much new ground on the territory of curriculum innovation, opened up lasting relations with students, and been vigorous in preparing the minority for public examinations. Much of this was compatible with my hopes for comprehensives but despite this I had a growing unease about my own practice. The arguments against the schooling system were well known and rehearsed by me, but I had felt that comprehensive schools might begin to alter the social and political results of the selective system. But, gradually, the way in which I defined my own activities, normally describing myself in terms which had elements of 'subversion of the *status quo*' and 'commitment to the kids', began to look bizarre. This was in comparison to how my day was actually spent.

My public statements zealously upheld the idea of comprehensives, the practice of mixed-ability teaching, the differences between a 'moral' and a skill education and the need to correlate thought and action. Typically, this was upheld by both staff and pupils, in that often unselfconscious connivance which is mutually supportive. My private feelings, on the other hand, were being irritated in a way which was singularly difficult to isolate. It was not just frustration with the system, or anger at the waste, but rather a feeling of dishonesty or irony at my own performance. But slowly, the very time that my experience was creating for me, as opposed to the frenetic rush of the teaching day in the first few years, provided a possibility to pick at the nits in my consciousness.

Chief among these was the increasingly custodial quality of my daily task. Anyone who has read the concerns of some of the early exponents of state education, or heard their echoes in the Black Papers, will have little doubt about the control function of schooling.[1] In personal terms, though, it can be very easy to develop a 'soft' mode of control, whilst being highly critical of authoritarianism, often only a difference of style. If one stops at the end of a day and attempts to quantify the amount of time spent in coercing, preventing and valuing student activity, then the more radical rationales begin to look more like apologies. This can be dramatically obvious in the 'moral' and behavioural arena, but can be most insidiously effective in the strategy-and-aims style of teaching.[2] Much of this posits a certain model of critical, autonomous and informed beings as its aims. Then, by its simplified learning theories and all-pervasive strategy, often prevents any real thrust in that direction. Teacher, course and kit between them absorb any real initiatives. The values of integration, much lauded, are often confounded by the RE teacher, history teacher and geography teacher, all doing their bit; in this way, firmly underscoring the division of labour and commodity characteristic of knowledge.

Infusing all this was a feeling that, in biographical terms, the students were not being excited. Interest and enthusiasm could be, and were, generated for some, but only in the compartment of time and space allotted to them. There was the disappointment that even these temporary heightenings of experience were not being translated into a working vocabulary, a way of coping with the world. They had a lack of status as events, compared to the evening or weekend happenings, not as a kind of subcultural defence, but because qualitatively they did not compare. Everyday life was better, and school experience was only relevant as an inferior attempt to prepare for a life style already sensed by most. This deterministic characteristic was perhaps the most depressing, as the treadmill carried a generation past on their long initiation ritual, from the school to the labour market, with little facility for what Paulo Freire calls 'conscientization',[3] or the power to recognize and name oneself in place and time, thus having a part to play in one's own destiny.

These feelings will be familiar to many, both teachers and taught. Schools described as 'anti-entropic feedback systems',[4] 'inferior learning environments' or 'manipulative institutions' are familiar critiques now. Equally, the irony of the gap between teacher beliefs and self-identifications, and between teacher practice and results, is well known. But, given the political and institutional constraints, the lack of finance, one's own ambivalence, and the sheer size of the cultural process, what should one do?

I was in the middle of perhaps the most over-subscribed area of the curriculum industry — the historical/economic/social studies field. Here, one, was inundated with exhortations to teach birth control/housing/third world/black studies, to follow the latest 'primrose path', the teaching kit, to whatever ends it prescribed. By rummaging through this ragbag of offerings to clothe ROSLA pupils, I came across the Nuffield/Schools Council Humanities Curriculum Project.[5] This was a prestigious and well-advertised attempt to provide a resource and a method for the New Era of ROSLA, and if anything made me read the glossy brochure, it was the suggestion of interest in method. The research group saw ROSLA as being of critical importance, but felt that, without an increase in experience to match the prolongation of school time, the whole effort would be a paper tiger. They reckoned, none too originally but accurately, that the reluctant or alienated learner would be the largest problem for many teachers. They would obviously constitute a challenge to many dimensions of school life, and the team felt that educational strategies could be adopted to meet this strong reaction to school. To this end, a five-point plan was developed, advocating the handling of value issues in the classroom: that the teacher should be neutral; that the mode of inquiry should be discussion; that this discussion should protect divergence; and that the teacher should have responsibility for quality and standards. In this way, every student would be 'given access to a complex cultural inheritance, some hold on his personal life, and on his relationships with the various communities to which he belongs, some extension of his understanding of, and sensitivity towards, other human beings'.[6]

Such noble and radical sentiments often grace the ends or beginnings of descriptions of work and curriculum. Equally often, they are contradicted by the assumptions which lie in strata within such schemes of work. This Humanities Project for me had many such shibboleths, not least the faith in discussion as a tool for enlightenment, or the hope that the neutral chairman could avoid being intrusive when he had responsibility for quality. Particularly, he could choose the material for discussion from the teaching packs, and terminate or direct the conversation as he saw fit. *Plus ca change!* The project also seemed to be modelled on a sedate, democratic model which seemed a far cry from the collective energies and perceptions of a group of school leavers. They would often be well versed in each other's thoughts and social lives, and bring their prior personal likes and dislikes into the group. Status would be well delineated already, and opinions probably judged by that, rather than by the intrinsic worth of a comment. But, despite the liberal-democratic gloss and overly intellectual medium, the project had one feature that distinguished it from the rest. It attempted to muffle the teacher, by turning him into a chairman without views, albeit with potentially omnipotent powers to direct through procedure or style! This theoretically placed the onus on to the students, and renounced the didactic approach of much teaching — the one-way informational procedure, or that peculiarly emasculated tool of investigation, the socratic dialogue, much beloved of school teachers.

But, this characteristic apart, my reasons for adopting the kit were cynical. It was well documented and advertised, and to jump on the bandwagon, you need the vehicle. My wishes were vague, something to do with creating an exciting context, but this was not a recipe likely to appeal to my colleagues, wary of both innovation and ROSLA. To get the blocks of time I needed to escape from the 'must get on with it' syndrome, and the finance to energize the ongoing activities within the course, I needed a platform. The Humanities Curriculum Project provided this. Political lobbying, the spectre of ROSLA, and the fortuitius non-appointment of an Audio Visual Assistant, provided the timetable blocking and finance required for an open-ended venture. All too often, curriculum innovation is allowed to die for lack of funds and time appropriate to its methods. Timetabling, particularly, is an area of huge significance within the school, and must be understood to enable alternative suggestions to be put.

I had to make certain decisions on how to present this as an option to the students. Traditionally, the various heads of departments spoke to the whole year or each form in turn, outlining in glowing terms the meaning of their subject, its attractions, and possible significance for the future – usually its examinability. The whole ritual was enacted quite seriously, departmental credibility and prestige demanding a certain promotional fervour on the one hand, and the last attempt to find that better life at the top of the school imbuing the pupils' choices with real seriousness on the other. Although this could range from an attempt to find a congenial passage through, to sometimes incoherent attempts to create a meaningful bundle from that mid-career jumble sale. The formidable task of piercing the atmosphere of rhetoric with a suggestion of how Humanities might work was almost insurmountable. Firstly, I did not really know, and, secondly, the brave new world of neutrally chaired groups, initiative, and that ubiquitous educational panacea, video, was meaningless to them. Equally, it was hypothetical to me! In fact, the only two things that raised much reaction were the prospect of 'visits', a yawningly empty concept in itself, and the thought that some money was available to the course. Even this last word was problematic, for I had no neat sequential structures to offer. Any attempts to fill in the possible meaning worried me as preemptive. The whole hazy process of attempting to communicate these unfamiliar ideas underlined the paucity of that process which seems to dominate schools talk – not discussion, dialogue or demonstration, but plain teacher-dominated 'blah'.

So far, I have attempted to outline, impressionistically, some of my unease at my then current practice, and the tortuous political and educational strategies that had to be adopted to attempt something different. The very vagueness of my aims was both vindicated by a philosophical wish for the students to play a major part in forming them, and also deprecated by me on account of its all-purpose amorphousness. It could absorb failure under the guise of something else, and this fear was to remain throughout the year. Whether this was a vestige of the objective approach, or the need for rigour in perpetual assessment, I could never quite disentangle.

On that first morning in September, the group assembled and ironically fulfilled the hopes of some staff that it would take up some of the malcontents. It was a formidable collection of tough, talkative, energetic fifteen-year-olds. Many already had their eyes set on employment, and were angry at their enforced year in school, typical cannon fodder for curriculum innovation and suggestive of the status of such changes in both the eyes of the staff, and perhaps the pupils, at least until it was sampled, and then still seen as 'lower' because of its non-examination characteristic. I attempted, somewhat tentatively, to suggest what might happen in the coming year. This uncharacteristic reserve on my part, the 'energetic' part of my image being more typical, unsettled them slightly. Was I bluffing? Was I letting a hundred flowers bloom, only to cut their heads off when revealed? Was I doing my job? This last question underlined the passive role they were used to, and also stirred many doubts in me. Not least if it took ages to achieve any momentum, could I resist intruding? The atmosphere tended to be a slightly disbelieving cynicism over the possibility of them playing a part in the school day in anything other than a disruptive role. My job, their experience, and the classroom layout all militated against this end. For many of them, school was firmly demythologized as a place of opportunity or creativity. Often, their failures had been personalized, officially or by themselves, though one or two felt that the school needed failure to succeed. So it was with somewhat jaundiced eyes that they regarded my efforts to outline a new strategy, and and invite them to manage the tactics, at least as an opener.

I suggested that we would have discussion groups for one of the half days, and we would record these on video for our own delectation. Also, I mentioned that I would not participate in the discussion, but would be a chairman. This latter suggestion was accepted gleefully, although majority opinion was that it would be boring. But, as they had no other suggestions, and I had not planned anything else, we decided to go ahead. The collective decision making was decidely 'tinny' at this stage, with them not trusting my will, and me not trusting my will! The urge to launch into something was overwhelming, a mixture of ego, the glass in my door, and our collective training.

So, during the next session, I cleared the room and set up the video-camera in one corner and a circle of chairs in the other. A small enough thing in itself, but important in helping to create a sense of difference. When the flood of bodies had settled selfconsciously in the chairs, taken up their pieces of paper with some figures concerning marriage and divorce, the tape recorder was switched on. The ominous click of that switch was to produce the same response for the next three weeks, almost complete silence! Instead of conversation, a fascinating proliferation of diversionary tactics was to be seen. Continuous yawning, stretching, staring, sleeping, and hair chewing produced hilarious viewing on the videotape, afterwards — the first few times anyway! All this, I felt sympathetic towards, but very frustrated over, dying to revert to norm and embroil myself in this dynamically static situation. It was a worrying time, for I had decided to be very regressive as chairman. Soon, I was wondering who would break the silence first, me or them? Certainly, I had underestimated the strength of group dynamics in this situation. It all seemed a far cry from the Project's ideal-type group, with its common ideals and tolerance of others' opinions, earnestly chewing over controversial issues. It was rendered all the more strange by the actual consistency of the group and their normal energy in conversation.

Our general concern in the group was 'Relationships Between the Sexes', and I remember distinctly the piece of 'evidence' (project jargon) which first prompted the group to speak at length. It was a double cartoon by Gilray of the nineteenth century, entitled 'Harmony Before Marriage' and 'Marital Harmonics' — a kind of before-and-after sequence; full of symbols and rich with meaning, this caught their attention. For a long time, they performed a verbal autopsy on the cartoon, and then one or two of them began to generalize about marriage. This was to set the trend for the year, with some of them beginning to realize the difference between the particular and general, not least the potential of the latter in shaping the world. Others remained suspicious of rational dialogue, arguing that to develop an argument from premise to conclusion was no more than a long-winded way of asserting, so why bother? I felt myself that this latter argument was sometimes lazy, an unwillingness to reveal any of the complexities behind a statement. But if there was a genuine investment in the premise, why should they reveal it to a group anyway? 'Creative Writing' and this kind of discussion have got to happen in a trusting context. Equally, I felt sure that the conceptual was a way to find out how things work, but often was more to do with information than with hierarchies of thought. But how was this information to be made available, without stifling their own opinion? To some extent, this remained an unresolved dilemma, silence often being the result of introducing some evidence into the group. This was not because the conversation was the kind of 'circular familiarity' that Bernstein describes as a type in his early essays, but because the evidence replaced teacher. Even contradictory authorities often had the same effect, but by the end of the year there was a growing awareness of the plasticity of fact and the motives implicit in its presentation. A small step, perhaps, towards looking behind the verbal structures with which our society is supported, and how their own experiences could be related to or amputated from the body politic.

A great deal of energy within the group was dissipated by intragroup sniping and dissent. Not surprisingly, to take a group of fifteen-year-olds and place them into a face-to-face situation was to produce tensions. In the more traditional classroom, groups that do not like each other can avoid any contact, 'baddies' at the back and 'goodies' at the front. Here they had to sit in close proximity, and, with no prior consensus as to the group activity or habits of tolerance, trouble could easily flare up. Certainly, part of the group were 'geezers', in the operative vocabulary, and they dressed to fashion, used the shifting phrases of the London language with facility, and regarded many of those who differed from them as 'poofs'. This label could cover anyone with even vestigial remains of school uniform, spectacle wearers, briefcase carriers, and those with short hair. The sum result of this was that certain members of the group became isolated and threatened, and, as a result of this, opted out. Once, after a fairly vicious piece of group cruelty, I intervened strongly, and produced a kind of enforced grudging tolerance for a few weeks! I remain unconvinced that discussion with these numbers can hope to achieve much mutual understanding or tolerance, though, done rigorously in conjunction with other more concrete experiences, it can help to illuminate positions. Compared to the teacher-dominated sessions in even the most enlightened classroom, it can offer a possibility for students to generate and test views. It can even begin to develop a sense that the words spoken have a power, if only to shape what was to go on in the other part of the course.

This change of responsibility meant that a great potential for abuse, as well as of use, was revealed in such a context. As confidence and trust grew in me and in each other, things were said at such moments which were transformed into ammunition the very next. Perhaps I was too regressive a chairman, but, having seen the early videotapes and marvelled at my own power within the group, I decided to remove myself even further from the course of events. Gradually, eyes stopped flicking towards me and confirmation ceased to be sought. Parallel to this, I developed more courage to allow what my teacher sense dictated as irrelevancy to develop or die, or to allow a silence to continue, refusing to accept responsibility for it in the group, Though here, as in any human group, some were more glib than others and could dominate the conversation. One boy spoke but once all year, and that was to mutter 'shit' when his chair fell over.

There were certainly times when my lack of participation enraged the group, not least when discussing topics within education which led to them becoming hopelessly enmeshed in analysis of our school. Here, they would appeal for adjudication on points of opinion, but I refused to give, although the discussion could well continue outside with me very much included. In the final term for the last six weeks, I deliberately began to participate when discussing aspects of work. They both resented this and enjoyed the relief of my support, and, having got used to the right of opinion, were much tougher in their arguments with me. Particularly, they would not allow the balanced view, but wanted my real position. But despite this, it lacked the zing, the potential for surprise, of the neutrally chaired groups: it had suddenly become comfortable for them.

The other major aspect of the course was covered by the vague label of 'ongoing activities', unplanned, unpredictable, and often jettisoned halfway through. Most of these originated directly from the discussion groups or planning meetings in the other sessions. They began with a series of question-naires, conceived, drawn up and duplicated by the students, on questions of sex, morality and marriage. Then, armed with instamatic cameras and tape recorders, they proceeded to pillage and pry the private views of the local populace. Feeling that this was too local, they proceeded further abroad to Hampstead, Soho and Regents Park, in an effort to contrast predominantly working class views with upper class, as they saw it. They kept a complete record of people's answers, and photographed their interviewees, thus building up their own resources. One or two of them tried to correlate the results in terms of sex, age, jobs, and so on. I always tried to make the complete process available to them, so they edited their own tapes and printed their own photographs. Little that was new concerning views on sex appeared, but the process of collection and interpretation, backed up with the learning of skills, was an exciting start.

Even this fairly conventional use of the locality and its people as a resource presented problems in terms of the school's system and the outside world. Often, as things were planned and executed on the day, the usual notice was im-possible to give, and it was only really because I was a head of department that I got away with this flexibility. Also, there is very real responsibility for students who go out in your name. Often, boys were stopped by the police, or the school received telephone calls from the station asking for information about four boys who had obviously stolen tape recorders. Obviously, a great deal of trust is needed here, or long-range control, and basically, although I did not mind time off for a cup of tea and a fag, I did object to no interviews being done. But any pedagogy which wishes to use the surrounding London environment has to come to terms with unfriendly adults, unsympathetic police, stupidity on the part of the students, and so on. It is one's own responsibility.

Another, and sometimes easier, way to tap society's resources is to arrange specific visits to all kinds of people. On the whole, we attempted to get 'celebrities', as the 'man in the street' had already been drained dry. Among our scalps were Leo Abse, Trevor Huddleston and Mary Whitehouse. These experiences were salutary, demythologizing screen images and, thanks to the unpatronizing honesty of some of those interviewed, gave the students a sense of their own intelligence. The warmth and humanity of Leo Abse and the utter straightness of Bishop Huddleston on questions of sex and morality, made a deep impression. Perhaps the best moment was with Bishop Huddleston in his offices in the Commercial Road when, on the subject of pre-marital sex which the Bishop had already made some seemingly near heretical comments on, one of the students after a long and thoughtful silence asked 'Do you ever have wet dreams? 'An obvious question after Huddleston had explained his views on chastity, and the boy was puzzled by this seemingly asexual creature. He got a very straight answer but the anecdote epitomizes the openness of some of these interviews, compared to the often taboo-riddled school discussion. People are often willing to help in this way and, if the meeting is small and the dialogue open ended, it can be a very potent experience indeed.

Whilst still investigating sexual relationships, moral and the rest, the students decided to try and use the video-camera to produce a Monty Python skit on aspects of sex roles, deviance and marriage. The classroom was turned into a studio with some working the equipment, some writing sketches, and some prancing around in drag, whilst others improvised scenery and visual aids. They rotated these jobs and began to work more as a group, even if the quiet ones tended to be the stooges in the various sketches. This lasted for six weeks and quite by chance culminated in an appearance for them on 'Real Time' by courtesy of the BBC. Though much to the latter's shame, this landmark in British television was not screened until the 'witching time of night'! A great deal came out of this venture, not least an appreciation of other people for what they could do and an unexpected traditional bonus of a great deal of writing, often cooperatively done.

The section of the year which scrutinized education was dominated by one thing — the students themselves teaching a full day in their old primary schools. This development arose from the first discussion group when there was a unanimous feeling expressed concerning the irrational nature of much teacherly authority. They rounded on me at break with this and I suppose that I threw something of a challenge out to them: that if they found themselves in a classroom situation they would probably be pressurized into irrational poses very quickly. The logical thing was to realize this, and to that end I telephoned some sixteen different primary and junior heads. To my surprise, most were willing, enthusiastic even, to have their old pupils back in a helping capacity.

Once they were ensconced I began to tour the schools to watch them in action and talk about the experience. Their scope of activity varied with the degree of trust accorded to them, varying from the highspot of two very rough diamonds teaching Nuffield Science to six-year-olds with 'borrowed' equipment, through to an increasingly morose Greek boy who was only entrusted to listen to two small children read to him, both better than him! Many of them, though, thoroughly enjoyed this experience — not least by being treated as adults by the staffs, using the staffrooms and having tea break with them. Perhaps more significant was the relaxation it afforded in not having to maintain an image, being gentle and kind without fear of mockery and using their minds to try to understand how to teach the barely comprehensible. Some felt constricted, usually due to the limits placed on their activities by the schools, but others became indispensable to the point where a permanent job was suggested, if possible, as an auxiliary. This new sensation, in schools at least, of being considered valuable, allied with the freedom of travelling to the schools from home by themselves, had a marked effect. They found the change in roles challenging and many of them were to become 'difficult' in other lessons at school where they expected a corresponding level of relationship.

The actual strategies adopted on this course were a joint endeavour, and though in themselves or taken separately they were nothing unusual, the combined effect was to be significant for many of the students. They talked a year later about the course and their primary feelings were expressed in terms of a release from a claustrophobic routine, a sense of freedom and trust and recognition of some joint endeavour, of something approaching equality, with an adult. Equally, a great deal of confusion was expressed about some of the 'official' Project descriptions which I had occasionally used. I as a neutral chairman was muddled with me as me in the other sessions. The actual label of Humanities produced peculiarly constricted definitions of 'the subject' which open-ended description of experiences usually confounded. This underlined heavily the habit of corralling a variety of experience into a subject box. Their pragmatic reaction to this professional closed shop was often more incisive than the collusion that their language produced. This often perpetuated accepted definitions and assumptions almost by habit. 'History', 'geography', and then 'humanities', were accepted commodities with official salesmen, but at least now some of them felt that they had seen the production process — the mystique was gone.

The year was exciting for me and for them. We had shared the sometimes odd sensation of dismantling roles and creating a new and shared context. At times we all reverted to norm but at the end of the year the prime feeling for most was of having constructed new definitions and relationships within the heavy and overbearing 'reality' of school. This sense of being able to impinge instrumentally on 'given' realities was perhaps the most radical insight of the year. Obviously, in hard Weberian terms of knowledge being recognized by its 'objective test potential', the year was low status, but, in terms of being party to the construction of a series of knowledge, then the year was significant. Almost all this group could have been described as 'alienated learners', and it seems indisputable that schools must strive to provide creative and positive contexts for this kind of student. From this experience, it seems that this can be a disturbing, and sometimes painful, development, but one which schools must encourage, if they are going to make manifest any of their platform ideals. If not, schools, for many students, will have rendered themselves thoroughly redundant.

Notes

1 See the *Black Paper: Fight for Education,* edited by C. B. Cox and A. E. Dyson (Critical Quarterly Society, 1969). See also *Black Papers* 2 and 3.

2 A good example of this is R. W. Taylor, *Basic Principles of Curriculum and Instruction* (Chicago, University of Chicago Press, 1949). This was reissued as an Open University Set Book in Britain in 1971.

3 P. Freire, *Pedagogy of the Oppressed* (Harmondsworth, Penguin, 1972).

4 Neil Postman and Charles Weingartner, *Teaching as a Subversive Activity* (Harmondsworth, Penguin, 1971).

5 Schools Council/Nuffield Foundation, *The Humanities Project: An Introduction* (London, Heinemann Ed. Books, 1970).

6 Ibid.

Chapter 12

An experiment in the teaching of Physics

Anthony Hoskyns

Introduction

Pupils are not involved and interested in what they are doing in lessons. Boredom, indiscipline, under-achievement and truancy are the results of this failure, in grammar schools and inner city comprehensives alike. School-based research being encouraged by the ILEA, which concentrates on what actually goes on in classrooms, indicates the extent to which pupils want to work if they are able to understand everything that they are asked to do.[1] It has shown that understanding is a complex process which we must know more about if much of what is being done in schools is not to actively inhibit the use of an individual's mind which is the basis of understanding for him.

In this chapter I describe the issues which have emerged for me in trying to plan and execute in the classroom a course of physics for 300 students in their fourth and fifth year, in order to try to satisfy students who really want to understand what they are doing and to enable them to take a CSE, O level or A level examination at the end.[2] When a student has opted for physics he has an initial expectation which he can only articulate in the light of what happens when he is involved in the classroom work. It is essential that the structure of the course should aim to fulfil and direct this hazy expectation by incorporating any experience that I, as a teacher, may have gained of the way in which a student's interest in the subject can be caught and maintained. I create the structure of the course by getting clear in my mind what the students want from learning physics, and what I ought to be doing so that they can gain a sense of what practising physicists are about. The physics that emerges as real through students being helped to understand everything that they do is different in quality from that which stems from an examination-based course where the content of the course is a commodity which will advance the career of the student. The process through which the physics of our course is established is a humanizing one which enhances examination work as envisaged in the Nuffield courses. It is in facing up to issues of this kind that the structure of our Physics course takes form.

How the course began

I began eight years ago with the Nuffield scheme and taught it straight from the printed material.[3] At the same time my main emphasis was to allow students to feel at home in the laboratories and to try to find out what they would find useful in the facilities available. School buildings are scandalously under-used in those communities which most need the basic facility they offer – space – because headteachers and schoolkeeping staff are frightened of the local community, who are not then encouraged to use the specialist facilities of the building. I have become convinced that students want to be able to use laboratory facilities outside lesson times. To open them enables students in tower blocks with very little space to have a place to go to which is theirs and caters for them as human beings with things they want to do because they have been introduced to the possibility of doing them. Youth clubs with coffee bars and organized sport or non-vocational classes assume that a leisure activity is a passive minimal affair. Young people also need to be able to spend a long time on serious and intellectually stimulating things which can be pursued in a relaxed atmosphere.

I opened the labs in the lunch hour and after school and pursued a policy of reacting to whatever the students suggested with a 'yes' rather than a 'no'. I introduced a number of routines and activities which I dropped if students rejected them and kept if they were enthusiastic. The atmosphere in the lab was not right, so I fitted a hi-fi amplifier and speakers into the lab with a radio and turntable; some pupils actually found it easier to work with Radio 1 in the background, while others started to bring their own records. We started a record loan club. As I got to know the students (especially in the evenings when they came up to work in the Youth Centre) I decided to build on the success of the music and make available other facilities which could be loosely allied to Physics. We introduced a loan service for equipment at the weekend. We designed and built radio controlled cars and introduced photography with a permanent dark room. We built a discotheque and used it in the school hall and local clubs. We encouraged those with an interest in electronics to build and test circuits out of *Practical Electronics* and similar magazines. We got some guitar amplifiers and cabinet speakers and let groups of two or three students use a room to practise with microphones and tape recorders in the Youth Centre in the evenings. I discovered that the computer terminal was free of charge after 6.30 p.m., so that students could run programmes up until 9.30 p.m. I got four people from Imperial College to help with the cars, the computing and the electronics in the evening. A number of third-year undergraduates came during the day and in the holidays to study the experiments in the Nuffield Course, to help students doing them and also to improve that section of the course for the following year. They responded particularly to the informality of the lab and the music and the confident way in which our pupils could talk about the difficulties they were having with the Physics.

These sort of facilities, which have developed over a number of years, are based upon an initial attempt to create the right atmosphere for mutual confidence between pupils and teachers. It is not particular innovations (music, model cars, etc.) that are important as any kind of magic formula. What is important is the continual effort to create a rich rather than a dessicated environment – one in which the activities and initiatives of the pupils and teachers are stimulated rather than stunted, and one above all in which pupils have time to explore and familiarize themselves with equipment, ask questions and regain the confidence their earlier experience of schooling has so often removed.

Nuffield Physics for all

In the Nuffield course, although great emphasis is placed on the pupils doing the experiments for themselves, each experiment is designed to teach a very specific and often trivial effect rather than to allow for genuine experimentation. In many cases the equipment which has been designed specially for the course has considerable potential, yet the course itself puts it into a straitjacket. I decided to ask the students from Imperial College to concentrate on the Nuffield materials to establish what might be done that the coursebooks did not suggest, whilst working at the same time with our pupils in the labs.

We began with optics and waves. The students' supervisor, a research physicist, was excited by the Nuffield equipment and continually stressed that they should use it to study how images are produced from the object and concentrate on them. It was most important to begin from what the student actually observed while doing the experiment and not worry about whether he had 'got the right answer'. A good experiment should produce (1) interest and involvement by the person doing it, and (2) a flow of observation and questions which lead to an understanding of it.

As I gained confidence in this approach I realized that the importance of the visits from the research physicist was that he released me from a mystification of Physics which leads to a fear of suggesting activities in which students may ask questions one cannot answer and need help with anything they are doing. Listening to him, one learned that phrases such as 'fuzzy image' and 'is that a shadow or an out-of-focus image?' were the real language of these experiments. For me now the study of objects which are creating or reflecting light and the images they produce means actually looking at them with my eyes. The theoretical rules contained in books, such as ray diagrams, angles, the bending of light, its diffraction and nature, are all tools to help me explain the real phenomena. Even the very few who are to be professional physicists must be allowed long exposure to basic phenomena without being stifled by ideal or formalized descriptions which destroy real understanding and force one to pretend to an insight one has never been allowed to acquire for oneself.

Currently our optics course uses pinholes, lenses, mirrors, prisms and a laser as an introduction. We study the telescope and microscope as in the Nuffield text. We do photography, learning to use a camera (aperture, shutter speeds, etc.) and doing our own developing and printing. We strobe and photograph pucks on an air table and golf balls falling under gravity. There are enlarging facilities which we share with the Youth Centre. We have a booklet duplicated by ourselves called *The Science of Photography* which pupils keep at home, and there is the chapter on optical instruments in the textbook which they also have at home. The optics course this year was two hours a week, and a term's work was constituted as follows:

Week 1	Light sources, shadows
2	Surfaces, reflection, screen
3	Colour
4	Images and the pinhole camera
5	Refractions (smoke box, fluorescein, etc.)
6	Images and a convex lens
7	Magnification
8	The eye

(For 6 and 7 we used large filament lamps and 7d lenses.)

After half-term we issued a typewritten sheet:

UNIT OPTICS

This half-term you are asked to do the following work: Question Book III: 44-45-47-48-50 and 54-63 inclusive

The Camera:	Learn how to load and use the Camera
	Take a film
	Develop it and make contact prints
The Telescope:	Ask for two lenses, an eyepiece and objective
	Set them up as a telescope and use it
	Use and explain the reflecting telescope
The Microscope:	Ask for two strong lenses

Anything you write under the above headings should be shown to me so that I may see that it is what you really want to say.

Within the framework of this term's work in optics students are able to study images with no strain. But instead of boredom setting in by lesson 6 or 7, the switch to photography is good for them intellectually and satisfying as a teaching technique. The change in lesson routine is all important if they are going to understand the various methods that they can use gradually to begin to conduct their own learning with confidence.

The Nuffield course is weak on electricity and particularly electronics. Four ideas emerged. (1) The fine beam tube is a wonderful tool for enabling students to see how to focus a beam of electrons and deflect it with magnets or a coil of wire with AC or DC through it or an electric field from two plates set across the beam. The principle of an electron gun and its application in valves and cathode ray tubes, in the oscilloscopes they use in the labs and the television tubes they have at home, is a more important area than simply getting notions of the mass and charge of an electron. (The Nuffield course suggests that the fine beam tube should be used exclusively for measuring e/m by a difficult and relatively uninstructive and artificial method.) (2) We found that pupils actually wanted to learn the techniques and the elements of circuit design much more than they cared about ending up with a radio or an amplifier. (3) They were also interested in doing their own repairs on cassette tape recorders, transistor radios and hi-fi equipment, etc. (4) They enquired about mains wiring in their homes.

We decided to develop a whole section of the physics course to cover electricity and electronics to include AC mains and domestic wiring. I worked on the mains and someone from the Post Office Research Department came to work on the electronic circuits; another physicist from Imperial College came on one evening a week to assist anyone who wanted to repair his own electronic equipment, in the belief that helping people to do their own repairs would demystify much of electronics in the process.

It has taken over five years to apply all that we have learned in informal classes in the evening to the main course for all the pupils in the fourth year, and we have not finished yet, especially as the wealth of material on electromagnetic effects in sound and communication has hardly been touched. The research worker from the Post Office worked directly with large numbers of youths in the evenings. He was impressed with their sheer interest in electronics when they first met him, which led him to want to strip the subject of its complexity and jargon and design work for them which would satisfy their need to know and understand. It was from him I learned that our pupils were interested in what he was trying to do with them because they really wanted to understand and were dissatisfied when his explanations were not good enough. He discovered that the requests to build amplifiers and radios were an excuse to get into electronics. We decided therefore to work from scratch on a series of circuits they would be able to build, designed in each case to teach them the basic circuits used in electronics and some of the concepts involved in understanding them. We decided to be driven only by their approval and his determination to make what was done the best electronics possible in terms of design and explanation, because these were what the pupils seemed to take most pleasure in. It was fascinating to watch how he worked. They started by learning to solder properly, make good solder joints, to lay out circuits neatly and take a pride in their work. In the five years he designed fifteen basic circuits which pupils could take home, mostly using a 9 volt battery.

Each year I used what he had produced and reported back to him, bringing pupils who were having difficulties to see him in the evenings. By concentrating on those with difficulties, we were able to see how the content of the course, the instructions and explanations, could be improved until a format was established which the students were able to work with. Their delight in being able to take the circuits home, the confidence of the pupils in electronics and their interest later in the sixth form is evidence of the value of curriculum research taking place among the students who are going to use it. Once the original research ceases teachers and pupils are just beginning and the course grows, in contrast to an impetus rooted only in the teacher which slowly dies from a rigid published format. The principle of development is therefore that each holiday or previous term should be a period of intense discussion of what is to be done in the next term or half-term. In this way, what the pupils need becomes central to the work of the following term.

The rest of the course is growing in the same sort of way. Heat engines and kinetic theory began with the model cars; we are now working, still in the evenings, in the motor vehicle workshop trying to get a serious understanding of the car and motor cycle to inform a rule of thumb approach to repairs, especially as many of our pupils may well be motor mechanics if they do not go into the GPO. We begin with the notion that gases are molecular and the molecules move. We do the experiments on pressure using a vacuum pump and U-tubes. We start engines — steam engines, jet engines, rockets, model engines with propellers clamped to the desk, and a two-stroke engine mounted on a motor mower. Everyone starts and uses them. The models are diesel. The two-stroke runs on a mixture of diesel and oil. We go to the railway area near the school and everyone has a go at driving as well — we have two old mopeds. We fire off trainer guns which give a massive kick using blanks. We do some work on heat. There are lots of thermometers about and pupils get used to measuring temperature, they make little junction thermometers with two different metal wires and a galvanometer and calibrate them. We use kilogrammes of water and aluminium to open up the idea of specific heat. We go skating and ask what is happening.

Behind all this we are finding out how an engine works: two-stroke/four-stroke, diesel/petrol. We have three-dimensional overhead projector models of two-stroke and four-stroke action. They are good dynamic models and are out in the lab all the time. Finally, pupils mount the model engines on a wooden trolley, which they have designed themselves with wooden wheels, and try to measure the thing's velocity. And we start on a unit of mechanics. The Nuffield experiments on pressure are superb and reinforce notions of the kinetic explanation of the engines used in the previous unit. The mechanics is a crucial part of the bridge between learning how to understand through involvement with experimental situations during the first year of the course, and a slightly different approach where I, as teacher, suggest that learning about speed, velocity and momentum is important for any serious study of physics.

We study pressure: collisions using different sized billiard balls thrown across the lino in the main assembly halls. We do a lot of work on pendula, springs, densities and strobe effects. Our students like to optimize every minute and in this section of the course we use accurate balances and calculators, electronic timers and ticker timers, so that everything we work out is an actual measure of some constant for this spring or that substance and can be checked in a book of constants.

By this time we are well into the fifth year where we cover seriously a number of specifically examination topics:

Static electricity, electroscope, Van de Graff generator
Radioactivity
Waves
Millikin's experiment
Diffraction
Interference and the wavelength of light
Electrons and the fine beam tube
Astronomy
Bromine diffusion, Brownian motion (kinetic theory)

With the confidence gained from a year of their own experimental work, they can begin to enjoy the rigorous approach and like the style that goes through a piece of work in the lesson and requires them to write it up in the text.

They are good at doing this because in the first year of the course they have been encouraged to wait to get everything right themselves. They catch on very quickly to everything we do, and frequently read a lot outside the formal lessons. The electronic circuits they are building can be beautifully done. We are able to send them to Imperial College to test the circuit and get expert help in understanding it. Similarly, those who made cars built beautiful models. They have confidence. They are then able to tackle the final leg where we issue to them past papers and they prepare for the O level or CSE.

One curious principle has begun to surface as a result of developing the curriculum in the school; that is the inhibiting effect of published materials. In our course it is the discussion of the work on optics, etc., that provides the continuity from one year to the next, not the published materials. With the electronics now so good that we have circuits and explanations fixed and publishable, the element of discussion as to how we are going to do electronics in the autumn term is different. There is not the same drive to establish what we are going to do, and that could be bad. There is no doubt in my mind that as soon as a course is fixed, it is dead, of use only for suggesting one or two individual experiments or ideas. The inhibiting effect of a pre-set course is paradoxically set against the enriching effects of the resources which go to make it. They need to be there and then forgotten as the new term's work is considered in relation to the current year's pupils and the teachers' accumulated experience.

The relations between science and technology in physics teaching

Quite clearly, one of the things we have been doing in rethinking the experimental basis of teaching fourth and fifth year physics is to explore the relationship of scientific theory and technological reality. It is only by relating scientific theory to a live technology that we can get a proper perspective on the theory which enables us to distinguish what are the theory's essential basic concepts. If theory is taught simply as a body of rules, the basic concepts are often given much less weight than the detailed nuts and bolts. In optics we found that the essential concept to concentrate on was the image. Once the student becomes thoroughly familiar with this idea he can begin to understand everything about light and its behaviour. This is much more important than laboriously memorizing the complexities of $(SIN\ I)/(SIN\ R)$ to describe the refraction of light. It is basic to our course therefore that students should be exposed to machines and instruments not simply to be trained in their manipulation (as might happen in any secondary school) but in order to understand the underlying principles behind them.

A boy who had studied the telescope picked up a microscope some months later and said to me: 'What lenses are there in here?' I said, 'You can see the eyepiece at the top.' He said, 'I suppose there is an objective down the bottom there.' This is the result of a real process of demystification. The concepts are basic and difficult in the sense that they must be established through prolonged contact with them in an atmosphere which allows them to be thought about over a period of time. In realizing that the same concept can be equally validly applied to other phenomena they know of, they undergo an intellectually exciting experience.

The sort of dishonesty that is prevalent in modern physics teaching at school and university level must be stressed because students feel it deeply even though they cannot articulate it, and it generates the sort of boredom I referred to at the beginning of the article The kind of physics described in this article is much more intellectually satisfying and difficult, where students are continually asking questions and learning through serious and concrete experiments. In this sense it is an advance on the rest of physics teaching through which so many of us were able to become physics teachers and even physicists. This approach is in sharp contrast with many 'academic' physics courses where the priority given to quasi-mathematical generalizations obscures the need to understand the phenomena. The mathematics I want to use with my students arises out of the experiments we are doing. It may be simple arithmetic or involve calculus, but it is not imposed. The science I do with students which fulfils them as human beings arises out of those topics in which they are enabled to really understand something which they did not know about before. They can be serious about their work and enjoy it because they are able to be serious. A rule seems to be emerging that the experimental work, which does encourage understanding of what is happening, should be based upon a live technology within the framework of the methods of physics. Often in any subsection of work the approach will be reversed or mixed up.

Motor car engineers, photographers, those involved in building and the electrical trade, radio engineers and even sportsmen are not encouraged to think about what they are doing and often have little confidence in their own ability to understand it. However, teachers who take their students' problems of understanding seriously may well confront real difficulties in practice; those in authority want competent and docile technical labour, not people who think.

Our unit on electrical installation which we call AC theory is an interesting example of a link between physics and a thriving technology where the elements of 'pure' physics are enriched by considering them in the context of wire and components available in Woolworth and very much a part of the 'Do it Yourself' scene and the building trade. It is a recent addition to our course and has arisen out of my amazement that an introductory course of physics at O level only touches on this whole technology, yet stresses many aspects of the so-called theory upon which it depends.

Building mains circuits throws up basic problems which it is immensely valuable for students to formulate and have answered while they are working on them. The problem is 'why are buildings wired as they are?' The sort of questions which arise indicate the wealth of physics that is learned if it is possible for the students to establish answers with the help of the teacher in the lab either on an individual or in occasional more formal lessons or in answer to questions on the board. Below are a number of problems which have arisen as students built lighting, heating and bell circuits.

'Why is there always an earth terminal on every fitting, even though it is now usually plastic?'

'How do you wire one switch upstairs and one downstairs to turn on and off a bulb in the hall?'

'Is neutral earth? if not why not?'

'Why is there a voltage between neutral and earth?'

'What are the reasons for using a ring circuit for wiring mains sockets? Why do you need thick wire to carry larger currents?'

'How could you suppress a light switch clicking over the hi-fi at home or in the lab? Why does this happen, anyway?'

'Why do regulations allow as many outlets as you want on one ring as long as it serves an area of not more than 1000 sq ft?'

'What currents do all the different wattage bulbs and heaters, etc., draw and how can you work them out? What is the resistance of each filament?'

'Is it better to use single wire or stranded in house wiring generally? When would you use each?'

'How do you pay for electricity and interpret a typical electricity bill?'

'Why use a ceiling rose and terminal block so much?'

'Why don't you get a shock from a mains tester screwdriver?'

Remember, all of this is in the middle of building circuits that work from a mains fuse box.

The conduct of the lessons

The most important thing that I have learnt is that students want a positive, enjoyable experience at each lesson. They want to do something interesting straight away and also to know that it is physics and not just an attempt to interest them. They want to understand what there is to do, and understand each thing they do. They want to succeed. They want to be able to show to others what they are doing, not necessarily directly, but through some obvious device like being able to talk about what they have done, or even show round the results. This enables them to respond concretely to the odd comment from parents ('Don't you ever do any homework?') or the possibility that an older brother or father might help them. It could establish a new kind of relationship with people they know outside school at a level they have seldom experienced. They want to be able to say that they are doing O level, especially when other youths living in the flats or the community are doing so. They need confidence that this is not another fantasy which on tackling they are going to fail. Occasionally there is something on television (Horizon, Open University programmes, etc.) or in the papers that they understand because they have done it, seen it, or used it in the lab.

Once the planning of the course is not primarily concerned with the examination, it becomes a serious and difficult problem to decide the content and the techniques that should be available to students. The questions and problems which they confront with each experiment they do become the focus of my desire to satisfy their enquiries. The prime importance of enabling students to really understand everything they do becomes the criterion for all my own activities as a teacher.

If I am going to be able to help students to question and talk, and gain confidence, then I must care about the experiments and lessons that I choose to give them. They will gain in confidence if they feel I have chosen an experiment which arises out of their reaction to what has happened before. Their confidence will grow quickly if they notice that I have developed a routine which enables them to find out quickly what they ought to do but leaves the detailed conduct of the experiment to them, where the planning that they are capable of enables them to demonstrate their own ability to themselves and to me and to organize their own learning.

If the student is to be enabled to do what he can in the planning and executing of an experiment or other work, I must learn to provide minimum instructions that everyone can understand at the beginning of the lesson. Equally there must be an established routine to give each student the confidence that he can ask questions and get swift unambiguous help at once when he needs it. *He must be able to get at me – this is the working rule of the lab.*

Someone may perhaps say, 'Surely it will need a teacher with massive experience to operate this system'. On the contrary, the reverse is the case. Since it has grown out of repeated practice, it is an example of simplified routine. If the instructions to the student are clear cut, if the routine is to read them, if common difficulties are anticipated with a note on blackboard or worksheet, the teacher can learn to deal quickly with any question. Students get used to what is going on and build into their own plan surprisingly generous reactions. If they see the teacher under pressure they will wait, and begin writing about the experiment. They will often want the student having the most difficulty to get help first; they always respond to a system they recognize is as fair as possible.

The choice of subject matter and the way in which each lesson is introduced to students constitutes prelesson planning. The lesson routine then becomes the establishing of a route for helping pupils with any question they may ask, noting any comments on the lesson that one hears, and beginning to think how the next lesson could compensate for any needs which may be beginning to be exposed. Someone says, 'Can I write up my last experiment?' 'Yes, of course.' I realize that it would be a good plan to devote the next lesson to writing up and letting people who had difficulties repeat the experiment.

The course as it develops gives a double security to myself and the students. I know that if I follow the principles outlined above students will feel able to use their own ingenuity to get the work done, which means I do not have to plan every stage of the class's activity and am released to answer questions and help with the work they are trying to get done. This sensitivity on the part of the students frees the teacher and arises out of sticking to the original structure, doing experiments which are presented in a way which allows students a chance of doing them themselves.

This is the heart of the concern which the teacher must bring into the classroom. It depends upon a single-mindedness in caring about those things which are most significant for a student's experience in the classroom. This is the practice of teaching which emerges in response to the realization that students want to understand everything they do, want to be involved and interested in their physics, and want to grow in confidence in their own ability to use what they have learned in their relations with others, and bring to what they are learning their own experience.

There are two key notions which emerge from studying a course that is successful in attracting students and involving them. They are crucial to any formulation of a course structure, and need setting out clearly.

Confidence: Students do not expect to succeed in a flashy competitive sense. They must be enabled to know that they are successful by the support they get from the teacher and the other students, and from gaining a sense of what they have achieved after each lesson.

Understanding: Confidence comes from understanding what you are doing. This is the heart of teaching, and students judge the success of their classroom experience by the confidence they can feel in the teaching used to help them understand. I cannot divorce the idea of planning a course as a teacher from the community research in the evenings at the Youth Centre. It is in this informal context that we have learnt something of the problems of understanding confronting anyone engaged in studying physics and some of the conditions under which it is made possible for students. The way in which I structure the classroom environment affects how the students are enabled to understand. I have learned that, since they want to understand, if the right means are available, they will use them as they need them. This is what I mean by enabling students to construct their own learning where they can. The areas in which they can do so are quite definite. A youth is incredibly sensitive about his own strategies for understanding. His means of understanding are his own and if any habit of mind is challenged or ignored he would prefer not to understand.

Tackling 'understanding' in the *doing* of the lesson

Understanding is a process that is full of contradiction. A student must be free to pursue understanding in a way that is best for him. He cannot do it if all the information he needs is not available as he wants it. If it is all too easily available from the beginning, he is swamped, he cannot select, and he is bored. If too much is left out in the initial instructions, for instance, he cannot relate what he is required to do with anything in his experience. I place great emphasis on structuring the introduction of any new piece of work to enable the student to engage it in his own way and at the same time succeed. I cannot overemphasize the importance of this. It accounts for a lot of our failure with individual lessons. I begin by deciding first what I want the students to do. I then write down what I am going to put on the board in order to get them going. I study this very carefully. It must be short, yet in embryo be a blueprint for a whole lesson. Anything the student might know, or if he doesn't could easily find out must be left off the blackboard, leaving only the skeleton.

At every lesson the instruction is refined. Here is an example from the section of the course on Heat.

HEAT ENERGY
Find an *immersion heater*
Heat up 1 kg of water, then 1 kg of aluminium
Measure: Temperature
　　　　　Voltage
　　　　　Current
　　　　　Time

This at first included a circuit diagram, and the instructions for what measurements to take were detailed and I have a number of similar examples. The points to make are that this is only useful in connection with the students I am now teaching because it arises out of what I know of them and what I have done with them. They will arrive at the lab. 'What is an immersion heater or whatever it's called?' 'A kilogramme would be 1000 cc wouldn't it?' This example illustrates how easy it is to nip the seeds of boredom which arise out of lack of confidence. There is no point in using an immersion heater until you know what it is. If it is there ready and all you have to do is switch it on it is a mystery and the whole exercise is boring. My answer to the question might be 'It's a piece of wire that heats up – there's one in the cupboard over there.' He gets it. 'I've got one like this in my fish tank'. I then add, 'Make sure it's in the water before you switch on or it will overheat and maybe burn out.' A number of students have arrived by now. They hear the conversation; I do not have to repeat it with each one. In fact, when I did this there was a lot of trouble over using multimeters, one as a voltmeter, one as a current meter. As a result, the lesson spread over nearly three weeks, with students setting up the circuit and then drawing it out in their own way, so that they can wire it up again. They have made no accurate readings. This will come later. The investigation grows quite differently to the way I envisaged it. It is a much richer experiment that I realized. Real problems emerge. As students connect up to the central low voltage unit with outlets on the desk, all the readings change for everybody. We decide to heat for over half an hour, taking voltage, current and temperature every five minutes. Students are working out the resistance of the heater, and noticing how current and voltage change. I find that they need calculators and I have put on to the board underneath the initial instruction

$$v \text{ (volts)} \times 1 \text{ (amps)} \times t \text{ (sec)} = E \text{(Joules)}.$$

It is odd that the circuit diagram to help them build the circuit prevented pupils from being able to become involved in setting it up. It confused them and prevented them from feeling free to do it themselves. Once it wasn't there, they tried, they asked me, they asked each other.

As a teacher, I want to face a number of questions. When and why does a student need to generate his own route through a series of procedures in order to become involved in an experiment or piece of theory? I now find with older students who have worked on a course for two years that they sometimes like to have a lesson demonstration and talk with a title and key words on the board.

They go away and write it up at home or in the next lesson. This is how they want to tackle theory. They write it up in their own words, often very briefly and sometimes with incredible insight. They bring it to me, I read it, and we discuss it there and then. Why the need for a gap between discussion and writing? Why the willingness and ability to engage in such an abstract and creative intellectual process? Why is this a so much better way to learn than reading about it in a textbook and paraphrasing that?

It is so much easier to teach when all this is happening that it is obviously worth my while to be able to understand it and help it happen. It seems as though a ground rule might be: 'Whatever there is to be done which a student can do himself, the classroom routine should be structured to enable him and encourage him to do so.'

It is this that gives the student confidence, particularly if it is extended to include encouraging him to ask questions because he knows that this is part of the routine of the classroom and encouraged because it enables him to understand what he is doing.

In order to provide this facility, I have to choose what work I am going to ask the students to do. I must think about the instructions I will put on the board and have ready a clear interest in the question and, if possible, a discussion or answer. In the above example, such questions arise as: 'What are those bubbles coming up from the heater?' 'Why doesn't it work?' 'What is all that muck, why is it blue?' 'Why does the voltage keep on changing and the amps?' 'Are they changing together?' These arise all the way through the lesson. It is important that the students know that their raising the questions and establishing the answers represents their learning Physics and doing very well. It is up to me to tell them this and explain to them how successful they are. 'That was a good question.' 'Are you clear about what you think the answer is?' 'Write it down and I will check then whether you really understand it.'

A note on writing

The existence of a student's written work, if it has been freely produced, represents the only assessment that I need. Writing of this sort is therefore a crucial part of the structure of a course and needs to be planned for. The following exchange is very common: 'Can I write up before I do this work?' 'Yes, of course, the paper is over there.' 'What shall I write?' 'Just anything you have done.' 'Oh, is that all'; the student then gets on. This is because he is being allowed to write in a creative way and in a way that he needs but believes that there must be something more to it, something beyond him. After all, many students have low reading ages and no success in English classes. Copying and other devices are a student's main experience of writing, and he needs confidence to know what he could do is wanted. Indeed, it is the real intellectual activity.

If I want to stimulate writing of this creative calibre, the student needs reassurance and a course structure in which it is acknowledged as an essential feature of the classroom routine. This means that I must think out exactly what I say when the student seeks reassurance by asking 'What can I write?' If I reply, 'Surely you know what to do. First describe the experiment — actually what you did. Draw a diagram, mention anything you noticed, etc.', I prescribe the form of the writing, and it is worse than requiring him to copy. It is extraordinary that the first form of reply, 'Just anything you have done', stimulates a clear, often a beautiful piece of work.

Conclusion

I have laid great stress on the instructions I give to students when they arrive for lessons, how I choose activities for them, and my approach to writing. These decisions all depend on assumptions about processes of understanding about which we know little. This is of course a long-term problem, but one which sociologists and others must tackle with teachers in the classrooms where they work. In the classroom context any researcher will be forced to consider the practical, administrative and social questions which confront teachers and pupils every day. If a course is to be experimentally based, and available to *all* pupils in a large comprehensive school, not just a selected O level group, will it be too expensive? Will wanton damage to equipment and the cost of repair be too onerous? Is it right to leave preparation for the examinations to the last three months? Can the choice of which examination to take really be left to the pupils themselves? Does the prospect of teaching all the 300 students of a year in non-selected groups involve too much work for the teacher and lab technician? Is it, as my account has implied, really possible? What of the disruptive pupils and those who want to simply sit in the lab and talk about football? What of the fighting that can erupt when twenty fifteen- or sixteen-year-olds are compelled to be together with very little to do?

As any practising teacher will know, these are real questions without easy answers. What I have tried to do in this paper is to describe, very practically, what I have learnt in eight years teaching and developing courses in the same school. Above all this has been that pupil difficulties in understanding what they have to do in lessons and the subject matter itself are basic to all the questions raised, and underlie what are experienced as disciplinary and administrative problems. I would go on to argue that many problems of truancy and bad behaviour are best confronted by starting with a central concern about pupils' understanding, because that is what they care about most. They want to learn, but often feel frustrated in not discovering ways of going about it, and express their resentment in disruption and destruction. This is not to say that different schools do not have specific difficulties which are related to their particular situation, or that overcoming them will be quick or easy.

Suggestions for 'survival procedures'[4] and pleas for specially trained teachers [5] and a middle class intake to 'leaven the lump' avoid the real issues. They are solutions proposed by headteachers which reflect a policy of containment, and, in that such a policy is unlikely to interest or involve the pupils causing their concern, they are doomed to failure. What *is* needed is for heads and LEA officials to give support to those teachers actually in the classroom and to give them the encouragement and opportunity to explore new ways of involving students. Teachers are often unsure of what they want, and rigid timetables which are administratively convenient do not help them to face their uncertainties. The school keeper keeps the school locked whenever possible, wasting both money and resources. The hierarchical organization of schools concentrates accountability at the top, and inhibits classroom teachers from being able to participate in initiating changes, or voicing their genuine complaints.

The career structure for teachers is increasingly away from the classroom and contact with pupils. Administration, pastoral work, teachers' centres, and the Inspectorate are all 'big business' and secure prestige and rewards in the educational world. Classroom teachers do not need more people to administer them, nor do they require 'retraining'. What they need is relevant classroom based research and direct and easy access to resources, both human and material. Most important of all, they need to feel they are, with colleagues, in control of what happens in the classroom and the school so that they are free to develop work in conjunction with pupils.

The theme of this article has been that for me *pupils' understanding* is the key issue, and that tackling it should not be avoided or explained away in terms of shortage of money or resources, real though these issues are.[6] I havefound that students of fifteen and sixteen want to do Physics and that once a pupil's wish to understand is recognized by both teacher and pupil, many of the so-called discipline problems disappear, which is not to say that there do not remain some pupils who find the whole context of the school impossible.

It is not easy to assess how successful we have been, though our criteria of success, which are based directly on eight years of working with nearly 2000 pupils, are clear. They want confidence in themselves, and the chance to discover that science need not be some mystery quite beyond them. In the process of gaining this confidence, they discover the relevance of their own capabilities in writing and handling calculations. In other words, I am suggesting that in so far as our students find their Physics both stimulating and rewarding, literacy and numeracy become integrally involved in the students' own activities, rather than problems for yet new committees of inquiry. If in addition the work done leads to some motor vehicle work, engineering, electronics, astronomy and photography becoming available in the school in the evenings as a way of extending the community's access to facilities, then any extra resources will repay themselves twice over, for why should 'leisure' activities be restricted to sport and discos alone?

Notes

1 The research upon which this paper is based was funded by the Cognitive Studies Trust, which was set up by the Inner London Education Authority in 1972, and assisted by the same authority's Oracy Project.

2 Science Department, Sir William Collins School, London NW1.

3 *Nuffield Physics,* Books 1-5 (London and Harmondsworth, Penguin/Longmans, 1970).

4 Michael Marland, *The Craft of the Classroom: A Survival Guide to Classroom Management in the Secondary School* (London, Heinemann, 1975).

5 Margaret Maden, *Any Questions,* BBC Radio 4 (February 1976).

6 Of course, if so much money was not spent on high salaries for administrators in the schools and in the education offices, and expensive media resources and teachers' centres which are not easily accessible to classroom teachers, we might find that many of the financial constraints were more fictional than real.

Chapter 13

Media studies : alternative or oppositional practice ?

Richard Collins

Among the major shared assumptions of contributors to this book is a belief that the education system is a principal agency of socialization, in which students and staff learn and internalize the value and behaviour systems of the containing society.* We also assume that there are contradictions within the system, and in the relations between the education system and the society it serves. For example, what the dominant class prescribes for education in the 1976 Public Expenditure White Paper, cuts of £618 million, is opposed or contradictory to what 'education' regards as its best interests, and the best interests of British society. And 'contradictions are hopes'; the education system is a social institution that does not 'fit' perfectly the interests and demands of the dominant class in Britain. It enjoys a limited autonomy (although it is decisively inflected towards the reproduction of the ideology of capitalism), it has contradictions and potentialities within it, which those who work in education as active agents in its processes, and whose work is an important determinant of the kind of knowledge and view of the world produced and reproduced in the education system, may work on and lever away at.

The education system is a major institution, or apparatus, whose internal relations (e.g. between pupils and teachers and senior and junior staff) and relations to society require change, if social relations generally are to be transformed. It teaches a view of the world which, by and large, naturalizes and legitimates existing relations between capital and labour, social classes, male and female, etc., and so reproduces these relations, which are necessary conditions of capitalist production and the way we live now. Education, then, is a 'consciousness industry', whose force in reproducing the ideology of the ruling class is perhaps rivalled only by mass communications, 'the media'.

In this chapter I want to investigate some of the claims which have been made for the introduction of study of mass communications into schools, in terms of the effects which mass media study may have on relations within school, and on social relations generally. There has been a beginning to mass media study in schools and colleges in Britain. Of what kind? To what end? Is it a good thing?

First, it is necessary to say that the study of mass communications, the cinema, broadcasting, the press, is not well established in British education. In higher education, institutions offering courses in the study of mass media can be

* Part of this chapter was first published in *Screen Education*, No. 12, and is reproduced by permission of the editorial board.

166

counted on the fingers of one hand, and in the school and FE sector, the subject has rarely achieved the status of a timetabled and examined subject; rather, an individual teacher may slip in classes, which spring from his or her own interests, to a liberal studies or ROSLA course.Within British education there is nothing of the scale or prestige of American journalism, film, or communications courses, or of the corresponding German work in Zeitung or Kommunicationwissenschaft. Penetration of mass communications study into schools may be measured by the number of students who, in 1974 and 1975, took O Level in Film Study: 385. To these should be added those who, in perhaps 100 schools, do a CSE Mode 3 in Film Study. Scant though Film Study is, there is nothing in other areas of media studies to compare to these figures, no O Level, fewer CSE courses, and, as Ed Buscombe says in his 1974 survey of television teaching, 'a positive attitude towards media education is always in the minority'.[1]

Why should there be a positive attitude towards media education? *Teaching London Kids* says in issue No. 4 on media education:

We feel that teachers need to be taking a more positive attitude towards these cultural forms. We ought to be attentive to what children make of their viewing and listening experiences, and to be encouraging children to analyse the process by which the media communicate, the 'how' as well as the 'what'. Children and teachers need to be aware of the ideology implicit in conventions which they may well take for granted, and of the political and economic structures within which the media operate.[2]

This statement is, I think, representative of the 'progressive' arguments for media education, and rests on three principal assumptions: that the experience of children should enter 'school knowledge'; that 'child-centredness' is a necessary element in the organization of school knowledge; and that mass communications are largely agencies of mystification, a 'consciousness industry' which constructs a view of the world masking its real nature and which requires 'demystification' in school. I broadly share these views, and want to go on to discuss ways in which the mass media have been taught and studied in school and what I think would be a 'positive attitude to media education'.

Until recently, the work which constituted virtually the only acknowledgement of the existence of mass communications in British schools was that springing from the pioneering work of *Scrutiny* in the 1930s. *Scrutiny*, [3] principally F. R. Leavis and Denys Thompson, offered a conservative critique of the mass communications consciousness industry, a critique which entered education as an inoculation of pupils against the guiles, blandishments and false consciousness of mass culture. The high water mark of this approach was probably the NUT conference in 1960 on 'Popular Culture and Personal Responsibility', and Murdock and Phelps[4] show that this is still the most practised approach to media studies.

To say that one of the principal thrusts of the *Scrutiny* critique was to examine, attack and propose reconstruction of the *institutions* of mass culture is perhaps surprising and paradoxical for the reader of the 1970s, who looks at the tradition of cultural criticism stemming from Leavis and Thompson's work of the 1930s through the spectacles of the 'personal responsibility' enshrined in the NUT conference title, and the later shift in Leavis and Thompson's own writings, i.e. Thompson's invocation of Angus Maude,[5] and FRL's *Nor Shall My Sword*.

Consistent loci for *Scrutiny*'s attack were the educational system, mass communications, particularly advertising and the press, agencies of official state culture, e.g. the British Council, and, in an unfocused but explicitly anti-Marxist way, capitalism itself. A concern with the relations of production was never very strong in *Scrutiny*, but its hostility to capitalism and espousal of a vague Utopian communism provided a consistent, although imprecise, perspective to the central focus of the critical endeavour, that of fighting the pervasive forces of mass society (whether exemplified by H. G. Wells, C. P. Snow, Bloomsbury, the Book Society, or the Sunday Papers), which were taken to signify fragmentation, alienation and the stunting of human potential, and as vindication of the superiority of social organization around the 'organic community', which preceded mass society. *Scrutiny*'s task and the problem it defined were in fierce opposition to 'mass civilization', in the name of:

> A culture expressing itself in a tradition of literature and art, such a tradition as represents the finer consciousness of the race, and provides the currency of finer living, can be in a healthy state only if this tradition is in living relation with a real culture, shared by the people at large. [6]

And, parodoxically, of manifesting its opposition by striving to create an élite 'minority culture' at one with the English literary tradition, able to test the current 'currency of living', but denied, in the post-lapsarian, post-industrial revolution world, any 'living relation with a real culture shared by the people at large'.

As Perry Anderson says, *Scrutiny* was unable to escape the epistemological trap it dug itself;[7] lacking any adequate analysis of contemporary social relations, *Scrutiny* was unable to define a way forward in the transformation of culture it so dearly wanted. There was clearly concern about the development of monopoly capitalism, e.g. in Thompson's 1973 introduction to *Discrimination and Popular Culture:*

> Imperial Chemical Industries, for example, has a capital of over £1130 million, Burmah Oil and Conoco together are capitalized at £1200 million, while the Ford Motor Company has assets of £2140 million, and 317,000 employees. Such firms have a near monopoly, and, in the case of the public corporations of this country, a complete monopoly of the goods and services they are concerned with, or share it with a few other giants. So, it would be very difficult, for instance, to break into the markets for chemicals, cars, electrical goods.[8]

However, concern was manifested in a hopeless strategy of pitting an increasingly embattled personal discrimination of cultured individuals against the enemy. The tragic disintegration of Leavis's own work into more and more petulant and contradictory rhetoric stems from this fundamental insurmountable contradiction in *Scrutiny's* analysis. Indeed, the major absence defined by Anderson in British intellectual life, the lack of a theory of society (and which he sees Leavis,

Scrutiny, and literacy criticism as trying to fill by pushing beyond boundaries of strictly literary or aesthetic discourse by engaging with notions of totality like 'culture', 'civilization', 'community') claimed *Scrutiny* as a principal victim.

Scrutiny, then, saw culture and society as determined in the last instance by the relations of production, by the legacy of the industrial revolution, but increasingly directed its attention not to the specific mediations and operations of that fundamental determination, but to the institutions and practices in a realm where the stroke of the final determination had, supposedly, not yet struck – the realm of culture. Between the 1930s and the 1950s, the attention which the journal gave to, *inter alia,* education (Crusoe's articles on public schools, Knight's on training colleges) and mass communications (Thompson and Grigson on advertising and the press, Hunter on cinema) shifted to fetishizing literature as a distinct, autonomous and superior entity. It is this patrician and fundamentally censorious later view of the mass media, innocent of any coherent view of the formation and relations of cultural institutions, consciousness, the containing society, and their reciprocal determinations, that governs the construction of media studies, exemplifed in the NUT conference, and manifested in the attempted inoculation of pupils against some of the major interests of themselves and their families.

Scrutiny deserves a look, not only for its major historical role in determining the scope and focus of study of mass media in British education, but also as an exemplary cautionary tale. In arguing for the place of media studies in British education, I don't want simply to argue for a fetishized spot in the weekly timetable, where classes investigate and compare concentration of ownership of the press in Britain, the United States, or the Federal Republic of Germany, or to raise pupils' level of 'visual literacy' (although these would be something), but rather to assert that what is critical in what is taught and learned is understanding of the sets of social relations in which knowledge of mass communications and the study of mass communications, their structure, and ways of signifying, has a part. There is great danger in arguing for a particular area of study, and for specific limits to the subject and syllabus; of abstracting knowledge about a crucial agency in the determination of social relations (which I believe mass communications to be) from its place in that network of relations. To argue simply for a place in the timetable for media studies is to argue for no more than superficial modernization of the school system, while preserving intact the existing relations between teachers, learners and knowledge.

Changes, however, in the intellectual formations of British society, and in the school situation, particularly the raising of the school leaving age and the 'problem' of ROSLA students, substantial spending on audiovisual hardware and 'resource-based learning', and the 'child-centredness' of the post-war radical strain in British educational theory and practice, have produced new possibilities and different practices in media studies.

Two of the most important ideas, which have been regarded as broadly progressive and making for change in post-war education, are those of 'relevance' and 'child-centredness'. Essentially, these ideas have supported attacks on the constitution of school knowledge as an initiation of the child into what R. S.

Peters calls 'public tradition', mediated through an extremely reified categorization of knowledge. The entailments of constituting school knowledge as a set of discrete subjects, preoccupation with 'standards', hard knowledge and civilization will need no rehearsal here: Michael Young's definition (with perhaps the rider that there is a bias towards a particular kind of 'unrelatedness' in the academic curriculum, towards a positivistic construction of knowledge)[9] aptly characterizes the tradition against which educational change in Britain has been defined:

> Literacy, or an emphasis on written as opposed to oral presentation, individualism, or avoidance of group work or cooperation, which focuses on how academic work is assessed, and is a characteristic both of the process of knowing, and of the way in which the 'product' is presented, abstractedness of the knowledge, and its structuring and compartmentalizing independently of the knowledge of the learner, finally (and linked to the former), is what I have called the unrelatedness of academic curricula, which refers to the extent to which they are 'at odds' with daily life and common experience.[10]

Media study, in so far as it has been espoused by progressives in British education, has been taken up, because it offers contradictory possibilities to those of the academic curriculum and its schooling in the 'public tradition'.

J. Grealy, for instance, argues, in an article largely concerned with establishing school as part of the ideological apparatus of the state, that media studies are well suited to challenging conservative constructions of school knowledge and authoritarian classroom relations:

> The subject as a closed system of knowledge can be undermined by the stress laid by media studies on the continuity between what the pupils study in the classroom, and what they watch and use out of school. Also, the normal hierarchical way of teaching, information conveyed from teacher to passively receptive pupils, is very difficult to sustain in a media studies course, with its emphasis on practice, as well as 'theoretical' teaching.[11]

It is to the question of practice, as opposed to 'theoretical' knowledge, that I want to turn. In media studies practice is seen as offering an aspect of 'child-centredness' to a subject which, although evidently part of the child's world through his or her consumption of television, radio, press or cinema, has its abstract features, and involves the acquisition and understanding of knowledge outside 'daily life and common experience'. Further, child-centred educational practice is seen as breaking radically with the customary hierarchical and authoritarian relations of school. Child-centredness, and its necessary relevance, rewrite the 'hidden curriculum' or so the arguments go. Practice, the use of film, tape recorders, and particularly television equipment, in programme making and exercises, has come to constitute part of the accepted definition of media studies, and has been 'naturalized' as part of the subject area.

It is difficult though, to generalize about practice: facilities differ, and those available in British educational institutions range from a colour television studio, through a single television camera with monitor and VTR (videotape recorder), to still camera and tape recorder, and facilities go far towards defining the kind of work that can be done. One major argument for practical work is that, in programme making, students experience situations analogous to those of professional media workers, and that this experience of programme making informs understanding of broadcast television. Clearly, the analogy has pertinence, in so far as the facilities used by the student are like those of the professional. The argument loses force when one video rover stands in for White City Television Centre, although simulations and games like 'Radio Covingham',[12] in which participants play the role of journalists on a local radio station, and receive inputs of news agency handouts, listeners' letters, interviews, press releases, etc., which they order into a news programme of predetermined length, offer interesting possibilities with the minimum of equipment.

There is a variety of ways of 'doing practice', between which I think it is important to discriminate. For there is, it seems to me, no guarantee that working in this way will necessarily have the progressive implications that Grealy and others find in it. For practice is often constructed as an *imitation* of broadcast television, and child-centredness does not necessarily oppose reproduction of these dominant forms of seeing and ordering the world, and the view of the world inscribed in the way professional broadcasters do things. To construct television study and television practice on a premise of child-centredness is to invite the reproduction of the relation of dominance between interviewer and interviewee, aspiration towards perfection of programme production, and disappointment when work does not equal that of professionals, with consequential reinforcement of the mystique of professionalism and the authority of the BBC and commercial companies. These professional practices, of course, are learned by children in consumption of broadcast television, whose specific conventions naturalize themselves as a definition of television, and will be reproduced in child-centred classroom practice.

'Doing practice' has, perhaps, three major rationales:

1 Practice as an artistic form and end in itself.

2 Practice which takes television (or whatever) as a mimetic system, which presents information without fundamental transformation of the information in the process of reproduction. The end of this mode of practice is the acquisition of the technical skills necessary to use television (or whatever other medium is in question) as an audiovisual aid, the contents of which have a one-to-one relation to the real world which it represents.

3 Practice as an instrument of study. Programme making as analogy or simulation; exercises in the systematic variation of conventions to determine the specific effect of particular conventions.

The first rationale sees the producer(s) of programmes as an artist, a privileged creative individual (although, when production is performed collectively, the individualistic ideology is usually salvaged by constructing the collective

171

hierarchically, with a director, who 'makes' the programme), who expresses himself (and it usually is 'himself') through the artefact and its production. Much broadcast television is like this. Its fullest definition, and, one hopes, its nadir, comes in Ken Russell's programmes named after other artists, *Elgar, Mahler,* etc. In broadcast television the élitism of this procedure is naked: in education the intrinsically individualistic and élitist notion of the artist is dressed up in populist clothes. Lightweight portable television equipment, e.g., the video rover (or, in another medium, simple and cheap reprography of written material), makes possible, it is argued, a new form of self-expression, uninhibited formally by heavy studio equipment or the baggage of *The Grammar of Television,* [13] and liberated from the expense of studio production. For the video freak, there are limitless possibilities of personal statements, creativity, demanding no legitimation beyond 'I did it', 'I like it'. This form of practice constitutes everyone behind a video rover as an artist, or behind a Xerox machine as a Pulitzer, and maintains the privileged status of the role, while purporting to democratize it. Central to this form of practice is a necessary anti-reflective and unanalytical stance towards the rhetoric of the medium in question (i.e. its signifying codes and their articulation). Indeed, this is part of the point: art objects, whatever they be, videotape or marble, are by definition removed from analysis and the province of reason to a realm of instinct, feeling, the subjective, personal, and artistic. This seems to me to be the antithesis of study, and hostile to the production and dissemination of knowledge.

The second rationale constitutes the medium used as transparent, that the process of representation is one of unmediated reflection of an anterior world. And, again, this is a view which is current among media workers; the dominant ideology of broadcast television is governed by the naturalist fallacy of television offering a window on the world. It seems to me that study of the mass media must have, as a principal concern, definition of the specific structuring and organizing properties of the media, of the ways in which information represented on television, or in a newspaper, has been transformed in the process of representation. For instance, the nature of reportage operating as a system of exclusions: television excludes phenomena temporally, by shooting a world of infinite duration for finite periods and by editing, and spatially, by using particular camera and microphone positions, angle of view of the camera lens, or angle of acceptance of the microphone. This kind of emphasis would confront directly one of the most pervasive mystifications and legitimations of contemporary broadcasting and journalism. Unless the conventions and mediations of the television system are articulated and brought into consciousness, or, to refer to another medium, the news values of journalists foregrounded, then study of television or newspapers cannot be said to be performed. Practice without attention to the mediated nature of communication subverts this articulation and bringing to consciousness, and opposes proper media study.

The third mode of practice seems to me to be educationally the most appropriate kind, and involves simulation exercises, or the systematic variation of elements in a message. For example, one might hypothesize that the convention of 'voice over' may be an important determinant of the meaning of a television

172

message; this hypothesis can be tested by varying the elements in the message, using silence, voice over, music, narrator in or out of shot, etc., in a particular exercise. I say 'exercise', because other definitions, like programme making, assimilate the activity to the category systems of modes 1 or 2. Even if a programme is presented and conceived as a simulation, it may be difficult for participants to think themselves outside the terms of the simulation situation, and constraints which are present solely to strengthen the desired analogy between imitation and the real thing, rather than as natural or necessary elements. For example, programme making which follows the organizational patterns of broadcasting may offer insight into the relations between members of the broadcasting hierarchy, or it may also 'teach' fallaciously that a director is necessary to programme production, and that he is 'responsible' for the programme.

The third mode of practice, then, specifically constitutes itself as an instrument of study, interrogating the structures and conventions of programmes, the codes and their articulation in variations of elements of the message, and questioning professional practice, and the production situation, through simulation. Problems of practice, though, are not solely or simply theoretical, for the dominant tendency in the provision of video equipment to education is to place the instruments of *reproduction,* not production, in the hands of teachers and learners. Thus, the provision of AVA and video equipment in schools and colleges tends to enforce patterns of reception and consumption, not of production and origination. We have more television receivers, videotape recorders and slide projectors than we have microphones or television and still cameras. The emphasis and implicit rationale is akin to that of early education: teaching reading, not writing, learning to be an object, not a subject. Raymond Williams, in *Television: Technology and Cultural Form,* [14] makes this connection very neatly, saying that literacy was one of the defining characteristics of élites, often of a priestly caste, just as 'media literacy' remains the prerogative of a contemporary élite, what Nicholas Garnham called 'The New Priesthood'. [15]

Given the way contemporary mass communications enforce a skewed pattern of production and consumption, a subject/object relationship between the new priesthood and the laity in the living room, it is tempting to applaud all efforts to redress the balance, and to put the means of production into people's hands, to enable children, community groups, or just anyone, to get their hands on a video rover, and do their own thing, even if it is a 'practice one'. But such strategies are open to the danger of constituting themselves as alternative, not oppositional (to employ a distinction of Raymond Williams, see *New Left Review* No. 82), [16] i.e. they become activities which 'can be tolerated within a particular effective and dominant culture'. Indeed, one could claim that pressure to consume (more video rovers, more film stock, more hardware) actually strengthens the dominant culture, and consolidates the position of Kodak, Philips and Sony (buying a state capitalist Praktika, or a Co-op Tandberg makes little difference).

Doing your own thing with a videopack is a questionable advance in media literacy, although it is an activity that has its champions. Staying at home, the argument runs, and gaping at the tube in the corner, equals reading 'the media';

cheap portable television equipment enables people to 'write' electronically, and to become literate in the medium. In some sense, of course, that is true, and an advance. Being able to write electronically is better than merely reading. But, one asks, who writes, who reads, and what is written and read in the new formation? In what sense are the existing powerful relations of knowledge and control changed? I don't think wider dissemination of television equipment will very much change the relations of production and consumption of information, which are overwhelmingly dominant, those between broadcast television and its audiences. After all, the means of production of radio have been public for a long time, and tape recorders have never been so cheap. Neither a great social and political change has ensued, nor greater understanding of the conventions and techniques of communications through recorded or broadcast sound.

Another of the current practices wrapped up under the heading 'media literacy', which I want briefly to consider, is that defined by Neil Postman in his *The Politics of Reading*. [17] He argues that literacy is a repressive force, that it makes 'students accessible to political and historical myth', that literates are obedient to the dominant classes and ideology, that, following McLuhan, print is an agency of 'political and social stasis', and that electronic media 'unloose disruptive political and social ideas'. This seems to me to be ignorant and mischievous. There is no evidence that an 'electronic circus', Postman's arcadia, would be less repressive than a print culture; indeed, what evidence there is points the other way. The electronic circus would diminish the plurality of information sources and communication systems, which distinguish print culture (see H. Marcuse's *One Dimensional Man*). [18] Given that the culture we inhabit, and that of the foreseeable future, demands literacy skills, if our aim is the augmentation of people's freedom, then argument against literacy is an argument for the possession of the most powerful sources of knowledge and control by a minority — a return to the priestly élite, having information as their unique prerogative. Postman's mistake stems from a simple confusion. Because schools and the dominant culture define non-achievement in reading and writing as denoting stupidity (clearly a strategy of oppression, and one which he rightly resists), Postman defines literacy, not the specific pedagogic practice, as repression. We may join Neil Postman in fighting the restrictive definition of intelligence propagated in the education system, while still affirming that literacy is a necessary set of skills. If media literacy is desirable, then, *a fortiori*, literacy is desirable.

There is a specific entailment to Postman's argument that he does not make explicitly, but which has achieved some currency, that non-achievers in the traditional communicative skills — reading, writing, drawing and painting — may achieve gratification and a sense of self-esteem, enabling them to approach the difficult task (say, reading) with a confidence born of achievement in use of photographic or television equipment. I simply do not have experience of this kind of practice, and do not know whether it works. I suspect that it works best (if at all) with equipment like Polaroid cameras, with which there is no delay in gratification, no time lapse between recording and playback. If this practice does work, it is clearly valuable, but may rest on some false assumptions, and implicitly propagate a fallacious view of electronic and photographic communication, and, therefore, should be treated cautiously.

The fallacy and false assumptions are those which underpin the instrumental use of television as an audiovisual aid (Practice 2), that electronic (and photographic) media of communication present an unmediated one-to-one image of the natural world. Acceptance of the non-achievers' photographs or videotapes as authentic representations implicitly accepts this realist fallacy, that the camera enables the user to make intelligible messages unproblematically. (Of course, actually, it is not just any photographic or electronic image that will be accepted, but only those which more or less conform to the criteria of composition, framing, choice of subject, sharpness of focus, etc., which we have learned to accept as 'true' or 'natural').

Any programme of media studies or media literacy has to attend to the dominant forces in contemporary mass communication, and any educational practice which does not attend to the BBC, IBA and the press concentrations, and challenges their hegemony of communication, will be 'alternative', not 'oppositional'. Practice has its place in this strategy, for, properly integrated into a programme of study, even programme making with all its attendant dangers of playing at artists, demonstrates that many skills, and much of the professionalism of the production élite, are non-essential. It is not difficult to make a television programme, and the sooner that is widely known and experienced in practice, the sooner the domination of the BBC and IBA will be more effectively challenged. Further, in programme making, or in exercises with video equipment, with tape/slide presentations, or with the simplest sequencing and juxtaposition of still photographs and captions on a storyboard, students learn by doing that there is nothing natural, inevitable, neutral, or impartial about sounds and images. Choice of a particular image from among others comes from, and propagates, a particular view of the world, a set of criteria as to what is, or is not, important. Inviting students to make 'neutral' and 'impartial' choices confronts them with contradiction, and provokes a recognition that it *is* a contradiction. I think that this is the single most important task in media studies, destroying the misapprehension which sustains and naturalizes the view of the world propagated by official mass communications, that any statement can be value-free, and from that new awareness, developing inquiry into which values are presented in a particular message, and into who produces and who receives the message.

Clearly, these matters may be approached through analysis and discussion of broadcast programmes, but practical work, the simulation, or creation, for students of analogous situations, and sets of choices to those experienced by the professional broadcaster, present the issues concretely and experientially, which, with students unused to analysis and abstraction (all British students?), makes for understanding. While one of my concerns in this chapter has been to qualify notions of child-centred and practice-centred media study, I do not want to suggest that the curiosity and excitement which students display when using equipment is not productive and valuable. Undoubtedly, it is. Equally certainly, the first sessions of practice have to be ones of having fun, playing at *Top of the Pops* or *News at Ten,* but some caveats remain, mimicking professional practice,

175

playing at artists, and so on, all seem to me to be opposed to study of mass communications that would produce knowledge about how the mass media's image of the world is produced, and of who produces it.

If practical work is used as an instrument of study, systematically varying television conventions – changing, for example, the framing and sequencing of images to show different versions of the same event, or, for instance, changing the roles and relations of the production crew, exploring hierarchical and non-hierarchical relations – then practice may reveal conventions precisely as conventional, chosen, not inevitable, cultural, not natural.

Finally, of course, after making programmes, one finds that there is nowhere to show them. You may have cracked the production problem, but distribution and exhibition remain the prerogative of the 'effective and dominant culture'. Say what you like, as long as no one can listen.

It has been suggested to me[19] that the idea of control of systems of distribution and exhibition by the 'effective and dominant culture' could be investigated within school, by attempting to establish a channel of communication within the school, whether radio system or magazine, or what have you, which, unlike existing channels of Tannoy, notice boards, assembly, etc., would not be controlled by the head. For how long and under what conditions would the new channel be tolerated? It seems likely that findings from this experiment would support the 'say what you like as long as no one listens' hypothesis. Dissent from or even challenge to, the prerogative of the dominant culture/head to set the agenda for debate, which may be tolerated when confined to small groups, is likely to be resisted when it is more widely disseminated.

What, then, is 'relevant' knowledge of mass communications? What is implicit in the question is the relation of school knowledge activities and skills to the containing society and culture, and the relation of the pupil to that culture. I well remember my first geography textbook, which made the subject relevant by taking the contents of the ideal bourgeois breakfast table – marmalade, corn flakes, bacon, eggs, tea etc. – and tracing their representative provenances. In doing so, the whole network of trading within the British Empire was naturalized, and teleologically vindicated by its production of a supposedly normative ample breakfast. Relevant knowledge indeed!

There is a dilemma between constituting school knowledge relevantly, i.e. fitting students for their place in capitalist society, in which case, school knowledge must be evidently usable and useful, and making an educational experience in which the knowledge acquired would (and, indeed, this would be its purpose and vindication) be hostile to the current British social order and experience. Irrelevant! About the pedagogic practices and construction of the syllabus which would be appropriate to irrelevant knowledge there will be substantial debate and disagreement, because what is at issue (as, of course, it is at issue in all discussions of teaching procedures and syllabi) is a view of society. Debates about relevance must centre on the question of how social relations should be ordered, on what knowledge is needed to achieve the desired order. Clearly, the production and mediation of that knowledge in the world we inhabit will be constrained by many factors, including properly and necessarily, student interests and expectations, and their need to survive in a capitalist, sexist and racist state. In my view, media studies have a place in this realm of irrelevant knowledge, concerned as they are with the understanding of a principal 'consciousness industry', the products of which go to form the view of the world of its consumers, and to carry a range of ideological legitimations of ruling class hegemony.

Clearly, a sufficient response to the imperial geography which coloured Ceylon red, and gave it the function of producing breakfast tea, is not just to predicate the possibility of Sri Lanka not coloured red (or even coloured a different red, what the palette of British mass communications labels 'extreme red'). To know the fallaciousness of the idea of neutral or value-free communication or institutions does not make the BBC other than it is. But knowledge of how things are, and that they could be otherwise, challenges one of the major legitimations of the ideology of the dominant class and culture, that their world order is the natural one. Knowledge produces a perspective for struggle for change.

The existing footholds of the conservative critique's 'inoculation' approach, and of practical work, are bases from which a syllabus concerned with understanding the modes of signification, organization and control of mass communications systems, and the functioning of the mass media consciousness industry, could and should be built.

Notes

1 Ed Buscombe's 'Television Studies in Schools and Colleges', *Screen Education*, No. 12 (Autumn 1974) p. 6. Society for Education in Film and Television, London.

2 *Teaching London Kids*, No. 4 (1974), p. 3.

3 *Scrutiny*, a quarterly review published from Cambridge between 1932 and 1963, reprinted by Cambridge University Press in 1963.

4 G. Murdock and G. Phelps, *Mass Media and the Secondary School* (London, Macmillan, 1973), p. 33.

5 Denys Thompson, *Discrimination and Popular Culture* (Harmondsworth, Penguin, 1973), p. 12.

6 F. R. Leavis, 'Under Which King, Bezonian', *Scrutiny*, vol. 1, No. 3 (1932), p. 207 (Leavis's first editorial).

7 See P. Anderson, 'Components of the National Culture' in *Student Power* (Harmondsworth, Penguin, 1969).

8 Thompson, op. cit., p. 9.

9 For positivism of coelacanthean vintage, see Terence Miller's (Director of North London Polytechnic) statements, reported in *The Guardian* (9 June 1975), that, *inter alia*, sociology has the epistemological status of alchemy, and grants should be weighted in favour of students studying 'hard' subjects like physical science, technology, etc.

10 M. F. D. Young, 'An Approach to the Study of Curricula as Socially Organized Knowledge' in *Knowledge and Control* (London, Collier-Macmillan, 1971), p. 38.

11 J. Grealy, 'Film Teaching and the Ideology of the Educational System', *Screen Education*, No. 15 (1975), p. 18.

12 'Radio Covingham', published by ILEA Media Resources Centre, described in M. Alvardo's 'Simulation as Method', *Screen Education,* No. 14 (1975).

13 D. Davis, *The Grammar of Television Production* (London, Barrie & Rockliff, 1960).

14 R. Williams, *Television: Technology and Cultural Form* (London, Fontana, 1974).

15 J. Bakewell and N. Garnham, *The New Priesthood* (London, Allen Lane, 1970).

16 R. Williams, 'Base and Superstructure', *New Left Review,* No. 82 (1974).

17 'The Politics of Reading' in N. Keddie (ed.), *Tinker, Tailor: The Myth of Cultural Deprivation* (Harmondsworth, Penguin, 1973).

18 H. Marcuse, *One-Dimensional Man* (London, Routledge & Kegan Paul, 1964).

19 By Roger Stephens.

Chapter 14

A free school `curriculum´

The White Lion Street Free School

'School knowledge', from the title of this book, is not an expression that we, at the Free School, are really familiar with.[1] Part of its meaning, at least, seems to be covered by 'curriculum', a word we do use, though in a rather special way. There certainly is room for some new thinking about school which might well require some new vocabulary. The comparatively new expression, 'the hidden curriculum', was the result of such thinking, referring of course to the important idea that the traditional curriculum is not all that is taught by a school. It may also 'teach' the morality, control systems, relationships and so on embedded in its own structure. 'School knowledge' seems to be intended to mean both the hidden curriculum and the overt one, and thus perhaps to refer to 'everything that may be learnt in school'. We feel that such a blanket concept is premature. Much dissecting has yet to be done before we can − if indeed we can ever − safely generalize about what could or should or might be − or even is − learnt in school. And, as for how this relates to what is 'taught' (whatever that means), . .

One of the ways in which we feel the Free School is fundamentally different from most schools is in the explicitness of its 'hidden curriculum': the extent to which this is planned and constantly reassessed by everyone involved. However, this chapter is confined specifically to a discussion of the School's formal learning programme − its 'curriculum', and is not intended to be a general account of the school.

We are anxious that this treatment should not be taken to reflect the balance between the two in the School itself in practice. [2]

It is possible to approach the problem of 'curriculum' (in the sense of formal learning programme) from what one could politely describe as an academic point of view. This tries to deduce answers from the nature of the concepts involved. Of course, one must be an expert in linguistic analysis in order to do this.

Another approach (ours) does the opposite. It questions existing concepts, though it does not necessarily do away with them. Below, we give a brief outline of our kind of questioning, followed by a description of some of what actually happens in the White Lion Free School.

Theory

Most left-wing criticism of schools today starts from the assumption that teachers could be doing lots of good things but for certain constraints. The constraints named depend on the author's viewpoint: they include exams, curri-

179

culum working parties, employers, parents, children, teachers, the mass media, capitalism, lack of money, housing, and many others.

We see things differently.

We start from the fact that the world is in a state of radical change; change far more rapid and total than anything that has gone before ('eco-spasm', Alvin Toffler calls it, finding no existing word strong enough to describe what is happening). We feel confused by the changes like everyone else (though some, especially those in what used to be 'positions of authority', are still afraid to admit it). Actually, we doubt if any mere human can grasp what is going on. So the 'Free School Philosophy' is not at all definitive. It is simply an attempt to see what kind of school, if any, might be appropriate to this changing world.

School, being one of the more self-conscious aspects of society's reproduction, has always been moulded by the rest of society. It only comes as a surprise to some people that publishers, employers, parents, economists, etc., can 'interfere' with school, when society is out of joint, as it is now. The whole idea of an institution set up to convey culture from one generation to the next implies a degree of consensus on what that culture is. (Question: How far must the consensus be eroded before the schools break down completely?)

The whole of the existing school structure flows from a once thriving, now dying consensus on what should be taught: information about the world stood still long enough to be written into textbooks by 'experts'. So school 'subjects' and 'subject specialists' were everywhere accepted. Clear social structures, within which individuals were obedient – to the boss, to father, to the vicar – made a hierarchical structure right for school, too. And so on.

Now, for reasons that we do not pretend to understand, society has broken up into a million bits and pieces, everything has changed, and schools are tossed back and forth on a tide of conflicting pressures. We are trying to step back from this situation. It is terribly easy to get caught up in local conflicts about which Social Studies syllabus to teach, how to get the head to agree to a PTA, etc. Teachers in ordinary schools love to tell us that *that* is where the real fight is. They're wrong. Getting bogged down in all that is just a way of avoiding the larger issues. This is no time for escapism. You only have to stand back for half a second to see that breakdown is imminent in our schools. Perhaps we can't prepare for it, but at least we can try. How?

Our procedure so far (and it may be updated any minute)

1 Waste as little time as possible on what is wrong with existing schools. True, one's criticisms are bound to be made in the light of a more desirable model (however vague). But this approach is negative. Besides, there are enough academics satisfying (?) their radical consciences by this means already.

2 Ask yourself to start with: what kind of school does society need now? Try the question different ways – e.g. What do people need to learn/know, etc., to operate successfully now, next year, in five, ten, twenty, etc., years' time? What would a Martian need to know to investigate Earth incognito?

What don't I know that I need? (Taking 'know' in the broadest possible sense – facts, attitudes, skills, dialects, experience, . . .)

3 Then ask how people might learn the things you think they need. Do they need systematic teaching, learning by doing, learning from a specific context (or hidden curriculum). Could society provide any or all of this informally, or is some specific institution, or perhaps a range of institutions, required? It may be that there are as many answers as there are different learners and learning needs.

4 Then approach the question from a particular, rather than a general, standpoint. Take your school, your own children – ask what they need (not what 'the school' needs).

5 The next question is not such fun. It is: Do you have any reason to believe your answers to questions 2 to 4 should be forced on other people? Or, put another way: What would qualify you or any other individual or group to act on those answers?

Nothing would. It is a fundamental characteristic of our fast-changing world that there is no agreement about what should be done, and so no basis for concerted action. But we cannot *do* nothing because the younger generations (and not only them) need help in coping with society; they need it all the more because it is changing so fast and is full of complexities that are not easily grasped. We also have to do something, because as a society we should try to reproduce the best parts of our life and develop our maximum human potential (wild disagreement, of course, about what that implies).

In the midst of this almost paradoxical state of affairs, the frightening tendency at the moment is for schools to be forced into the mould of whatever happens to be the most powerful local influence. Those who believe that society can only evolve in a mindless, organic way will presumably accept this as inevitable. We are convinced that an overall approach implying an overall direction of schools, however benign, is totally inappropriate in the world today, and is bound to be destructive.

What is needed is a new kind of institution that can reflect our kaleidoscopic world without illegitimately imposing values, experiences, or particular forms of knowledge or skill on its members. This is what we have tried to work towards in the Free School in White Lion Street.

Practice

If no one has the right to impose 'their' curriculum, is there any conceivable foundation for a learning programme? There has been a lot of talk recently about letting children decide for themselves what they want to learn. As anyone who has tried it will know, this is not a straightforward alternative (even with adult learners in some situations it does not yield a learning programme that satisfies anyone).

One difficulty has been that 'radical' thinkers, who recognized that the basis

181

for a traditional curriculum had been undermined, now wondered if the whole concept of 'childhood' was also obsolete. Free Schoolers, in particular, were tempted to believe that any guidance, formal teaching, let alone pressurizing of children, implied an 'inferior' role for them which was unjustifiable.

At White Lion Street we discovered early that though a few children knew what they wanted to do, most didn't, beyond a (usually) guilt-ridden conviction that they ought to do reading, writing and numbers.

The teachers therefore felt it was up to them to make some suggestions. We had several months' excitement producing a curriculum of our own, by asking questions like the ones suggested earlier in this chapter: What would a Martian need to know to operate successfully in Islington now? We introduced four main curriculum 'areas': bodies (biology human and other, health, sex, food, etc.), thinking (child development, family influences, decision making psychology), employment (including jobs for everyone, we hoped), and the future. We reckoned that any other topic under the sun could be included in one or other category − employment, for example, was to include everything about society and how it worked. We produced lots of material, working two or three teachers to an area − each group planning to fill two 'periods' a week for two to six weeks. The idea was that each 'area' should be offered (at a set time) once a week to two groups of children, older and younger. Since, from the start, no Free School activity was ever compulsory, no one, we hoped, would be forced to learn something in an 'area' which bored him.

From the teachers' point of view some of this was extremely successful: i.e. lots of children took part and seemed very interested − particularly in bodies!

But, however much we tried subconsciously to convey to the children why we had chosen a particular topic, we became more and more aware that our invention was unjustified. We might be more genuinely in tune with the special learning needs of Islington youth, than, say, the Associated Examining Board, but we didn't have any magic insights. Our choice of curriculum was determined quite as much by our own personal preoccupations as by objective assessments of other people's needs. This might yield exciting new material, but equally it might (and often did) not.

We had no more grounds for becoming curriculum authorities than anyone else. Was there any means by which a curriculum could be generated which would spread the responsibility while avoiding imposition by us or some outside 'authority'?

A similar kind of power sharing was precisely what we had been trying to achieve in other aspects of the school's life. We already had a quite complicated system of meetings, and consultations between parents, children and teachers. Should we simply put 'curriculum' on the agenda of the next Wednesday meeting? (Wednesday meetings are whole school meetings, to which a few parents now come regularly, at which everything is supposed to be decided.)

In fact the question 'What do you want to do/learn here? ' was often touched on in meetings, and was also the subject of frequent uneasy confrontations between teachers and children (sometimes these were friendly and constructive talks, but not often in the early days of the school's life).

It was obvious that a curriculum was too big an area, with too many individual facets, to be invented by a big meeting. But it was also obvious that the parents and children had got to be brought in on the direction of it, somehow.

At first we tried small special 'curriculum' meetings. We had a weekly meeting with the older group, for example, in which we hoped to discuss what had been done the previous week. During its short life it was dominated by guilty discussion of why they had done so little. We tried to get some feedback on what they liked and wanted, but our attempts mostly sounded like lectures. We also got some parents to join in teacher discussions about the four areas. The parents felt very selfconscious and made only the vaguest suggestions.

If meetings fail, what next?

From the first we had a system of 'allocations'. Each child was allocated, usually by his choice, to a particular teacher whose responsibility it was to follow his development, and to know him and his interests and problems well. The teacher was also to get to know his family, which he would visit at least once a week, though usually more (all teachers have an afternoon set aside each week for this and no one of us is allocated to more than ten children; with the under elevens, the allocated teacher is usually also the child's main, basic skills teacher).

The approach we are now trying to move towards revolves around an individual level of discussion, in particular that based on the allocation set up. An outsider looking at the school might think nothing had changed. No specific machinery other than small group or individual conversation has turned out to be appropriate for this highly delicate matter. We have on occasion used the formal device of a parents' questionnaire – when introducing a new sex education project for the older ones, for example. But mostly we just talk, question and discuss with children and parents. The aim is to be as explicit as possible, and to get them to be; to take nothing for granted, to keep the questioning going all the time in order to create a context in which parents and children can make real choices. This can be a tedious and nerve-racking process.

It's a very slow process, and we teachers must still take more than an ideal proportion of the initiative. Until more formal machinery can be used, when more parents and children are really involved in the process, we must try to prevent a teachers' oligarchy from developing. We need some rules of play. For example, we must always remember to ask, in relation to any learning offer, what need is it supposed to meet and how, how do the parents and children view it, and how can they be involved in meeting it themselves, how else could that need be met, what resources could best meet it (we must guard against regarding the Free School as a self-contained resource), and so on.

There are already signs that there are two kinds of formal learning programmes: what one might call a 'local consensus curriculum', and a personal or individual one.

In our school the 'consensus curriculum' – agreed in theory by everyone – includes reading, writing and number, and preparation for employment (what that means is not necessarily agreed). One might hope that the world was sufficiently coherent for that curriculum to be practically universal, despite the chaos in other areas. But we don't feel at all sure of that. Indeed, even in our own bit of Islington, the hopeless job prospects for most children, and their inherited lack of resources to move elsewhere, are rapidly undermining the grounds for any structured learning whatsoever.

The school must also generate hope, as well as a curriculum, but that is another story.

Besides the general curriculum is a mounting array of individual arrangements, some made with parents, some without. Someone wants to be a taxidermist, so various visits, jobs and projects are arranged for him. Another makes a skateboard with Phelen and his mother in the workshop, for his new craze. Two girls who want to be hairdressers are offered visits and projects and films on the subject – as well as some general questioning discussions with teachers and the local careers officer. And so on, in great profusion.

With eight full-time teachers and fifty children individual arrangements are easy (and before you dismiss the whole project as unrealistic, therefore, note that we can share the children out *because we share out the other tasks*: cooking, cleaning, admin, 'youth work' (because the school is open evenings and weekends), accounting, handling and raising money, public relations, and so on; there are no more trained workers in our school than in the average LEA school, and we cost slightly less than it does).

Two other points may be worth making about this kind of Free School 'curriculum'.

First, it is partly 'disposable'. Though the basic skill ingredient remains pretty constant, for the time being, little else does. Since we opened (in 1972) very few projects have been repeated – even the sex education course changed a lot. We expect this. If it did not happen it would probably be because we had ceased responding to the school's real context.

The second point relates to basic skills. Apart from the earliest levels, which are taught in a highly structured, 'old-fashioned' way, reading and writing are done as far as possible in the context of specific subjects, i.e. those suggested by the 'disposable' curriculum. And though we agree that the three R's are fundamental, there is also agreement among teachers and most parents on a wider range of basic skills (those parents who don't explicitly agree don't oppose either). These include talking, letter writing, map and timetable reading and other routine information extraction, telephoning and 'telephone research' (making the best use of information services and directories), and what we call 'London Belongs to Us', in which the skill is making use of the city's resources. These are pursued less systematically than the three R's, but persistently, as they arise as part of the real context of the school's operation.

This approach to curriculum, of course, implies subtle changes in the teacher's role, and in the qualities and training he or she may need. We have described ourselves often as 'enablers'. We are emphatically not subject experts, nor are we experts in the field of human knowledge able to select appropriate bits of it for our clients' consumption (parents are slow to accept this). However, we could be well informed about the resources for learning, about the whole range of books and other media people and institutions available to members of the Free School. We could help with the processing of this material for people who have not yet learnt to cope with the mass of it unaided. We could also, though here we need our danger-sensors turned up to full sensitivity, immerse ourselves in the lives of the families involved in the school in the hope that we may thereby make useful *suggestions* (nothing more) for learning projects. Above all, we must practise a certain awareness - literally selfconsciousness - in all our school activities. We must be ready to give and take criticism from other workers at our daily feedback meetings. We must be able to make straight relationships with children and parents, and to be consistent.

It may be worth outlining one of the more successful Free School projects here, as an example of a possible teacher role. Two teachers had been offering a project on the future of cities. Very few children had taken an interest. The local Council decided to have a meeting on the future of the area immediately surrounding the school - where all the children live. Research by the teachers revealed that the flats in which most of the families at the school live were likely to be knocked down by the Council. The session on the future of cities became one of the future of the immediate area. Advertised by the usual poster in the front hall, it brought in not only more children, but several parents from the flats. A discussion of the Council's literature on the area, which had failed on a previous occasion, now took fire. The parents commandeered some video equipment which the school had on loan for uncertain use and made a film in the flats, getting many tenants' views. The film was shown at the Council's local public forum. A week later the school filled with tenants come to form an association, for the first time for decades, of which a parent is also secretary. Many children were involved in this. One child's report of the first meeting appeared in a local newspaper. And so on.

Of course our initiatives don't all get so happily enmeshed with local circumstances. Without the captive audiences which teachers in conventional schools can rely on, the role of 'enabler' often feels more like that of education tout. We must sell our offers. We make posters advertising each day's attractions, and coming events. We must think hard about what visits, visitors and experiences outside the school would add to a project. It is perhaps important to note here that our approach to basic skill teaching is highly structured - some would say 'old fashioned' — as this is so far from some conceptions of a free school. We have behind us here the spoken, if inwardly uncertain, consensus of parents and children that these things are important (plus, of course, our own 'teachers' conviction). There is now a general understanding that everyone is supposed to do some basic skill work every morning. What that 'supposed' means is a matter of permanent discussion in the school. It is, of course, a fundamental part of our 'hidden curriculum', and not therefore a major concern of this chapter, though the two kinds of curriculum are not separable in practice. We know that the context in which the school operates is perhaps its most important message. The extent to which, and the way in which children are involved in school decisions, including how much 'work' they do, is basic. Briefly, our approach to both kinds of 'curriculum' is the same: talk, in the most explicit terms possible. We continually discuss with children and parents what they feel their responsibilities

185

and needs are or should be – particularly in relation to basic skill work. There is no straightforward formula, and certainly not, contrary to popular conceptions of the Free School, a situation in which 'it is all left up to the children to decide for themselves'. Children do need to make 'real' decisions if they are going to learn to think for themselves, but they may also need help with this to begin with.

In practice, virtually all the White Lion Street children work through graded programmes in reading, writing and maths, and no one pretends it is all fun. This approach, because it is individualized, requires more, not less, organization than an ordinary school, much to some of our visitors' surprise.

Although it is easy enough in theory to dismiss the traditional influence on curriculum as no longer well founded, how does it work in practice? Can we in the Free School really rely only on internal initiatives to generate our programme of activities? The answer is no, for two reasons.

First, an important existential point. The members of the Free School are part of the world. Their interests and wishes reflect it. They are subject to its pressures. We have not removed those pressures, only tried to mediate them through the people immediately concerned.

Second, if the free school, unlike most conventional schools, is to be a resource by means of which its members really can come to grips with the real world, it can't be an isolated institution. The whole basis of the comprehensive school ideology was the belief that schools should be self-contained watertight knowledge-containers. But knowledge is no longer self-contained. It doesn't stand still long enough to be packaged in this way. The Free School has got to be *really* part of its surrounding world, and this means that it must be sufficiently flexible to make the constant readjustments that world now requires (how this need can be reconciled with the need of all learners for a certain degree of stability could be the subject of yet another paper on the Free School).

So, to be more specific, one may object to the exam system but still recognize that the acquisition of O levels will increase some people's choice and control over their own lives (which is one of the aims of this Free School). So we run an O level course in conjunction with a local FE college. In fact the way in which, so far, this compromises the School's neutrality is the undue pressure it adds to some children's working. The content of the course (these are Mode 3 O levels in which we teachers have some say) has not, to our surprise, caused problems.

There are four other specific areas in which the school might be pushed into compromise by outside pressures. Only one actually exerts any pressure in practice. Our two main sources of money – Islington Borough Council and various charitable trusts (particularly the Wates Foundation) – could, presumably, have attached conditions to their contributions. They haven't. Both have been in close touch with us and seen what we were doing. We have been obliged by law to undergo inspection by HMIs. They, too, have simply approved what they saw (though they were careful not to comment too much on what was different about the School).

The immediate community (if it can be called that) around the school is a different matter. We have not tried to publicize the school, and rumours some-times circulate among some people not involved in it. There is a great deal wrong with life in our part of Islington, and sometimes that nutty school in White Lion Street looks like the cause of it all. There have been no specific incidents (yet) but we feel the need now to talk as much as possible to people locally and invite them to the school whenever possible so that they can see for themselves what is really going on.

There is one other highly significant external force with which we could choose to compromise – and, indeed, with which we have been trying to negotiate for some time: the Inner London Education Authority. We felt, and still feel very strongly, that small, responsive, locally accountable institutions, of which we are just one possible version, must be the pattern for the future. Also that such institutions must be government financed, but without the policy con-ditions of the present set up. The ILEA would fund the Free School now, but at the cost of much too great a compromise: we would have to become a special treatment centre for specially labelled children (truants, 'difficult' children, or some other scapegoat title). Fortunately there seems now to be quite enough general understanding of our importance for enough money, for the time being at least, to be forthcoming from elsewhere. And there seems good reason to believe that the ILEA connot deny the significance of what we are doing for much longer.

Notes

1 This contribution was finalized by a meeting of the following Free School workers and parents: Phelan Black, Bob Bollen, Sally Carr, Carrie Cox, Joan Degnan, Nick Doyle, Sue Field-Reid, Lucy MacKeith, Josie McDaid, Peter Newell, Alice Rainey, Alison Truefitt, Jill Wright.

2 Bulletins 2, 3 and 4 on the school's development and *A Handbook of Alternative Edu-cation* can be bought from the school, 57 White Lion Street, London N1. The school is open to visitors without appointment every Tuesday evening from 7 p.m. to 9 p.m.

Part 4: Exploring the limits to educational change

The focus of Parts 1, 2 and 3 has been largely on teachers' practices, both in accounts of how prevailing conceptions of school knowledge are sustained and as potentially strategic contexts for change. However, as we argued in our introduction, and as is brought out explicitly by a number of our contributors, a failure to consider the ways in which teachers' practices are embedded in interests and relations far beyond the school, let alone the classroom, is not only theoretically suspect, but certain to diminish the possibility of a critique of those practices providing the basis for realistic strategies of change. This final part, therefore, contains chapters which explore the assumptions and interests of some of those whose activities most radical teachers are likely to experience as constraining. They emphasize the importance of teachers' strategies embracing contexts much wider than the classroom, and point out how, once one starts to examine relations between teachers and curriculum developers, examining boards and publishers, the struggles of classroom teachers cannot remain separate from the wider politics of capitalist society itself.

The first two papers by Young and Gleeson, consider the relations between classroom teachers and the social organization of curriculum development, and indicate some of the ways in which these relations militate against the radical potential of even those projects which overtly challenge prevailing assumptions about education. Young focuses on the recent response by the Schools Council to criticisms that it has failed to encourage grassroots involvement. He looks at their proposals for local curriculum development in the wider context of Schools Council priorities and argues that, in effect, they minimize the extent to which control of resources can be shifted from committees to classrooms. Then, in a study of what is often thought of as the most radical of the earlier Schools Council projects, Gleeson suggests that the way in which the Humanities Curriculum Project attempted to 'bring controversy into the classroom' actually led to the neutralizing of such possibilities. In Chapter 17, Whitty takes examination requirements as one of the most frequent explanations of the difficulties of radical change given by classroom teachers, and looks at the attempts of some teachers to overcome this resistance through the development of Mode 3, or school-based, means of assessment. He points to the way in which, even when teachers are in a position to devise their own syllabuses and set and mark their students' work, they are restricted by the boards, who essentially invoke existing syllabuses as standards of comparison. Macdonald and Spradbery take two very different, but often neglected, groups, who are able to limit the possibilities of

189

educational change — publishers and pupils. School publishing is 'big business' and, as Macdonald's paper indicates, involves investment decisions which are likely to be based on 'what is currently used'. This of course confirms existing categories of pupils and knowledge, rather than offering opportunities for teachers to challenge them. Spradbery's account in Chapter 19 of the conservatism of a group of pupils about 'proper maths' reminds us that resistance to change in education must not be seen as just a question of dominant group interests, but of the much more embracing ideological context, within which schooling takes place. This is often expressed in the conservatism of subordinate groups like pupils and, in the William Tyndale case, working class parents, who take over and identify with prevailing ideas about 'proper education'.

In the final chapter Wright describes the attempt of the Rank and File group within the NUT to democratize the Union and the schools. He sees this programme as the necessary basis of any teacher struggle to transform education. His analysis of what he sees as the failure of the Rank and File movement outside the issue of teachers' salaries, provides any of us concerned with developing strategies for radical educational change with two crucial lessons Firstly, that the wider political struggles over the kind of society we want are likely to be as significant for achieving educational change as the more narrowly based struggles within education with which this book has largely been concerned. Secondly, that we must be aware, as is indicated in Wright's account of Rank and File's increasingly narrowly based 'economism', that a politics which neglects the ideological significance and human meaning of what currently counts as education can only replace one form of domination with another.

Chapter 15

The rhetoric of curriculum development

Michael Young

Neither local nor national governments, we are frequently reminded, can legis-late the content of what is taught in schools. Politicians and educational admini-strators are keen to point to the apparently privileged autonomy of the teacher in England in comparison to teachers in other 'Western democracies'. France with its highly centralized control and the USA with control associated with local School Boards are often cited as typical examples. As anyone who has studied the demise of radical educational movements, or who has attempted any-thing which challenged existing notions of 'what education is', will be aware, the reality of this autonomy is limited in scope and individualized in conception. Most teachers are left to themselves in the classroom and may even be able to choose the resources they will use, but a *group* of teachers who tried to influence which organizations were to be asked to the Annual Careers Convention of a London secondary school quickly experienced the constraints on collective auto-nomy. In making the elements of constraint less obvious to practising teachers this apparent autonomy actually obscures its reality and therefore any possibi-lities of change. It is the constraints, of exam boards and syllabuses (see Chapter 17), hierarchical school structures and headmaster power, parent and even pupil resistance (see Chapter 19), often expressed in terms of the massive inaccessi-bility of 'the system', that young teachers particularly confront. The likelihood is, whatever their political or educational radicalism, that they come to see these constraints as in some sense part of 'how the educational world is', part of 'what it is to *be* a teacher', rather than contexts of action. The objections to the inclu-sion of Marxism on the Birmingham Religious Studies syllabus, the public row which erupted when a Hertfordshire School invited an MP to address its sixth form on politics, and the closing of ranks that was apparent, for example in the *T.E.S.*, in opposition to what was seen as the extremism of the William Tyndale School staff and Chris Searle's work, are all indications of the narrowness of the scope of even the rhetoric of teacher autonomy. In the current context of pleas for 'public accountability' and the establishment of the DES's Assessment of Performance and Standards Unit to monitor school performance, the signs are that, in a period of educational cutback, opportunities for control through appointments, references and distribution of 'allowances' are going to increase. It therefore becomes even more important to critically examine the reality of classroom teachers' 'autonomy', and the relations between that autonomy and the kind of opportunities for teachers concerned to reform their classroom practice that agencies like the Schools Council claim to offer. Parallel to the

191

development of Mode 3 assessment there has been a shift in Schools Council policy since the publication of Schools Council Pamphlet 14 in 1974 towards an official encouragement of local curriculum development. [1] This can be seen as a response to criticisms of the Council's first decade of work, that in spite of its massive production of curriculum materials, it was often out of touch with classroom teachers' needs and only involved them on a highly selective and relatively passive basis. Gleeson's paper in this section illustrates this well in the case of the Humanities Curriculum Project, in which there was probably more attempt at follow-up and in-service training than in any other of the Council's projects.

Before looking more specifically at these recent developments, it is important to consider the way in which, since 1964, the teachers' own body (for, with its teacher majorities on all committees, that is what the Schools Council explicitly set out to be) has, through a virtual monopoly of resources for curriculum development, effectively defined *for* teachers the parameters of innovation. In examining the Schools Council and its recent proposals for local initiative, I do not want to assume that the Council's activities are, of themselves, necessarily significant, nor that the achievement by teachers of greater control of their work situation is a realistic possibility independently of wider movements for industrial democracy. On the other hand, this is not to say that Schools Council resources cannot be used to redevelop more 'oppositional' local projects, and perhaps more significantly, to develop a critique by teachers of the ways existing educational hierarchies are sustained by proposals which appear, superficially, to modify them. It is to this latter task that this paper is directed, and it is divided into three parts:

1 A critical examination of the establishment and priorities of the Schools Council as an agency specifically designed to assist teachers in transforming their practice. [2]

2 The 'local initiatives proposal'.

3 Some implications for alternative strategies for teachers.

The Schools Council was set up in 1964 'to keep under review curriculum and examinations', but at the same time not to infringe 'the actual as well as inalienable right of teachers to teach what they like, how and when', as one NUT spokesman put it at the time. [3] This was to be ensured by allowing teachers the freedom to choose whether they used Schools Council materials, and by ensuring a teacher majority on all its committees. I want briefly to examine some aspects of the way the Council's work has been organized and how the teacher majorities have been constituted, before trying to make explicit some of the assumptions about knowledge and education that have defined the nature of the projects that have been initiated. In light of the picture that emerges, I shall suggest that it has been difficult for classroom teachers, unless they happen to have been seconded on to one of the projects, to feel that the Council was 'teacher controlled', and, in spite of official denials, they do feel some pressure to use Schools Council materials. Because of the problems of rewriting national projects materials for particular contexts, and the lack, often, of adequate reprographic facilities and secretarial assistance in schools, teachers specifically involved in curriculum innovations can feel that the Schools Council inhibits rather than encourages them, by diverting resources that they might be able to make more use of *in* the schools. Pamphlet 14 which recommended more teacher participation can be seen as a somewhat belated attempt to respond to this situation.

There are three aspects of the organization that I shall refer to.

(1) Up till 1973, 91 out of the 125 projects were located in universities, and only three in schools, which would seem to indicate an unquestioned assumption that curriculum development *for* schools is best located outside them (in universities), — thus institutionalizing the separation of theory from practice.

(2) Of the first 125 projects, twelve of them cost over £100,000; and accounted for nearly half of the total expenditure. We can only speculate on the significance of the priority given to large-scale 'national' projects. It is perhaps not surprising that the committees allocating such large amounts wanted some evidence of results, and that this should be experienced by project personnel as a pressure on them to produce published materials. [4] Only by 1974 in the pamphlet that I referred to, did the problem of who the Council's materials were reaching become a public issue. For curriculum development to be less about the production of materials for teachers and more about teachers' access to resources that they can use involves recognizing the limitations of the large-scale project as a model. However, the Working Party on Dissemination whose report became Pamphlet 14 had no such doubts, as is indicated in the following extract from the report:

> We have confined ourselves very largely to the present situation of the Council as a central agency funding national projects. . . . This seems to be required by our terms of reference . . . we did not feel that any of the problems of dissemination were so intractable that, in themselves, they challenged the idea of national projects.

(3) The chairmen of the main committees and senior officials are drawn almost without exception from DES and LEA officials, higher education staff and headmasters. [5] Senior appointments are made therefore on the basis of administrative or academic experience rather than any very direct contact with the problems and needs of classroom teachers. As the initiative and responsibility for innovation and allocation of resources is located outside the context of the classroom it is not surprising if many teachers, like the ones Gleeson refers to in Chapter 16, find the Council's work largely irrelevant and relating little to their needs.

It is in the context of these features of the Council's organization that the implications of the teacher majorities on the committees become significant. Three things are apparent. First, the teacher majorities are very small, so effective control depends on very regular attendance. Secondly, teacher members come from five different unions, often in competition in other contexts. They have therefore to act as a concerted body rather than as union representatives, if the majorities are to be effective. Thirdly, teacher representatives on the critical committees are usually union office holders or permanent officials, so the question becomes: how representative are they, and how much contact do they, or can they have with their members in local branches? If one recognizes the problems facing teacher representatives, and their lack of time to study all the relevant documents, the importance of the committee chairmen and senior officials becomes apparent. The possibility of the union representatives being accountable to their members becomes even more questionable when one considers that the NUT, by far the best represented union, has no official policy on curricular matters at all. To do so, as a senior union official explained to me, could be seen as infringing the 'rights' of individual headmasters and teachers. This is clearly a very individualistic notion of autonomy and depends upon a tacit consensus that, broadly, there is general agreement about 'what education is': it leaves teachers able to do little more than respond passively to initiatives from elsewhere — project directors, academics, Council officials and publishing companies (over twenty now publish Schools Council material). We can gain some indication of the nature of this consensus from the writings of Council officials. Caston, a former joint secretary, in addressing an audience of head-masters is quoted as saying:

> The Council has no authority over teachers. It may, indeed I hope it does, carry a certain amount of professional consensus, and a great deal of the kind of authority which comes with organized knowledge.

What is *organized* knowledge and *who* is asuumed to be suitable to do the organizing is again taken for granted in the introduction to Working Paper 33, *Choosing a Curriculum for the Young School Leaver*. The author writes: 'At the outset there was no firm intention of producing a report of the Conference for the public . . . for there were no authoritative speakers present, only people working on development projects'. It would seem that both the control by teachers and the consensus within which this control is expressed are both deeply embedded in traditionally hierarchical notions of who has the right to speak and be heard.

Both the style and content of Schools Council projects exemplify similar assumptions about education to those I have suggested are expressed in its organization. I have suggested elsewhere that it may be useful to divide projects into two kinds. [6] First there are those that depend on 'academic expertise', so that the problem of those involved in such projects becomes finding ways in which pupils and teachers can adapt to existing academic notions of 'knowledge' — mathematical model building in Geography, and the increasingly biochemical character of Biology are typical examples. Secondly there are those projects which reflect a pre-Schools Council tradition of the Inspectorate which relies on identifying the 'good practice' of teachers. The latter have all the appearance of drawing on practising teachers' experience. Consider for a moment a not entirely hypothetical case — a group of English teachers engaged in some novel sixth form work on Black studies, or exploring new ways of developing language use by twelve-year-olds. After a visit by a Schools Council project director, the next thing they know is that their work appears anonymously in an integrated humanities pack, or in a paperback on the language of children in school. Inevitably, though not intentionally, the authorship of their work has become that of the project director. It is difficult not to see such a process as confirming for teachers that their own work has nothing directly to say to a wider public unless it has been picked out by some official expert, thus making active collaborative production by groups of teachers the exception rather than the rule.

Both of these project styles view the classroom teacher as a relatively passive resource, with the initiative lying elsewhere. Ten years after the Council had been started a Working Party on Dissemination and In-Service Training [7] felt it necessary to suggest 'increasing the involvement of teachers in the *creative* side of project work'. Among its recommendations were that 'teachers' opinions should be important in influencing the Council's choice of areas of research and development (No. 34), and that the Council should 'Look for opportunities to fund developments arising out of teachers' activities and ideas' (No. 35). It was thus clear that even in its official publications there was a recognition that whatever concerns the Council represented, they were not primarily those of classroom teachers. Two months later the Programme Committee, effectively the Council's final executive decisioning making body, agreed in principle 'to consider, for grant purposes, initiatives from individuals or groups and such local projects as might be judged to have wider interest' (Schools Council Report 1974-5). An unsigned article, 'Schools Council and Local Curriculum Development', appeared in the Council's house magazine, *Dialogue*, in 1975 and by the end of the year nine local projects had been supported, costing just over £92,000 – less than one eighth of the year's expenditure specifically devoted to curriculum development (as distinct from examinations).

Though the very limited funds devoted to 'local initiatives' indicate that the proposals suggest no dramatic shift in policy, the conception of 'local development' they represent is important to consider as it is a concrete expression of the circumstances within which teachers might become involved in initiating development. The first thing that is apparent is that nearly half of the funds devoted to local projects in 1974-5 were allocated to enable local dissemination centres to be set up – presumably in order for *existing* materials to be more widely available, and thus perpetuating the teacher as a 'transmitter' of prepackaged materials. In the *Dialogue* article referred to above, which was probably the first attempt to inform teachers of the shift in policy, the Council is on record as wishing to 'respond to increasing interest and activity at the grass roots' and it is from the proposals in that article and the documented experience of one of the first local projects, the ILIS [8] group, that I wish to consider what obtaining resources for local initiatives might mean to a group of teachers.

The proposals start by distinguishing between 'curriculum development that is an integral part of the daily task of the teacher' and 'that which is undertaken as the specific task of groups of teachers *drawing on knowledge or expertise'*. It is quite specifically the second kind of local curriculum development for which funds will be made available. Inevitably one can only speculate on the limited evidence available, but what seems to be involved is how the Schools Council's funding procedures generate a hierarchy between 'knowledge-based' and 'practice-based' curriculum development. This makes it likely that local initiatives that are funded are likely to be abstracted from the contexts of practice, as some aspects of the ILIS example referred to below suggest. It also suggests that teachers seeking funds will be encouraged to give their proposals something identifiable as a knowledge base, presumably 'curriculum theory', so that proposals will tend to conform to a particular style. [9] It is presumably in this way that the programme committee members can decide whether or not a particular proposal 'can be *shown* to be of value to teachers beyond the locality'. [10] It is explicitly stated that following a series of local meetings any proposals would go through the normal Council committee procedure. This would seem to add to the likelihood that a 'local initiative' would be spotted as valuable by the Council only if it stemmed from a national project or could be recognized as looking like one. Evidence on the experience of the ILIS project would certainly lend support to this view. As ILIS Chairman Jack Whitehead writes:

> It has taken one of our workshop groups eighteen months to formalize Schools Council support. The procedures which were used for large-scale national projects were imposed on local developments. By their nature, local developments demand a rapid response. To impose this structure on local developments will, I suggest, destroy the possibility that this form of development can be successful. [11]

Elsewhere in the newsletter, Eric Green, ILIS Secretary, reports how they were obliged to follow the general conditions laid down in the Schools Council Handbook for Grant Holders, which insists, *inter alia*, that representatives of the relevant national committees − in this case the subject Advisory Committee for Science − must sit on each local consultative committee. Certainly one group of teachers, those associated with ILIS, experienced the cumbersome and unwieldy Council procedures, which appear quite inappropriate to the variety of problems local initiatives are likely to confront.

If the ILIS experience is more widely reflected, it appears that the Council is able to draw on a variety of procedures to 'control' the local initiatives that they sponsor − presumably on the grounds that it is their responsibility to ensure that local projects 'benefit the whole education service'. It is therefore likely to be delay, frustration and endless committees that any local group seeking Schools Council support is likely to encounter, unless sufficient numbers of groups like ILIS, and the Wiltshire Science teachers, press for modified procedures for local projects.

The professional consensus that has pervaded the Council's work is certainly not in danger of being challenged by those who obtain grants for locally initiated projects. Furthermore, it seems likely that any remotely radical initiative, such as a project in association with local trades unions on industrial democracy, would be dismissed through one of the Council's 'consultative' procedures. On the issue of industrial democracy, there seems little reason to suppose that the 'professional consensus' will be challenged by the recently launched Education and Work Project, sponsored jointly by the Council with the CBI and the TUC, even if those involved are willing to actively encourage local initiatives between

196

shop stewards, teachers and employers, and give each local group a free hand in how they decide to work.

Conclusions and implications

I have suggested that in a variety of ways the Schools Council, in spite of its explicit concern with innovation and improving classroom practice, has, in the way that curriculum innovation has been conceived, confirmed rather than enabled teachers to transcend existing educational categories and hierarchies; its subject advisory committees sustain the divisions in the traditional school curriculum, and provide the framework within which 'integration' is considered, and it is these 'subjects' as in the recent series of sixteen-plus projects, which still get the bulk of funding. The distinction between 'academic' and 'less able' or 'non-academic' children, which is something taken for granted by most teachers, has been institutionalized through separate projects, which assume that different kinds of knowledge are suitable for different kinds of child. Mathematics *for the majority* and Geography *for the young school leaver,* whatever the particular merits of their project materials, presuppose a static model of a society in which 'the majority' have distinctive and defined needs or interests. Similarly, the whole programme orientated to that euphemism for educational failure, 'the young school leaver', takes for granted an education system which forces a large section of pupils to legally remain in school when neither they nor their teachers can find anything either would recognize as valuable to do. If we turn to the way Schools Council priorities are defined and projects are organized, then I have argued that, similarly, though less explicitly, a tacit consensus on conceptions of knowledge and hierarchy is confirmed, as much in the way local initiatives are encouraged as in how large national projects are supported. Not only are the parameters of innovation defined, but also what is to constitute legitimate 'participation'. Grass roots activities of teachers are seen as important, but they are, by definition, *not* experts in 'curriculum development', so the terms of their participation are severely limited. The limits in practice on the active participation of classroom teachers are in stark contrast to the Council's professed aims 'to increase the involvement of teachers in the *creative* side of project work'. This may, however, point to far deeper hierarchies, not restricted to education alone, that prevailing models of curriculum development express. This paper has presented a critique of the Schools Council's monopoly of over 'innovation', primarily in terms of the ways it has confirmed existing educational hierarchies and excluded any real possibility of widespread teacher involvement in the transformation of curricula. However, educational hierarchies are not embedded in education alone, and the classroom teacher's sense of isolation and impotence is not so different from that experienced by those who work in many other contexts. For teachers to develop strategies that might shift the resources of the Schools Council in any significant way, may well involve a challenge to the ideology of teacher's professional autonomy *and* authority which the Council's work has so successfully upheld. Teachers who seek sources of support outside the profession are likely to confront severe forms of resistance both within the schools and within the unions, though the very successful pack of local history materials. *If it Wasn't for the Houses in Between,* [12] which was sponsored by the NUT quite independently of the Schools Council, indicates that even within the unions there are possibilities. The implications of any challenge to the 'professional' authority of teachers are far reaching and not necessarily radical. [13] However, such a challenge by teachers, which would involve not only parents, but social workers, trade unionists associated with the range of employment in any area, and others, is likely to be one of the strategies which might enable the development of conceptions of curriculum development that might really transform educational experience.

Though I have emphasized in this paper the constraints which teachers experience, or are likely to experience, rather than the alternatives they might develop, the Schools Council is a monopoly rather than a monolith. The ILIS group and the Wiltshire Science Teachers among others have obtained funds, and others can learn much from their and others' experience. The small but not insignificant shifts in policy would not have happened if those who control the Council had not felt the need to offer at least a token response to criticism by teachers. Likewise a further shift which would involve more resources for local initiatives and a recognition that the procedures laid down for national projects are quite inappropriate for encouraging such initiatives will not come through critical papers like this but through the efforts and struggles of teachers and those they can develop links with outside the schools. It is to the importance and possibilities as well as the difficulties and limits of these struggles that this chapter is offered as a contribution.

Notes

1 *Report of Working Party on Dissemination and In-Service Training (1972-3).*Schools Council Pamphlet 14.

2 An earlier version of some of these ideas can be found in M. Young. 'On the Politics of Educational Knowledge', *Economy & Society,* vol. 1, No. 2. (1972).

3 At a recent House of Commons Arts and Education Subcommittee, the 'teachers' right to fix the curriculum' was directly questioned. *T.E.S.* Report (2 April 1976).

4 This point is brought out in M.D. Shipman's *Inside a Curriculum Project* (London, Methuen, 1973).

5 These details are all available from the Schools Council's Annual Reports.

6 See Note 2.

7 See Note 1.

8 Independent Learning in Science, whose coordinator is Eric Green, Countesthorpe College, Leicester.

9 For example, the aims/objectives framework as expressed in the Wiltshire Project on Mixed Ability Teaching in Science — see Schools Council Project Information Centre.

10 Schools Council and Local Curriculum Development, *Dialogue 20.*

11 *ILIS Newsletter,* No. 7 (August 1975), obtainable from the Secretary (see Note 8).

12 Prepared by a group of Hackney teachers and published by Centerprise, Dalston Lane, London E8.

13 See Note 3. It is perhaps ironic that it was the Conservative Chairman, Miss Janet Fookes, who suggested that teachers might have a 'vested interest' in controlling the Schools Council.

Chapter 16

Experiencing a curriculum project

Denis Gleeson

In this chapter I intend to discuss a particular conception of humanities teaching which is reflected in the Humanities Curriculum Project, and to consider the ways in which such conceptions have come to have meaning to a small group of teachers in a comprehensive school. A feature of this chapter is that it draws attention to the ways in which the potentially radical forms of inquiry that are embraced by the HCP may not become realized through the methods it advocates. It is not the intention, however, of this chapter to raise criticisms which might throw the baby out with the bathwater or to deny the ways in which those working with the Project come to perceive pedagogic relations differently. Indeed from my own experiences of working with the Project, interviewing teachers, as well as supervising student teachers, it is my impression that the Project makes apparent to many humanities teachers the particular dilemmas of seriously exploring the nature of controversial inquiries within the existing social context and organization of schooling. Nevertheless, I want to argue that whilst existing conditions of schooling may repress such alternative conceptions of pedagogy, there are ways in which certain assumptions within the Project act to neutralize its radical possibilities, and to render its conception of school knowledge as meaningless as those narrative processes of education to which it is addressed. Furthermore, I shall discuss particular issues associated with such large-scale curriculum developments and consider problems and issues involved in developing alternative conceptions of curriculum change.

Background

The HCP emerged against a background of curricular change in the 1960s which advocated the need to 'structure' the learning environment in which innovation takes place. [1] This concern with 'structure', often referred to as the New Social Studies movement, reflects a reaction against conventional Social Studies and Civics courses in the 1930s, 1940s and 1950s which were perceived as being poorly organized and too loosely defined. It has been argued that such courses were characterized by a lack of content, clarity and rigour, and that under the ideological veil of social relevance they sought to uncritically introduce pupils to civic awareness and responsible citizenship. [2] The HCP's concern with structured inquiry methods which address issues of didactic teaching style, narrative pedagogy, the examination of evidence and emphasis upon rules of neutral

200

teaching (chairmanship) in many ways reflects the particular concerns of this movement.

The processes through which such a national curriculum project emerges within the school curriculum cannot therefore be perceived in a vacuum or as distinct from those conventional processes of teaching and learning to which it is critically addressed. The concern to legitimate such an alternative view of humanities teaching rests upon a number of assumptions concerning the existing conditions of school practice, and as such suggests a number of important issues for exploration in the politics of school knowledge. In the first place there is the need to explore the ways in which the assumptions of curriculum developers relate to the experiences and views held by teachers working in the school, and secondly there is the need to identify the ways in which teachers redefine their conceptions of school knowledge through working with such a project.

Teachers' experiences

In this section I wish to put forward some criticisms of the Project as expressed by a small group of humanities teachers, who, although sympathetic towards the intentions of the Project, had lost much of their earlier enthusiasm for its methods. Initially the teachers were attracted to a number of important features of the Project which supported existing humanities work in the school. The teachers pointed generally to such features as:

1 It generated discussion amongst staff concerning the aims and approaches of inquiry-based learning.

2 It served to support claims made by the teachers that the organization of school work should be more related to the contexts and conditions in which pupils live.

3 It raised questions and hopes that research and discussion concerning the nature of authority and power in humanities teaching would be as much concerned in influencing the organization and social context of the school as it would be in influencing pupils' critical relations with the community.

An important claim of the Project is that there is a need to link the kinds of controversial issues generated in Humanities work to their related contexts both within and without school. Such an approach to the questioning of authority, for example, would imply that the activity of teaching and learning is concerned with examining possibilities for exploring the relations between classroom processes and the existing contexts in which school knowledge is organized. It further implies that traditional distinctions between what goes on in classrooms, in schools and in communities, become blurred in the processes of open-ended inquiry. Furthermore, such an approach holds the promise that teaching and learning in social studies are 'for real' rather than being simply a process of transmitting and acquiring knowledge 'about' the social world as if it were an entirely 'out there' thing.

For teachers to take seriously the radical implications of such an approach the contradictions and dilemmas in which they have to work become quite explicit, and cannot be taken lightly. A number of important issues arise both in terms of their relations with their pupils and in terms of their relations with the social organization of the school. For example, the Project's particular attack on authoritarian processes suggests ways in which teachers and students may openly question features of oppression which influence freedom, and not least of all those features that exist within the contexts of school practice itself. Discussions concerning 'Power and Authority in Education' may focus upon the nature of school subjects, discipline, decision making and democracy, and cannot readily be divorced from the everyday life experiences of teachers and pupils within the school nor can they be conveniently compartmentalized to the four walls of the humanities classroom where such talk may be tolerated.

It would appear therefore that such an alternative conception of pedagogy holds important critical implications for the social organization of the school. However, I want to argue that this is not necessarily realized in the conditions of practice, and cannot be simply explained within the existing narrative conceptions of school organization or in the failure of teachers to take the aims of the project seriously. Rather, through the following accounts of the teachers, I wish to explore the ways in which features of the Project's methods reinforce existing conceptions of school knowledge and act to interfere with the teacher's particular conceptions of critical social studies teaching. In the following comments we may observe a tension between the teacher's notions of radical humanities teaching and his experiences of particular aspects of the Project's methods.

John: HCP isn't controversial enough . . . quite often there isn't the emotional nexus . . . if you like . . . with the situations which are being discussed . . . frequently discussions emerging from HCP materials become forced . . through the method of chairmanship . . . in the abstract . . . I mean . . . you know . . . many of our pupils live in bad housing conditions . . . but frequently it seems as if the method maintains a kind of protective blanket . . . if you like . . . which prevents the kids from being perhaps as critical of these conditions as possible . . . it makes relations a bit formal . . .

D.G.: Um . . . protective blanket . . . is that a feature of HCP or something else?

John: Well . . . um . . . I had a chat with some of the kids who constantly opted out . . . they pissed off and you know . . . didn't want to know . . . I had a long chat with them . . . in the bog . . . and they were very cynical . . . very cynical . . . and they said . . . well . . . you know . . . um . . . it's all very well . . . the HCP discussions . . . but so . . . so what! . . . it doesn't get you anywhere . . . I know they were suffering from a kind of um . . . ah . . . a lack of understanding of practical procedures for involvement and for changing situations . . .

and ... in a sense they see HCP as removed and abstract .... Radical humanities teaching has got to mean something through its links ... with a practical exercise ... it's got to be linked to an outcome that can be shown to be effective ... I mean practical ... action-orientated ... critical work ... where they're working in a position of being politicized .... HCP material can't stimulate this ... they can't ... because frequently materials are seen as uninteresting ... O.K. sometimes interesting the kids say ... but they say so what ... a lot of material they find meaningless .... It's far too impersonal ... removed.

Such comments would appear to include a number of observations stressing the need to consider the ways in which the development of alternative conceptions of pedagogy cannot be separated from factors relating to the social context of the school. In the first place John draws attention to the ways in which particular aspects of the Project's methods (chairmanship, evidence, neutrality) may render inquiry work as abstract an activity as those pursued in other subjects in the curriculum. Secondly, his reference to alternative conceptions of humanities teaching, based upon such criteria as 'practical involvement in change ... practical exercise ... politicization ... action-orientated ...', suggests quite explicit criticism of the existing abstract, removed and subject-centred nature of schooling. Teachers who work seriously with such a project may have to consider much more closely the relationship between its methods and the practical situations in which inquiry is generated. This might well imply conflict as teachers and pupils find that the action-orientated nature of such inquiry learning suggests a radical requestioning of narrative conceptions of school knowledge and traditional assumptions concerning the relationship between school knowledge and community activity.

The awareness of such dilemmas highlights the contradictions in which *all* radical teachers find themselves when confronting change. It is a critical awareness which recognizes the political nature of school knowledge and questions the assumptions upon which traditional conceptions of knowledge are organized and sustained. The risks are great and there is a need to recognize that the nature of particular forms of critical questioning creates conflict and may attract authoritarian repression. It is the case, for example, that conservative and dominant ideological beliefs in education seek to maintain the spurious myth that education and the teacher's role is not concerned with political processes. Teachers who question such assumptions, in the contexts of the learning situation, become only too aware of their potentially 'deviant' position. The following comments expressed by Mark suggest ways in which he is able to utilize features of the HCP to legitimate and support his political conceptions of teaching, whilst at the same time redefining aspects of the method relating to neutrality.

Mark: Whether I'm actually keen on HCP as it was originally devised or whether I just see it as an important educational need which can be met partly by HCP as its set up and partly by adaptation within the school ... like the use of the time for careers work ... outside

visits . . . work with drama . . . music, etc. . . . What I really like about
it is that it offers the opportunity for a very informal situation where
the teacher is very much playing a non-dominant role. . . . I don't go
along with the ideal of a neutral chairman entirely . . . because I think
many of our kids require taught background information on certain
topics and areas . . . they need a great deal of direct help and guidance
with their written work . . . and advice and positive direction on political issues relating to jobs and work. They haven't got the kind of
background information on issues relating to work and choices . . .
inquiry-based learning may be OK when kids have some idea of where
they're going . . . many of our kids don't . . . they don't have the kind
of access to that knowledge. . . . I think the real issue is that . . .
having said that . . . the teacher doesn't use the situation as a platform
to impose any particular ideology or axe on the kids . . . so long as the
teacher doesn't abuse that position of power which the teacher inevitably has . . . because the kids are interested in his opinions . . . that's
the real issue . . . I think. . . . If you've got a project that's thought
about these problems and got down on paper . . . um . . . as HCP
had done . . . it can act as a guide to people . . . particularly new
teachers. . . .

Within the activity of working within the Project, Mark redefines his own
conceptions of impartiality and political education through his relations with
pupils, whilst, at the same time, using HCP as a support for his own particular
approach to teaching. Such an account not only reveals the way in which a
teacher may handle the controversy attached to such an approach, but it may
also suggest the ways in which such a project may draw attention to particular
dilemmas involved in humanities teaching, as well as offering some elements of
'sponsored' support. However, such a view is not one that is entirely endorsed
by Dave who argues that the use of resource evidence, neutrality and rules of
chairmanship, obscures the issues of critical understanding and 'interferes'
with classroom relations.

Dave: One thing that comes to mind is that . . . I find the materials not
controversial enough . . . a kind of woolly liberalism . . . the packs
don't reflect adequate examples of polarized views at all . . . in
fact . . . I found quite often the materials provided very little to argue
about . . . I mean . . . you introduce a topic . . . and perhaps the kids
have had this liberalizing approach already pumped at them by telly,
radio, magazines . . . they've become immune to it . . . they're open to
coming to consensus more than anything . . . and bang that's the end
of it . . . the kids want action and to see themselves involved in seeing
changes going on. . . . OK, HCP would agree with that . . . but you
know if I'm doing some work with the kids and they say 'Well that's
wrong in'it, sir?' I say what I think . . . . I don't give nine different
views or throw the question back at them.

D.G.:   Are you being neutral or impartial according to HCP rules, then?

Dave: No, course not ... but then many of my kids are shat on by land-
         lords ... by the council ... high rents ... harassment ... you
         know ... I mean society doesn't treat them impartially ... you can't
         look neutrally at these issues ... the kids need info ... often ... to
         know how to cope ... handle ... manipulate ... etc.... Look, there
         are no four, five, etc., ways to look at the housing question ... there's
         one ... people who get shat on ... they need knowledge to protect
         themselves ....

D.G.:   Yes ... um ... how do you hold back in discussions in those embar-
         rassing silences, for example?

Dave: Ah, yeah ... with those pregnant pauses ... I call that sliding off the
         hot seat craftily....

D.G.:   Hot seat ... ?

Dave: There ... there always seemed to be a point where the kids wanted to
         know what I thought ... it's phoney to avoid answering ... that's
         what I meant by sliding off the hot seat ... the thing is ... you're in a
         small group ... a personal group of fifteen kids ... its a personal
         situation ... you can't avoid ... once kids know you as a person ...
         and like you ... they want to know what you think ... you can't
         avoid this involvement ... you can't be impartial.

As with other accounts, Dave points to a view of school knowledge which suggests that education is not simply concerned with learning *about* the social
world, but that it is equally concerned with developing strategies and approaches
involving pupils in influencing change — classroom knowledge being perceived as
'useful' rather than as 'neutral'. In this sense Dave draws attention to the tension
between notions of impartiality and his involvement with the political issues
facing his pupils. A concept such as neutrality is perceived as meaningless both in
terms of his relationship with his pupils and in terms of the housing conditions
in which many of them live. Whilst the Project advocates the need for teachers
to explore the many sided nature of social issues, impartiality and chairmanship
are not perceived here as useful procedures for creating the kind of dialogue and
trust necessary for the exploration of crucial issues. Although the project also
points to the dangers of teachers foisting their political views upon pupils, it may
be the case that the issue of 'imposition' may hold other interpretations. In this
case the teacher is suggesting that there are circumstances in which pupils require
additional positive guidance and information in support of their expressed views.
He perceives the teaching situation as not simply the interchange of views in discussion but also the consideration of strategies and approaches which may help
students to act on their developing awareness. In this sense the term 'imposition'

takes on another meaning which may suggest that whilst pupils are aware of the social conditions in which they live, they also need a good deal of guidance and support for exploring possible alternative avenues of action to influence, and perhaps change, those conditions.

A feature of the accounts so far is that they point to the lack of relationship between key areas of the project (neutrality, evidence, chairmanship) and the particular views which the teachers hold of social studies teaching. One explanation for this is that the assumptions of the curriculum developers are not adequately grounded in the contexts of practitioners' experiences. A particular problem associated with centrally constructed curriculum developments is that they separate off persons in the activity of constructing curriculum. The planners and seconded teachers most often operate from the removed context of the university and relate to selected trial schools in an experimental role in which ideas are tried out and evaluated. Although classroom teachers are involved in such experiments their participation is often of a token nature and is certainly not significant in decision making processes. Indeed an important aim of the Project is that teachers are 'inducted' into it. However, being 'inducted' into a process very often implies that one is there to learn rather than to question the assumptions of the experts. In circumstances where teachers experience the use of Project tools (evidence, neutrality, chairmanship, etc.) as alien, there is a real sense in which their classroom relations may become adversely influenced.

Jane: I suppose I was too selfconscious about being impartial, that because I was working through that I became less sensitive to the kids' feelings than I would have been normally and they were very conscious of this ... there'd been always before a group feeling of mutual warmth and giving which the kids were very aware wasn't there because I was trying to withdraw and be this neutral figure, and they became as a group hostile .... I could feel group animosity being directed ... at not necessarily me, but what I was trying to do ....

D.G.:   What did you feel about this?

Jane: Well I felt a bit let down and *really* sceptical about the induction course. I remember on the course that I felt very intimidated by the guy who chaired our discussion group .... I felt certain vibrations ... you know ... as if he knew something about me which I didn't know ... I mean the impartiality bit took warmth away from him and he appeared cold ... you felt that the silences were designed to intimidate ... his expressionless face gave him a kind of superiority ... I don't really know ... but I can see that my kids reacted more honestly and openly to what they thought ... I understand their hostility better now.

This account would appear to suggest that both the teacher and the pupil experience this 'new' method as alien to their existing relations. Whilst it may be true that such a statement is indicative of a teacher 'under threat', reacting to alternative demands, it is equally the case that the experience of induction into the style of teaching is seen as oppressive. When asked to elaborate on what she saw as important to her teaching relations the teacher replied as follows:

Jane: I feel it very difficult to distance myself from people ... distancing yourself from the kids can happen using this method.... It's not only a cop out but makes them resentful.... I don't like the idea of holding back on relationships ... you know ... I mean ... it's possibly rather ill advised in fact ... you know ... increasingly to be so ... but I think that in the same way that the children make themselves vulnerable. ... I have to respond in the same way ... I feel hiding behind impartiality wouldn't be fair....

It would be very easy, of course, to dismiss such an account as an example of one of those 'authoritarian' teachers to whom the Project is addressed, but my own feeling is that such a viewpoint expresses as much sympathy towards the experiences of the pupils as it does to the teacher's rationalization of her own position. Her account stands on the grounds that she perceives her criteria of teaching as being *different* to those advocated at induction conferences.

The emphasis upon developing standard rules of procedure in such a large curriculum project generates inflexibility towards teachers who wish to redefine or construct different rules. Teachers sympathetic with the Project's aims often experience induction into its methods as artificial and contrived. In the following comments Margaret draws attention to the 'Catch 22' dilemma of acquiring the correct method:

Margaret: I felt it wasn't very real, somehow ... as if the kinds of teaching situations and discussion settings looked at there were kind of very different to those I meet.... I mean some of the films we saw ... they didn't ring true ... I felt the kids were specially picked in ideal situations.... I mean in my groups at school things didn't run like that with everyone courteously waiting for everyone else ... there were very long silences ... times when the kids couldn't make anything of the materials, and they said 'so what'.... There were times when everyone wanted to say something and you know ... the shouting would escalate ... all that one could do then was to adopt an authoritarian role and shout 'Quiet!' ... I felt that the films at the course had been of an ideal situation and presumably the kids were aware of being filmed, and on their best behaviour. It wasn't real....

D.G.: But presumably the course only attempts to use these 'ideal' films as a guide to generally indicate what such teaching might look like?

Margaret: Yes, OK, but I felt I was looking in on a style of teaching which was

207

alien to me. . . . Being a teacher . . . I mean your style . . . is I think influenced by who *you* are . . . and on how the kids relate to you . . . and vice versa . . . learning someone else's style doesn't help you to develop on your own strengths. I mean . . . watching some of the 'ideal' films made me think the teachers on display were expressionless . . . they looked rigid and formal . . . the atmosphere in these discussions was respectful but stilted. The teacher in one looked like a praying mantis!'

D.G.: Did you make these views known to other people on the course?

Margaret: Yes . . . I mean quite a few other teachers expressed scepticism . . . but because I think most teachers who bother going on such a course are sympathetic to the kinds of things HCP is trying to do . . . I think anyway . . . it was difficult to push the issue . . . after all we were there to learn how to use the method. I did feel that the more outspoken teacher critics were 'sat on' by some course organizers as well as teachers. . . . You know . . . it was as if . . . if you criticized such progressive stuff . . . in front of advisers, inspectors and HCP people you'd be seen as an example of those fascist teachers the whole show's addressing. . . .

D.G.: What do you do then?

Margaret: Well, though I'm sympathetic to HCP I've become very sceptical. What pissed me off about such conferences . . . or when the Project people come in to see us teach . . . was that they always had a better answer to the teachers' criticisms. It's not as if people here are against the principle of things, is it? It's almost as if the early project workers were like evangelists . . . you know one came in to see me teach . . . and make tapes. . . . It was like Catch 22 . . . every time I expressed a reservation about the method . . . she explained it away on the grounds that I wasn't operating the thing properly.

Whilst it may be suggested that the teacher has made an overtly literalist interpretation of the rules implied in the method, it is undoubtedly the case that many teachers have given up working with the project because they feel that the procedures are beyond their reach. From my own experience of such induction courses my inclination is to feel much sympathy towards Margaret's viewpoint, recognizing that induction 'workers', inspectors and advisers, in their enthusiasm for generating new ideas, often intimidate the teacher in vulnerable circumstances.

The processes by which teachers experience curriculum innovations as external constraints coming from 'out there' raise a number of critical questions concerning the assumptions upon which national curriculum projects operate. There is a tendency for curriculum developers to assume that the educational system acts in a systematized fashion, in that once ideas have been fed into it from the top (inputs of structured materials, resources, methods) these may then be processed through various channels to the grass roots at the bottom (output: classrooms). Such hierarchichal assumptions of 'development' assume a split between experts and classroom teachers. Furthermore, the assumptions in such a model imply clear distinctions between the ascendancy of theory at the top and practice at the bottom, which largely ignore the ways in which the nature of educational practice generates and informs theory. Evaluators who share such assumptions, and who seek to monitor the success and failure of projects, may wrongly interpret obstacles and problems to progress in terms of the poor performances of teachers rather than as a critical reflection of the constraints in which they work. In other words, such notions of curriculum development create disjuncture in the relations between theory and practice, which ignores the possible ways in which classroom teachers may have significant things to say concerning processes of innovation and curriculum change.

Although HCP generates important discussion concerning the aims of humanities teaching, and draws attention to the dilemma of teachers working with 'alternative' pedagogy, its particular model of curriculum development (and methods subsumed within it) imposes constraints which fail to actually support the teacher within the contradictions of his work. Teachers who seek to take the aims of an alternative pedagogy seriously find it holds critical implications both in terms of their relations with their pupils and in terms of potential change within the school. Such teachers operate within politically vulnerable conditions, and it is essential therefore that support be given to them in the contradictions in which they work.

There is a need therefore to consider alternative strategies for curriculum change and teacher education which are based upon the close working co-operation of classroom teachers, teacher educators and researchers. This implies that existing hierarchichal distinctions between planners and practitioners should be re-examined so that teachers are more fully involved in constructing alternative conceptions of pedagogy in a shared relationship with educationists, pupils and researchers. The recently conceived Ford Teaching Project attempts to address itself to this question by suggesting:

> With a few notable exceptions curriculum designers have failed to support teachers grappling with the problems that curriculum presents in the classroom. They have tended to underestimate the stresses and strains which attend the necessary changes in role relationships . . . for both teachers and pupils, too easily assuming that changes in pedagogy can be brought about by merely changing content and materials.

Whilst it may still be too early to say what kind of impact such an approach may hold for developing alternative conceptions of school knowledge and the political problems involved, it certainly points to the need to examine distinctly different conceptions of curriculum innovation and change based upon notions of collaboration within the learning context as distinct from innovations which are externally 'grafted' on to schools from *outside.*

However, this process is not simply one of generating the collaboration of practitioners in the field alone, but must necessarily incorporate equally the questioning of assumptions and practices implied in those changing relationships as they relate to alternative theories of school knowledge and the social context of the school. The Social Education Project, for example, makes important reference to the ways in which alternative conceptions of teacher-pupil relations have important implications for both the social context of the school and the relationship between school knowledge and everyday life. The Project approaches an alternative to those conventional Civics or Community Studies programmes which have traditionally adhered to the hazy aims of creating social awareness, but which have more often than not uncritically introduced pupils into the accepted order of things. It suggests that social education is as much concerned with helping teachers and pupils to develop skills and strategies for controlling and influencing both community and school as it is with generating social awareness . Emphasis is placed upon the ways in which teachers and pupils may critically research social action within and without school, in the attempt to both critically understand and to tentatively construct theories and strategies which may influence such social forces. Williams and Rennie suggest:

Basically social education of this type is dependent upon a relationship between pupil and teacher which is democratic. They are colleagues, jointly seeking answers to questions about the problems and challenges of the immediate school and community. Responsibility for control in the classroom is shifted gradually from being principally that of the teacher to a joint responsibility of teacher and children. [4]

Both writers point out, however, that such programmes of collaborative action research cannot alone transform political inequality within the community, but must be perceived realistically alongside other forms of struggle. Their suggestion, however, that the 'identification of problems, initiation of action, must come from within the community and not be imposed from outside: it must come from 'us' not them' — suggests quite clearly that the struggles within education against the conditions that produce and reproduce alienated knowledge are not to be seen as dissimilar from related types of social critique and action found elsewhere.

Notes

1 A particular feature of the 1960s concern with 'structure' relates to the establishment of 'new' rigour in humanities and social studies teaching based upon the underpinnings of social sciences knowledge. Both here and abroad writers such as Bruner, Rogers, Fenton, Lawton, and Cannon were but a few concerned with this movement. For a discussion of the 'New Social Studies' see D. Lawton and B. Dufour *The New Social Studies* (London, Heinemann, 1973).

2 For elaboration of this perspective see C. Cannon, 'Social Studies in the Secondary School', *Educational Review*, vol. 17, No. 1 (November 1964).

3 J. Elliot and C. Adelman, 'Teacher Education for Curriculum Reform', an interim report on The Ford Teaching Project, *British Journal of Teacher Education*, vol. 1, No. 1 (1975).

4 W. Williams and J. Rennie, 'Social Education' in D. Rubinstein and C. Stoneman (eds), *Education for Democracy*, Harmondsworth, Penguin, 1972.

Chapter 17

Teachers and examiners

Geoff Whitty

Considerable concern is often expressed about the influence which external examinations appear to exert upon the secondary school curriculum. Yet most research into assessment has been concerned with techniques of measurement and, in the case of examinations, with issues such as the reliability of marking or the comparability of grades between different examining boards. With a few exceptions, it has offered little insight into the social relationships between teachers, pupils and examiners which produce the grades whose reliability is being assessed. [1] It is, of course, hardly surprising that there has been little research in this area, since even those boards which boast a large measure of teacher participation are notoriously secretive in their operations. Access to their committee structures is generally restricted to 'insiders' whose loyalty to the organization limits their freedom to discuss their experiences and the administrative procedures of the boards have remained almost totally impenetrable. Most of the sociological work on examination boards has, largely for these reasons, remained speculative and it is still the case that, as Musgrave reported in 1970, [2] 'there are very few studies that look at the ways in which examination syllabuses are set or how they change in answer to new demands from the various related parts of the social structure'. The only substantive work to which Musgrave was able to point was in the field of technical education, though Carson has since given us something of an insight into a somewhat unusual attempt to construct an A level syllabus in the new curriculum area of Environmental Studies. [3] In the more usual case of examination syllabuses emanating from within the boards' normal channels, however, documentation relating to their construction often remains firmly in the 'confidential' category.

Despite the paucity of research into the activities of examination boards, there is no shortage of staffroom folklore on the subject. 'I'd like to do so and so, but what with the examination coming up . . . .' is a common refrain amongst secondary school teachers and one recent research study reports the constraints of the examinations system as amongst the reasons why some teachers opt for the 'freer' middle school field.[4] In the Scottish situation, R. F. Mackenzie has gone so far as to argue that 'there will be no progress in Scottish education until we have cleared our feet of the external examination system'. [5] One of the most common criticisms of examining boards is that their syllabuses force teachers to compromise their ideals and, in particular, to adopt a transmission mode of teaching rather than more pupil-centred work. [6] Teachers engaged in developing experimental curricula feel particularly exposed in this respect – if their work is non-examinable, it is likely to lack status; if they make it examinable they may be deflected from their original goals. This dilemma is clearly present in the minds of the Humanities Curriculum Project team who, at the same time as yielding to pressure to publish guidelines on the examination of HCP work, feel compelled to comment:

> If you have reserves about examining the Humanities Project you may, in the light of your study of these syllabuses, papers and comments, find evidence here to strengthen your position. Certainly some of the teachers' comments suggest that they are being pressurized to modify in the direction of a more formal pattern of assessment and teaching. If this is in any way indicative of what is happening throughout the country, it could mean that the status and structure of examinations in this country will prevent any effective implementation of the Project on a large scale. [7]

On the other hand, many people suggest that it is teachers rather than examination boards who act as a conservative force in the curriculum field. Hoste and Bloomfield comment that 'the disagreement between teaching objectives and examination objectives is frequently merely the difference in opinion between two groups of teachers', since at CSE level 'examiners are usually practising teachers and their proposals for papers are subjected to close scrutiny by teams of practising teachers'. [8] A local authority adviser, closely connected with one of the GCE Boards, went even further than this in suggesting to me that 'our more radical proposals always get thrown out when we put them to practising teachers'. Eggleston has summed up this point of view in the following statement:

> Curriculum in schools, though infinitely more varied than before, is still largely conceived within the existing social system. Moreover the constraints that kept it that way may seem to come not so much from curriculum development agencies and examining boards but rather from the teachers' own consciousness. [4]

This seems to imply that it is teachers' conceptions of knowledge and pedagogy which serve to maintain the *status quo* rather than the activities of outside agencies or even that the limitations which these agencies seem to place upon the development of radical alternatives are partly a figment of teachers' imaginations.

In general terms Eggleston's claim is not particularly contentious. Any efficient system of social control will, of course, tend to rely upon ideological rather than overtly repressive control of its agents. If the majority of teachers were to reject that conception of education which is reflected in our examination system, then it seems unlikely that the boards could of themselves maintain that conception. However, this should not lead us to the conclusion that the activities of the examination boards are irrelevant to that process of control.

Even the annual administrative demands of the boards are a sufficiently significant part of reality for any secondary school teacher to contribute to his conception of what schooling is all about. Nor should we assume that the examination boards lack the means to constrain the activities of those teachers who do reject their definition of reality and seek to challenge prevailing views of curriculum, pedagogy and evaluation.

However, many people would wish to argue that the minority of teachers who do seek to mount this sort of challenge need no longer feel constrained by external examinations. They would argue that, even if Mode 1 examinations often do place teachers in unwelcome straitjackets, the Mode 3 option offered by CSE boards and the special syllabus arrangements of some GCE boards have given teachers the opportunity to devise courses and assessment procedures commensurate with their educational aims. This is the position taken up by Eggleston and Holford [10] who claim that teachers now have the opportunity to reassert control of their curricula, whilst MacIntosh and Smith regard Mode 3 examinations as part of a general trend in examining which could facilitate the development of a freer curriculum in which curriculum development and assessment no longer act as hindrances upon each other [11]. Many teachers who have chosen to submit Mode 3 examination schemes have expressed similar hopes, as this quotation from a teacher operating a Mode 3 CSE and GCE Humanities programme indicates:

> Our early enthusiasm for innovation was in part sustained by the feeling that we couldn't possibly produce a course that was less motivating than the more traditional, single subject Mode 1 CSE examinations in the Humanities. . . . The breadth of content to be covered forced teachers to use an excessive degree of didactic teaching, thus stifling the pupil's initiative in the learning situation. . . . [12]

In this, as in other similar schools, the staff clearly felt that the syllabuses and assessment criteria for Mode 1 examinations interfered with the curriculum objectives of the school while Mode 3's were expected to offer greater possibilities for harmony between them.

The remainder of this chapter casts some doubt upon the extent to which such hopes can be regarded as justified. Based as it is only upon some initial fieldwork for a research project into the social processes involved in the construction and examination of Mode 3 CSE and GCE syllabuses, it can only offer limited insights into the ways in which the activities of the examining boards facilitate or hinder the development of alternative conceptions of knowledge, pedagogy and evaluation within schools. The evidence concerning the ways in which teachers developing Mode 3 courses experience the work of the boards is largely drawn from schools in the south of England working with three CSE boards and one GCE board. It is derived from the notes of guidance issued by the relevant boards to their centres, from a selection of syllabuses in the Humanities, Social Studies and Environmental Studies fields submitted to these boards, and from formal and informal contact with some of the teachers responsible for those syllabuses. Although limited in scope, the study did raise serious questions about the extent to which Mode 3 examinations do, in practice, offer greater freedom to teachers, and it is hoped that it will later prove possible to investigate the issues raised in greater depth.

None of the schemes under consideration here could properly be considered oppositional to the 'existing social system' but some of them do relate to curriculum developments which involve a substantial departure from the prevailing pattern of fourth and fifth year studies. There were relatively few substantial complaints about the boards' activities from teachers whose schemes differed from their equivalent Mode 1's merely in terms of syllabus content, but complaints increased where modes of assessment differed or where the examination was linked to a major piece of curriculum development. Thus, while this paper concentrates on ways in which teachers feel constrained by the procedures and demands of examining boards, it is not intended to suggest that relationships between teachers and examiners are in a state of perpetual conflict. A number of teachers had 'no complaints whatever' or 'no complaints, by and large'. The majority of complaints related to the boards' submission procedures and to the boards' apparent attempts to impose Mode 1 assessment criteria upon Mode 3 schemes in such a way as to limit the effectiveness of the sort of curriculum development to which they were linked. The response of the boards to some of the comparatively mild proposals for reform put forward in these schemes is perhaps suggestive of the fate which more radical alternatives, conceived in opposition to the existing social system, would have met. [13] It certainly suggests that the constraining influence which the boards exercise over curriculum activities is rather more real than some commentators have seemed to suggest.

Many teachers, including those with high expectations of Mode 3 schemes reported that in practice it proved less easy to escape from the constraints of Mode 1's than they had hoped. This difficulty related both to the problem of getting a scheme accepted in the form originally envisaged and also to the operation of the scheme once approved. CSE Board One, which had a reputation amongst teachers for being unsympathetic to Mode 3 schemes anyway, was felt in many schools to be less than serious about encouraging coursework assessments, continuous assessment and other alternative modes of examining. [14] This board operates a system whereby 'a restriction may be placed upon the grades to be awarded' so that courses 'designed for candidates of lesser ability in the subject concerned' would be limited to the highest award of a grade 3. This restriction could be invoked 'at the time of approval of the question papers' or '(in the case of schemes based largely or wholly on coursework) during the awarding procedure'. However, a number of teachers (Schools C, D and E) reported that such a restriction had been imposed or suggested at the time of submission of the scheme and there was a clear feeling that the rubric was used to justify this imposition in cases where the assessment procedures differed radically from Mode 1 norms in the relevant subject. They felt it was particularly applied in cases where it was proposed that there should be no terminal examination or where such an examination was to constitute a small proportion of the total marks. The aim of the restriction was 'to ensure that, in any subject, candidates do not obtain a grade more easily in one examination than another' but a number of teachers felt that the concept of easiness related to 'Mode 1 criteria' which were inappropriate to the aims of their Mode 3 schemes. The board's chief examiner reacted to a suggestion from a teacher at School E that pupils' 'community service diaries' might be submitted for assessment with the comment that 'You'd have a job to shove that sort of thing onto a marking matrix' and this left a clear impression that his school's curriculum objectives and the board's assessment criteria for Mode 3 were far from in harmony.

CSE Board Two, on the other hand, had a reputation for encouraging Mode 3 schemes. In general this board was felt to place less obstacles in the path of teachers submitting Mode 3 schemes but an incident at School A suggests that the criteria it adopts for assessing Mode 3 schemes are less liberal than they at first sight appear. At this school an error led to a pupil being marked absent from an examination which she had actually taken. The assessment scheme allotted 50 per cent of the marks to this examination, 50 per cent for coursework and the final grade on the basis of the aggregate total. When the error was discovered and the paper forwarded to the board, the candidate was awarded a grade 3 and this corresponded to the school's assessment of the paper. However, it was pointed out to the board that the final mark ought to have taken into consideration her coursework. On the school's assessment this approximated to a Grade 1 standard and would hence have affected her final grade. For almost a year this dispute continued but the board steadfastly refused even to see the pupil's coursework or discuss the case with the teacher involved. Ultimately the school was forced to accept the board's decision even though this involved ignoring 50 per cent of the assessment procedure which had been agreed. The confidence with which the board felt able to reach a decision on the basis of the formal examination alone casts doubt on its integrity in appearing to support a more broadly based approach to assessment.

The overriding influence of Mode 1 criteria was felt by teachers to be even more marked in the operations of the GCE Board. The different structures, traditions and concerns of the GCE boards were felt to make 'academic respectablity' a central issue in the board's deliberations about Mode 3 submissions, and at two schools (Schools A and H) there was a strong impression that this concern had been growing rather than diminishing in recent years. Certainly, a senior official of this board, commenting on a Mode 3 scheme at the submission stage, wrote 'obviously we could not allow continuous assessment to count for 70 per cent of the examination' (my emphasis) which illustrates the way in which Mode 1 norms tend to be taken for granted as the 'obvious' in the minds of the board's employees. Despite the often rehearsed arguments about the weaknesses of terminal examinations, it still remains inconceivable that an official would write 'obviously we could not allow the final examination to count for 70 per cent of the marks'! Easy comparability with existing practices dominates discussion of alternatives, even though many teachers report a reluctance upon the part of the boards to offer as detailed a justification of those practices as teachers preparing their own schemes of assessment are asked to produce.

216

The tendency to measure the acceptability of Mode 3 schemes by Mode 1 yardsticks also carries over into the implementation of moderation procedures. The board's report on the submission and assessment of special syllabuses states, for instance, that:

> In appointing [moderators], the Board looks for people with appropriate academic qualifications, and with suitable teaching and examining experience. The moderator should have an understanding of the kind of institution with which he will be working – preferably from teaching in a similar school or college; he needs experience as an examiner in Mode 1, because at the end he has to maintain the standards of the Board whilst applying these standards to different material from that present in Mode 1 examinations.

The suggestion that examining at Mode 3 involves applying the same standards to different materials appears to imply that Mode 3's will tend to differ from Mode 1's largely in terms of content, though many teachers adopting Mode 3's see this as the least important difference. On the other hand, the board's method of appointing moderators for such schemes seems to reinforce the board's rather than the teachers' point of view.

At the present time there is, of course, a shortage of people who adequately fill the board's stated requirements for O level moderators. In situations where the board had to choose between a moderator with Mode 1 examining experience and one with relevant teaching experience, it was felt by a number of teachers operating schemes with the board that the former usually took priority. In one case this led to the appointment of a moderator to an innovatory school (School B) who had not taught in a school of any type, let alone a 'similar' one. In another case (School A) it led to the appointment as moderator of the Mode 3 syllabus of a senior examiner for the very Mode 1 syllabus which the teachers had sought to escape in compiling their own scheme. In both cases, incidentally, the board rejected the schools' own suggestions of people who had had experience of operating similar Mode 3 schemes. In the first case this has not, in fact, led to the sort of conflict which the appointment seemed designed to create but in the second case the teachers have always felt that the moderator has sought to impose upon their scheme assessment criteria entirely inappropriate to it.

Another aspect of the GCE Board's activities also gave teachers cause for concern. A number of teachers felt that the board's administrative procedures seemed almost designed to hinder rather than assist curriculum development in schools. At School F, a new scheme for fourth and fifth year Humanities – described by its originator as 'meaningful and relevant' but certainly 'not radical' – was the subject of a Mode 3 submission to this board. The overriding feeling which the head of department expressed about his dealings with the board was one of 'frustration', particularly over the time which the negotiations seemed to take:

> I mean, I don't know how long it takes to tool up a motor car in industry or to get the production model on the line, but it's taken us almost four

217

years to achieve. . . . I mean, basically, the real problem as I see it is that the machinery for getting a Mode 3 O level through is not flexible enough for a large school that doesn't want instant examination but certainly wants examination within fifteen months of conception, so to speak. . . . I mean eventually there is this thing inside you saying, 'Isn't it better to submit the kids to Mode 1 exams, isn't it less trouble?'

This feeling that it might be less trouble to revert to a curriculum geared towards Mode 1 examinations was strengthened by his view that, by the time a Mode 3 scheme had been amended to suit the board's requirements, it was no longer a genuinely school-based alternative to the Mode 1 anyway:

It's difficult to say to the board, 'This is what I want to do', when in fact it's them that's offering the goodies. Isn't it? I mean, you can't go in a shop and say I want five pounds of green jelly babies when in fact they're only making blue and white ones. And that's part of the conflict that perhaps runs through the frustrations of all teachers of whatever exam. You know, that we're having to teach children for an examination which we don't think is strictly relevant. . . . They're not interested in teaching methods, your resources, they're interested in the assessment. And from their point of view that's reasonable . . . . Obviously one would feel enormously gratified if a team of board people said, 'Now listen, you want to do this, it's relevant, it's going to improve your teaching situation and in some situations it would be better than Mode 1. . . . Listen, let's have a look at what you're doing, talk to you, work out the problems in the school, look at what's going on, come for two or three days and see the situations and work with you and give you far more personal guidance. . . .' In other words, we'd say to *them*: 'Why don't you make a commitment to what we're doing . . .?'

The point being made, then, is not that Mode 3's are necessarily worse than Mode 1's in this respect but that their promise of being different is somehow lost. Many of the conflicts are, as this teacher recognizes, features of any external examination system. However, their existence within Mode 3 schemes — which seemed in theory to offer possibilities for avoiding at least some of them — becomes all the more difficult to accept.

These examples do little more than illustrate the fact that many teachers operating Mode 3 schemes feel that the examining boards place constraints upon them which force them to compromise their ideals. They further suggest that there is some evidence that the activities of examining boards do serve to maintain the *status quo* within school and that they do have the power to ensure that 'curriculum in schools, though infinitely more varied than before, is still largely conceived within the existing social system'. In the majority of cases, we can agree with Eggleston that teacher consciousness sustains existing patterns of curriculum but the response of the boards to the somewhat limited reforms proposed by the teachers whose views are reported in this paper suggests that they can act to quell the enthusiasm of those teachers who see the world differently.

This is not to suggest that there is no point in teachers attempting to devise alternatives to Mode 1 syllabuses, even though at least two teachers reported that their experiences made them ask 'Was it all worth it?' (Schools F and G) and a third went so far as to state quite categorically that 'It wasn't worth it' (School H). There is, in fact, some evidence that really determined teachers have succeeded in pushing through quite radical Mode 3 schemes against the initial opposition of CSE boards – as in the case of a Community Rights syllabus [15] recently approved by CSE Board Three – and there seems every reason for others to follow this example. It would, however, be simplistic to conclude that pressure from radical teachers could, by itself, achieve major modifications in the system of external school examinations. It must be recognized that the conservative influence of the boards is not purely a product of tradition or administrative and economic considerations – even if the public defence of Mode 1 is often couched in such terms as its being 'the most economical method of providing large-scale examinations'. [16] Examining boards do not operate, any more than schools, in a political vacuum and, rather than treating them as the source of all our educational ills (as R.F. Mackenzie seems to imply), it is vital to consider the ways in which they are related to other parts of the social structure. It is quite clear that pressures from outside either the schools or the examining boards have a significant influence on the activities of examiners and some of these pressures have become uniquely public in the context of the recent debate about a common examination at sixteen-plus. [17]

It is surely no coincidence that, at a time when increasing numbers of teachers are trying to exploit the radical potential which lies in the opportunity to construct their own syllabuses, Mode 3 has become a live political issue and a stick with which to beat the sixteen-plus proposals. Many of the early CSE Mode 3 courses were widely welcomed as an educational 'advance' because they offered ways of occupying otherwise troublesome pupils with the sort of 'relevant' activity which was designed to fit them into society. The experiences of School I suggest that courses which stress community 'rights' are altogether less acceptable to the boards than those which stress 'duties', whilst the comment 'We have enough trouble with the CSE trying to get employers to accept it as it is' has on more than one occasion been used to dismiss interesting innovations in both content and mode of assessment without discussion or further explanation. There do, however, seem to be some grounds for the belief held by teachers at School D that, with a CSE board, you can usually 'get what you want provided you make enough fuss' [18] and provided, in some areas, that you accept a grade 3 ceiling on awards. Yet, as soon as Mode 3 schemes have begun to make a significant impact on the GCE field, enthusiasm for the idea seems suddenly to have waned altogether and a concerted campaign has developed to limit their influence in any common examination at sixteen-plus. It is as if teacher control can only be tolerated for the assessment of those pupils who have already been defined as 'failures' anyway. The rhetoric of standards and comparability is swiftly invoked as soon as diffusion of control seems a real possibility in that area of the curriculum which the traditional guardians of educational 'standards' regard as significant. [19]

It is, however, evident that Mode 3 is seen as a threat to a peculiarly narrow section of that society in whose name 'standards' are supposed to be being defended. It is certainly hard to disagree with Mary Warnock that there is a danger in regarding 'schoolteachers as the final arbiters of what is, and what is not, educationally desirable', [20] but her own attack on the sixteen-plus proposals, and on Mode 3 in particular, seems to assume that the universities and the professions have some divine right to be the ultimate arbiters on that issue. The hypocrisy of this position has been exposed in the pages of the *Times Educational Supplement* [21] and it is instructive to notice that the very university academics who defend their own right to determine the 'educational standards' of the schools, regard any attempt to question their own concept of 'standards' in the universities as a threat to their 'academic freedom'. The hysteria which Mode 3 seems to be causing amongst employers, the professions and senior university academics may be seen to provide some evidence that a decentralized system of assessment poses a real threat to the entrenched interests of the *status quo* in society and, when a leading Conservative politician [22] has declared in public a preference for Mode 1's, it is scarcely surprising that a number of the boards have felt it necessary to abandon even the limited flexibility which they currently offer. It is perhaps not the incidents which are reported in this paper which are strange but, rather, given the pressures to which the boards are exposed, the fact that they should strike anyone as surprising in the first place. [23]

Thus, the attempt to develop more radical syllabuses within the schools must be accompanied by a campaign to open up for debate and action the whole system whereby what exists at present has become elevated to the status of an 'absolute' in terms of which all else must be judged. The struggle to develop a more flexible conception of curriculum, and to give teachers and their pupils more control over what is defined as educational activity, must be carried on in collaboration with those groups in society against whom the definitions currently sustained by examining boards tend to discriminate. The appeal to 'standards' must always be met by the question, 'Whose standards?' and the device by which the Black Paper brigade conflate any attack on particular standards with an attack on standards in general must be exposed as the ideological device which it is. Until examination boards are prepared to face up to such issues, their claim to be the impartial defenders of the interests of *all* children must be treated with some scepticism. [24] To expect them to acknowledge spontaneously the ideological implications of their current practice in the prevailing political climate is, however, to regard the educational system as detached from the 'various related parts of the social structure' and to treat examination boards, rather than the nature of the society we live in, as the major stumbling block to educational change.

Notes

1 See, for example, the research studies published by the Schools Council and the National Foundation for Educational Research. Among the exceptions is R. Hoste and B.

Bloomfield, *Continuous Assessment in the CSE: Opinion and practice,* Schools Council Examinations Bulletin 31 (London, Evans/Methuen, 1975), which offers a considerable amount of interesting interview data on how teachers and moderators experience the procedures of examining. A forthcoming Examinations Bulletin (No. 34: C. H. Smith, *Mode III Examinations in the CSE and GCE: A Survey of Current Practice*) should also be useful in this respect. However, the most interesting attempt to date to place examiners' practices in their broader educational and social context is to be found in J. Pearce *School Examinations.* (London, Collier-Macmillan, 1972).

2   P.W. Musgrave, 'Towards a Sociology of the Curriculum', *Paedagogica Europaea* (1970-1).

3   S.M.B. Carson, *Environmental Studies: The Constuction of an A Level Syllabus* (Slough National Foundation for Educational Research, 1971).

4   See C.R. Bornett, *The Social Relations of the Middle School Curriculum: Some Preliminary Observations* (unpublished M.Ed. Dissertation, University of Bath, 1975).

5   R.F. Mackenzie, 'Down with Moderation', *Times Education Supplement* (24 October 1975). Mackenzie, who was dismissed from his post as headmaster of Summerhill Academy, Aberdeen, in 1974 continued '(Having cleared our feet of the external examination system), the schools will be set free from the tyranny of the idea that education means accumulating mark-earning information'.

6   P. Taylor *et al,* 'Influence on Economics Teaching: A Study in Teachers' 'Perceptions' *Educational Review,* vol. 27, No. I (1975) may seem to throw some doubt on the extent of such views. This study of A level Economics teachers suggests that they regarded examination boards as the most powerful single influence on the *content* of their courses but as having little influence on their teaching *method.* It may, however, merely be that these teachers' conception of teaching coincided with that which others feel is forced upon them by the adoption of examination syllabuses.

7   A Dale and J. Elliott, *CSE (Mode 3) and the Humanities Curriculum Project: Some Examples of Current Syllabuses.* Since their comments refer to Mode 3 syllabuses, they to some extent offer corroboration of some of the statements reported in the present paper.

8   See Note 1 above. In *The Case for Examining Boards* (AEB, 1976), H. G. Earnshaw stresses the role of practising teachers within the particular GCE board for which he works. Other GCE boards stress, however, the importance of the non-teacher majorities on their governing bodies.

9   S.J. Eggleston, 'Conflicting Curriculum Decisions', *Educational Studies,* vol. 1, No. 1 (1975).

10 J.F. Eggleston and D. Holford, 'Recent Trends in Examining', *Forum* vol. 13, No. 2 (1971).

11 H. G. McIntosh and L. Smith, *Towards a Freer Curriculum* (London, University of London Press, 1974). The authors do, however, express reservations about the viability of single-school based Mode 3s.

12 This quotation is taken from D. Gleeson and G. Whitty, *Developments in Social Studies Teaching* (London, Open Books, 1976), where other similar comments may also be found.

13 Thus it seems unlikely that Mode 3s can become, to any widespread extent, a means whereby pupils can develop a sense of their capacity to be producers rather than consumers of culture. This optimistic hope was expressed by Graham Murdock in 'The Politics of Culture' in D. Holly (ed.), *Education or Domination?* (London, Arrow, 1974). The importance of his further point that ultimately this can only be achieved in the con-

text of a broader strategy of class struggle is even clearer in the political climate which prevails today.

14 As D.H. Board pointed out in the *Times Education Supplement* (13 February 1976), the idea that CSE boards cannot 'reject' a Mode 3 is a myth. In general, however, less extreme forms of discouragement tend to be employed.

15 For a discussion of some aspects of this case, see J. Fiehn, 'Sociology and Community Rights at CSE Mode 3', *Social Science Teacher*, vol. 5, No. 3 (1976).

16 The Joint Matriculation Board was reported in the *Times Educational Supplement* on 27 February 1976 as suggesting that, although a common system of examining should allow for some Mode 3 papers, 'Mode 1 will continue to provide a general reference point and to be the most economical method of providing large-scale examinations'.

17 See particularly the pages of the *Times Education Supplement* during Autumn 1975 and Spring 1976. This material could well help to reduce the speculative element in studies of school examing boards.

18 A similar view was expressed by a chief examiner for CSE Board One.

19 It seems clear that the division of labour is more finely controlled at some points in the class structure than others, and that the very process by which certain areas of the school's activities can be unproblematically treated as less 'significant' than others depends upon the continuing legitimation of unidimensional criteria of 'success'.

20 M. Warnock, 'A 16-Plus Disaster?', *New Society* (11 March 1976).

21 See the letter signed by twenty-one academics on 9 January 1976 and that from J. Dunning-Davies of Hull University on 16 January 1976. Richard Bourne's response to the former (23 January 1976) is very much to the point.

22 Norman St John-Stevas, the Conservative Spokesman on Education, was reported in *The Guardian* of 24 November 1975 as saying that 'the needs of employers ... were for reasonable objective assessment of ability. The great majority of both CSE and O level examinations were controlled by an independent examining board which defined the syllabus and the scheme of examination. This was much to be preferred ... to the mode by which both the syllabus and the assessment were devised by the school itself in accordance with standards laid down by the Board.'

23 Many of the GCE boards have publicly expressed reservations about the growth of Mode 3 schemes in the context of statements to support their own role in 'monitoring and enforcing standards' for the proposed new sixteen-plus examination. See particularly the *Times Education Supplement* for 27 February 1976.

24 Many of the available theories about the relationship between schooling and the reproduction of the class structure would certainly seem to suggest that teachers who entertain high hopes of the freedom offered by Mode 3s are somewhat naive. However, it is arguable that only experience of the sorts of concrete practices described in this chapter makes that relationship meaningful to those involved and helps to suggest appropriate strategies and contexts for intervention.

25 This is essentially the claim made by Earnshaw in *The Case for Examining Boards*. See Note 8 above.

Chapter 18

The politics of educational publishing

Gerard Macdonald

Textbooks have, traditionally, helped to define the content and fix the limits of legitimate educational knowledge. They have also helped to chart its ideology. In the texts of the early nineteenth century, for example, there are well-defined political themes. Whatever their ostensible subject, schoolbooks justified the existing social order. Toward the end of last century this open evangelism waned. Since then texts have been more concerned to describe the known world than to praise it. Neutrality and objectivity have replaced exhortation. Education is to be kept out of politics and, if we are to judge by textbooks, politics are kept out of education.

In this chapter I shall argue that texts are no more politically neutral now than they were in the past, though they may be more persuasive. I am not, of course, referring to party politics, but rather to the control that some people have over the lives of others. Knowledge, I assume, is a major component of such control. [1] Textbooks, as a main avenue of educational knowledge, are inescapably a factor in the politics of everyday life. It is, admittedly, awkward to use 'politics' in a wide sense when it is commonly used in a narrow one. But precisely for this reason we cannot abandon the word. To do that is to concede defeat in the perennial argument that what is 'political' cannot be 'educational'. Certainly where publishing is concerned the converse is true: what is educational is almost certainly political, in that it bears on the distribution of power.

Textbooks present a particular ideological position which can best be described as the politics of stasis. The existing order, whether natural or social, is presented as what Marx calls an 'exterior fatality'. Textbook knowledge glosses or ignores the extent to which our world is a human project. It does not help towards either real understanding or real alternatives. Resigned quiescence is no longer an overt message in textbooks. Instead it has become their hidden agenda.

It would be easy to explain this situation by following Marx further in his contention that 'the ruling *material* force of society is at the same time its ruling *intellectual* force. . . .' [2] Capitalist publishing firms are, in this view, unlikely to criticize an established capitalist order; their interests would lie with the commercial and political elite. I shall argue that, though the end result may be much the same, the process has in fact gone the other way. Elites have used educational publishers as one means of disseminating their view of the world. This is not, however, an exercise in deliberate propoganda. Elites, like the rest of us, believe that their vision of the world is simply the way things are. Their business is instruction rather than deception. The motivation is seldom wholly political,

223

even though the consequences may be.

The politics of educational publishing, then, are a good deal more complex than a simple transmission of elite attitudes. We need to take into account the fact that these attitudes are mediated by teachers; and teachers, at least in the present sense of the word, are not an elite group. Similarly, publishers have not always been an elite group either — though that seems to have made very little difference to the political effect of their publications. The notion of elective affinity modifies an otherwise simplistic relationship between the distribution of knowledge and of power.

The following sections take up these points in more detail. The first section describes the movement of texts from openly moral exhortation to apparently neutral presentation of fact — a neutral presentation which is calculated to foster attitudes not greatly dissimilar from those promoted in the earlier texts. Further, certain types of knowledge have always been thought educationally unsuitable for textbooks. Very often what is left out is material that might give learners more control over their own lives and, by the same token, threaten the contemporary political order.

The second section traces changes in the organization of the publishing industry and suggests some relationships between textbooks and their publishers. Publishers moved from identification with religious and educational groups to an independent affinity with elite attitudes. In the postwar period publishing firms have become generally larger, more businesslike and somewhat more open in their attitudes. This is reflected in a wider range of authors, more attractive learning materials and a broader spectrum of legitimate educational knowledge. The mechanisms of control, which still exist, are more diffuse. They operate principally through consensual agreement, between publishing and the upper reaches of the education system, on what should be taken as 'educational'. The third section looks at this postwar consensus.

The fourth section suggests some alternative ways of publishing which stand outside this consensus, and which might work outside the system of formal education altogether. The fifth section suggests a redistribution of curriculum development funds along these lines.

The ideology of educational publishing

Texts at the beginning of the nineteenth century, in almost every school subject, were pervasively religious. But the religious message was not there simply for the greater glory of God. It was a secular message to the poor, in favour of acceptance and resignation. This is clearly illustrated in Goldstrom's admirable survey of such books. [3] Sarah Trimmer, a prolific author, brings out many of the political undertones of the Christian message. One of her books was modestly entitled *The Servant's Friend, an Exemplary Tale; Designed to Enforce the Religious Instructions given at Sunday and other Charity Schools: by Pointing Out the Practical Applications of Them in a State of Service.* Here, as Goldstrom notes, Mrs Trimmer combines a desire that the poor should be pious with a firm resolution that piety should not interfere with wage labour. She describes a poor but pious woman who would not 'wish to be reading and praying all day long, because she knew it was the duty of poor people to labour for their food and raiment: she therefore resolved to continue to be industrious, and to go out washing and ironing, as she used to do.' [4]

Mrs Trimmer shared another common textbook theme: that laziness and unbelief brought the poor to their unhappy state. She observed in a further exemplary tale that if poor women 'would be industrious, cleanly, and good-humoured, so as to make home comfortable to their husbands — if they would bring up their children in the fear of God, and help one another to the utmost of their power, they would not want half so much assistance from the parish, or the rich, as they generally did.' [5]

Work might lead either to secular happiness or to divine approval, but it was not a path to social mobility. The worker stayed within his assigned station; neither industry nor education should lift him out of it. Another of Mrs. Trimmer's characters is a teacher who never forgot 'that it would be very improper to give her scholars a taste for things which were unsuitable to the simplicity of a country life'.

Nonconformist texts did not differ fundamentally from their Anglican counterparts but were, at times, more open in recognizing the ambivalence of their political message. This comes out in an interesting text, William Allen's *Scripture Lessons for Schools on the British System of Mutual Instruction:*

> The middle and upper ranks of society are more dependent on the poor, than without a little reflection they are apt to be aware of: it is to the labour and skill of the poor that we owe our comforts and conveniences: we have indeed a deep interest in the state of their morals; for as in every country they are by far the most numerous class, our personal security is very much involved with their moral qualities ... [Religious education] when made to extend to the great mass of the people, will do more to diminish crime than all the penal statutes that ever were or can be enacted; and, connected with the exertions of the Bible Society, and the system of Savings Banks for the poor, may be expected in the course of a few years to produce results in the highest degree gratifying to every friend of his country and his species. [6]

This religio-political stance was shown to be wider than any one denomination when state publishing started in Ireland. None of the existing texts fitted the Irish situation, so the commissioners for education set about producing their own. Initially these had something in common with Mrs Trimmer's work. We can trace the same admixture of morality and social resignation in the story, from the *Dublin Spelling Book* of 1819, of 'The Good Boy whose Parents are Poor'. This lad:

> when he sees little boys and girls riding on pretty horses, or walking with ladies and gentlemen, and having very fine clothes ... does not envy them or wish to be like them. He says, 'I have been told, and I have read, that it is God who makes some poor and some rich; and that the rich have many troubles which we know nothing of; and that the poor, if they are but

good, may be very happy: indeed when I am good nobody can be happier than I am.'

As the Irish series expanded its style changed significantly. The elevated tone remained, but the moral conclusions came to depend on this world as much as on the next. In 1825 the commissioners wrote of their series that 'whatever was of dubious tendency has been carefully excluded, while the merits of Vaccination, the treatment of Fever. the Nature of Savings Banks, and a variety of Knowledge useful to the peasantry are to be found illustrated in Works where they might have been least expected' *(First Report of the Commissioners on Education in Ireland,* 1825).

If any one description foreshadows the future of textbook publishing it would be this one: 'a variety of Knowledge useful to the peasantry ... in Works where [it] might have been least expected'. Of course, there were changing opinions as to what knowledge was, at any time, most useful to the peasantry. Toward the end of the century public virtues like patriotism were added, in British texts, to the more individual virtues of piety and industry. In 1867 Matthew Arnold's attention was caught by a text which apostrophized England in the following terms: 'She's not a dull or cold land,/No she's a warm and bold land,/Oh she's a true and old land/This native land of mine.'[7] But Arnold's concern was misplaced. The tradition of exhortation was, as we have seen, declining in importance. Much more significant was the tendency to draw elevating conclusions from 'factual evidence' − where, indeed, they might have been least expected. History teaching, for example, was a presentation of fact with an explicit or implicit moral purpose. Its aims, according to the 1896 *Suggestive Handbook of Practical School Method,* were

1 To trace the progress of the nation in political and personal liberty . . .

2 To trace the development of the social condition of the people . . .

3 To teach love of all that is noble . . .

4 To lay the foundations for knowledge of rights and duties of citizenship . . .

5 To foster love of country . . .

6 To exercise power of judgement, of compassion and of imagination . . . [8]

From the late nineteenth century to the present, with very few exceptions, learnng materials have followed this pattern. They proclaim neutrality. Their political stance is hidden and is increasingly hard to detect as we approach the self-evident truths of the present day.

The organization of publishing

Publishing firms have changed as much as the content of their texts. The earlier and more overtly moral books were usually published directly by their commissioning organizations: either religious societies or, in the case of Ireland, the state. The Schools Council is, in some ways, a modern version of the Irish commission. But, in the intervening century, independent publishing firms became increasingly important. The Education Act of 1870 extended their opportunities for profit. It did not, however, lead many firms to specialize in educational publishing. For the first half of this century education books were often seen as a supplement to a publisher's more respectable 'general' list — fiction, belles lettres, biography, and so on. This approach reflected a particular attitude towards publishing. It was a rather refined class of business for gentlemen with literary leanings. In terms of organization this gave a great deal of power to senior editors rather than, say, to accountants or managers. Editors have often been, or become, directors of their firm and have shown a high level of self-recruitment. The proportion of sons following the father's occupation 'compares with the highest mentioned in David Glass's *Social Mobility in Britain.*' Publishers are also 'disproportionately drawn from families high in the social scale' and 'are very highly academically qualified as a group . . . . We would expect the values of publishers, then, in view of these factors, to show some signs of their elite, academic origins.' [9]

In this period publishers most closely approximate Marx's notion that one part of the ruling class is a group of 'active, conceptive ideologists, who make the perfecting of the illusion of the class about itself their chief source of livelihood. [10] Certainly, directors of publishing firms tended to take a patrician view of themselves, of their more menial employees, and also of their educational lists. The latter could be a useful source of profit, particularly where a successful text could be reprinted year after year — at low cost and high return — from standing type. Such profits might subsidize a more esoteric general list. But whatever its economic uses, educational publishing remained a rather disreputable business. It was also, from the publishers' point of view, a markedly casual one. Manuscripts arrived from teachers who were willing to sacrifice their spare time to the hope of extra income or advancement; and editors chose among these offerings as much for the seniority of the author as for any intrinsic virtues in the manuscript. Even commissioned books were generally written in the author's spare time. Publishers' advances seldom allowed a teacher-writer to become a full-time author. The publisher matched this cottage industry with a correspondingly modest view of his editorial function. Advisers, usually indebted to the publisher in some way, would be asked to check the manuscript for suitability — which meant, very often, its fit with a particular examination syllabus. Beyond this, an editor might make suggestions for amendment, scatter illustrations through the text (or misplace them on art paper inserts), and prepare the typescript for setting. To go further was to go beyond the proper call of editorial duty.

We have identified two stages in which the educational publisher moved from commissioned evangelist to gentlemanly amateur. Since the last war there has been a third stage of increasing professionalism. This has been due to a number of factors, including: rising costs of materials and labour; wide changes in the educational market and corresponding changes in editorial staff; the need to consider non-print media; the costs of producing large projects of Schools

Council type; mergers and threats of takeover and American influence. Publishing has become a bigger, more orthodox, more rationalized and more corporate business. Rationalization, however, stops short of vertical integration. Authors are still usually professional teachers and amateur writers.It is interesting to contrast this with a survey of the American publishing industry, from which the following general picture emerged:

... editors, working on leads from salesmen or getting in touch with educators, collect 'authors' − ideally, from the point of view of sales, well-known educators from various parts of the country. After signing contracts, these authors provide anything from outlines to rough manuscripts. The editors then take over. Their work ranges from writing the textbooks on the basis of author outlines (usually revised by the editors) and obtaining critiques and suggestions, to rewriting rough manuscripts. The full resources of the publisher are now tapped. Production plans are made within established cost parameters (colour, paper quality, amount of illustrations, etc.); sales projections are made by sales managers who give opinions on whether any textbook taboos (involving race, religion, sex, etc.) have been violated which would prevent sales. The production staff, working with the editors, prepares the manuscript for the printers, and the textbook − perhaps five years after the decision to publish − is completed. The people who develop the textbook are many. The real author, in many cases, is in fact the editor. [11]

Clearly this is rationalization on a different scale from that of most British firms. It is worth noting, too, that the control of knowledge − 'involving race, religion, politics, sex, etc.' − is ordered differently, if not better. Mechanisms of control in Britain are more diffuse. They depend largely on a consensus negotiated between senior teachers and the publishing industry. This consensus has the virtue of allowing political control to be exercised on irreproachably educational grounds. It merits close examination.

The postwar consensus

Control over the content of learning materials is intimately linked with the sense which publishers make of their educational market. The postwar changes in education − particularly in secondary schooling − almost completely reversed publishers' editorial and marketing assumptions. Subject structure and teaching methods were called into question and sometimes radically changed. Boundaries shifted. Secondary moderns and grammar schools became comprehensives; single sex schools became mixed; the racial balance changed in many areas; and more pupils stayed beyond the leaving age, while increasing numbers of GCE students left for college. The notion of 'a textbook' was challenged; and, with it, a reliable source of publishing profit. Most traumatic, the examination system changed. Publishers could no longer settle their GCE texts and see the rest of their output as predictably subordinate. For many editors this period was one of considerable shock and confusion. [12] A working universe had to be conceived anew.

It is part of publishing's accepted wisdom that educational decisions are made elsewhere. The industry does no more than serve and follow. There is an agreeable humility about this proposition, but it is not true − as anyone who has written a textbook, or even observed the publishing process, will know. Publishers need 'educational' classifications in order to make commercial sense of a mass market. Since the education system is a bureaucracy, with a well-developed taxonomic propensity, it also needs to classify. Given this coincidence of interest it is not surprising that the postwar reclassification of pupils became a matter for negotiation between the industry and the education system. As a result, a spectrum of groups has become a proper object of publishers' consideration. There are, to take some examples: the 'integrated lower secondary'; the 'less academic'; 'early leavers'; 'upper and lower CSEs'; 'new sixth forms': 'special' and 'remedial' or 'sanctuary' children; 'EFL', 'ESL' and 'ESP' pupils; and, of course, the 'academic'. We have noted that it is in publishers' commercial interests − which need not, of course, coincide with their educational interests − to establish such categories. It is also in the taxonomic interest of the education system that publishers should do so. The fact that there are books specially designed for, let us say, 'remedial' children helps to establish that there are remedial children to whom the books are particularly suited. Teacher-authors who disregard these categories are, as a rule, either enlightened or dropped. Most teachers, though, accept the negotiated schema. Some do so almost in spite of themselves − as in the case of a teacher who, at a publisher's seminar, attacked the classification of children on the grounds that some of her 'middle range CSE pupils' had stayed on in the sixth and, eventually, gone to university. One or two had reached Oxford: 'they were, obviously, university material all along'. At the same seminar a Cambridgeshire teacher described the surprisingly good performance of pupils who were 'not at all A level youngsters − you would have taken them as two or three CSEs at perhaps grades B or C, on first meeting them'. In this milieu, and many others like it, publishing decisions are made.

The interdependence of publishing and education goes beyond specific common interests. There is a common universe of meaning. People move between the two systems. Authors and advisers, as we have seen, are likely to be practising or retired teachers. Editors, too, often have a teaching background. This has the advantage of establishing a shared language between publishers and their customers − and the disadvantage of reinforcing shared preconceptions. In this sense the trouble with publishing is probably not a lack of teacher influence. The problem may be that there is, of a certain sort, too much.

The notion that there may be too much educational influence in educational publishing needs some unravelling. The shared universe of discourse can be analytically reduced to a constellation of ideas, often poorly articulated and ill fitting. We can list a number of them without in any way claiming a comprehensive or even coherent pattern. There is, to take an arbitrary starting point, the idea of *correct description*: that there is a correct and neutral description of the world, though there may now be some dispute as to its detail. This idea is more prevalent in some subjects than in others, but it prevails with varying intensity across the curriculum. 'Things to think about', 'research exercises' and 'experiments' do not mitigate that impression. Related to correct description is the idea of *rationality* — 'immediately available functional rationality, rationality as it is thematizable in the everyday life of the individual'. [13] Then there is the idea of *componentiality* — that 'reality is apprehended as being constituted by clearly separable components which relate to each other in structures of causality, time and space'. These ideas lead to that of *apolitical neutrality*. Politics exist, but their more unruly forms are, in a sense, the product of delusion. Complete rationality and comprehensive knowledge would bring us to a correct description of things; political faction would disappear. Politics, therefore, are either ignored, studied as a constitutional model ('Wesminster is the mother of Parliaments'), or seen as an irrational and localized phenomenon in the same class as astrology or cockfighting. Where factional views are unavoidably introduced in texts, they must be in *balance*. A scrap of Fanon is redressed by a bit of Enoch Powell. No complete world view or intellectual model is presented. In this way the danger of indoctrination, or incorrect description, is avoided. In the same way *bias* is eliminated. Bias is the unbalanced expression of opinion, as in advertising, propoganda and the sensational press. Students should learn to recognize and discount bias in these quarters.

The teacher-publisher consensus reaches beyond the content of texts to the learners for whom they are intended. Here a central notion is that *only experienced teachers can write textbooks*, since *only they know what learners need*. This avoids the necessity, for publishers, of consulting learners directly and in depth. No doubt publishers are also swayed by the fact that teachers, not pupils, actually buy their products. The practice of not consulting learners and of not employing dissident outsiders means that *educational categories* are not threatened by empirical evidence. These categories are matched to *appropriate levels of presentation and content*. 'Lower ability pupils' are not only offered easier reading matter and more pictures: they are also given simpler and more concrete ideas, appropriate to their limited grasp of the world and brief concentration span. Other categories have their own particular needs. Finally, there is the idea of *transfer of knowledge*. This has survived various counter-ideas, including the formerly fashionable notions of 'activity learning', 'inquiry' and 'discovery materials'. In the real business of education, teachers and books tell, and learners remember.

Publishers and successful authors respond to this consensus with a well-developed system of pre-censorship. All sorts of things are either not suggested for learning materials or discarded after brief thought. The discarded matter is 'not educational'. For example, the writings of James Baldwin on race are not, in themselves, educational, since they are biased, often irrational, are not correct descriptions and are not neutral. Clearly Baldwin could be used, if at all, only in brief excerpt and probably balanced by a counter-view. A good author will understand this, and not embarrass either his publisher or, should the contentious material have gone into publication, his responsible colleagues. For the publisher the considerations of mass market and examinations doubtless enter his calculations. But they are not, I suspect, a primary factor. It is now more important for materials to fit with the educational consensus. Fortunately its criteria are, by and large, also those of the market.

There is no doubt that the postwar changes in education have, as a side effect, improved the quality of learning materials. They are more flexible than traditional texts, wider ranging, and more attractive. Authors are often younger and the area of legitimate subject matter has enlarged. We have noted the main area in which there has been little change. Learning materials are still too remote from their audience to increase a learner's control over his own life; and they are too misleading to help redress existing imbalances of power. No one, to take a random example, would learn enough from textbooks about multinational corporations to affect their influence, even in his own life. That is not, in the consensual view, an educational matter. Learning materials, to paraphrase an old saying, will give you any information except what is vitally necessary.

Some alternatives

Occasionally groups of teachers, working to some extent outside the educational consensus, develop their own educational materials. Such groups usually work outside the school day, drawing heavily on the time and energy of their members. Even limited funding would make a lot of difference to their work. It would allow for assistance with typing, with subediting, with illustration or design.

At some point these groups are inevitably faced with questions about the future of their work. Is it simply an exercise for those immediately concerned in the group, who share its assumptions and who will use any materials within that context? Or should the group's work be commercially published? Can members agree to their work being used in ways they might disapprove?

Quite apart from members' feelings, there are other questions raised by a decision to publish. A group of politically radical teachers may dissent from established educational wisdom, but may be much less willing to question its own assumptions. One sort of closure is often replaced by another.

Educational radicalism can be, in practice, a simple controversion of conventional axioms. For example, schooling relies heavily on the transmission of knowledge. The converse is that learners should find out everything for themselves. They are left, as Bruner says, to reconstruct the culture around them. Further, there are real questions around the issue of indoctrination. The fact that conventional teaching materials convey a particular ideology does not automatically make a counter-ideology desirable. Politically committed groups do not, in this context, always distinguish between critical and programmatic education. Apart from the gut opposition that the latter evokes from the educational establishment, politically programmatic curricula deny the more generous ideals of radical education — for example, the learner's right to choose among political alternatives.

As a final point, materials produced outside the commercial publishing sector may need further development if they are to be disseminated more widely. A teacher's rapport with his class is not easily transferred to a more generalized and mediated form. Successful lessons can make remarkably didactic pieces of print. Despite a number of attempts to disprove the proposition, there is more to publishing than having access to tabletop litho. The problem for radical groups is to separate publishing skills from the concomitant mechanism of educational censorship.

The answer may lie with the alternative publishers. They have demonstrated that, despite the daunting economics of quality printing, learning materials can be reasonably priced even without access to a mass market. Centerprise in London has published local themes and minority views without massive subsidies. The Writers' and Readers' Cooperative has explored other areas of alternative educational publishing. Michael Norton, and groups like Shelter or VCOAD, have experimented successfully with non-book formats. The time is probably right for more ambitious cooperation between radical teacher groups and alternative publishers. This sort of joint venture would serve that minority of teachers who want, and are institutionally free, to teach from an avowed and non-consensual political commitment.

Publishing by teacher groups is one answer to the industry's closure. But other initiatives are needed: for example, learning materials which are critical rather than politically programmatic. Assuming that schools will be with us for a long time yet, we should take seriously those values – independence, inquiry, autonomy – which are proclaimed in rhetoric and actively denied in practice. In other words, the political stance of schooling can be challenged by learning materials which accept its established values as well as by those which deliberately counter them. For example, history materials could move toward a more adequate account of the global and domestic havoc wrought by our imperial ruling class. Social studies, among many other possibilities, could do the same for the contemporary American and Soviet elites whose actions shape our present and future. Scientific texts could look at the world science is creating for us, rather than teaching quasi-scientific experiments to children who will never use them. Geography materials might abandon the task of conceptually fragmenting the world, in favour of assessing the structures of interdependence to which industrialism has condemned us. There are other possibilities within these and, even while we keep to the present organization of school curricula, within every other subject. Only within the educational consensus are these alternatives invisible; closure operates , after all, on both the inward and outward flow of ideas.

To develop alternative and mediated curricula we need to review the notion of *ad hoc* project teams. These have been rightly criticized in the United States as academic playgrounds. Schools Council teams in this country have not been widely acclaimed for their organizational achievements. But these criticisms reflect on the composition of teams rather than on intrinsic faults in the team method. We need to find out whether, with different membership and different aims, project teams can work outside the educational consensus. This would involve bringing together groups, for a specific time and purpose, with a deliberately diverse membership. Diversity does not mean recruiting different sorts of teacher: it means looking for people who will question what educationists take for granted; learners, for example, as well as those who have done their learning.

232

Whether or not schoolchildren are members of a project team, we need new ways of finding what learners think and need. Traditional research tells us as much about the researcher as it does about his subjects: validity, it has been noted, is a perennial victim of reliability. Such research is based on a fundamental misconception of human thought and action. Research has its own methodological consensus which, like its educational counterpart, works very well for a particular professional group — and rather badly for the rest of us. In educational research we now have a few models of purposeful work. [14] These are evaluations which have gained in depth as they have been limited in scope. This seems clearly to be a model for future alternative project work.

It seems natural that alternative publishing, of the sort outlined here, should dissociate the idea of education from that of schooling. Education out of school depends, of course, quite heavily on learning materials. We lack the informal networks to make them available and effectively used; continuing education in Britain scarcely gets lip service. Eventually publishers will pay attention to the gap between partworks and Open University materials. At present it remains yet another area for alternative educational publishers to explore.

Paying for alternative publishing

There is one main constraint on publishing for anything less than a mass market. This is the cost of development. It is almost impossible to finance development costs from profits. To do so is a recipe for conformity, as educational publishing has amply demonstrated. But if development costs are subsidized large markets become less important. Various forms of limited publishing — by LEAs, for example — have shown that experimental or short-run projects are possible where developmental costs need not be recovered.

At present almost all money for curriculum development in England and Wales is controlled by Schools Council. While this near-monopoly exists, any subsidy for new developments will mean a redistribution of Schools Council funds. This does not necessarily mean cutting off the old in favour of the new, or the conventional in favour of the heterodox. The Council is by choice a publisher of learning materials and, perhaps not by choice, is an inefficient and wasteful one. If the Council ordered its curricular priorities more rigorously and openly; if it exercised more control over the working of its developmental groups; if its evaluation schemes were more cost effective;and if it used commercial publishers as such, rather than as expensive printers, then its learning materials could be brought to publication at a considerable saving on their present cost. It follows from the present argument that such savings should be used to finance the development of alternative curricula— either from groups of working teachers or from project teams which can stand outside the educational consensus. [15]

There is, as a final point, some urgency about the provision of alternative learning materials. The further we decline economically, the more necessary it becomes to consider political alternatives; and the less likely it is that funds will be available for anything but the most basic and uncritical forms of education or training.

Notes

1 There is both a positive and negative control of knowledge in textbooks. In the positive aspect, knowledge is selected to emphasize certain values or a certain view of the world. Usually this is a view formed by wider and unexamined social demands – those, for example, of imperialism, industrialism, technocracy or bureaucracy. The negative aspect refers to the range of knowledge left out of texts, or out of the wider school curriculum. School children, as a result, are cut off not only from wide areas of knowledge, but also from many of the terms and ideas which could extend political dialogue. This is, no doubt, one reason for the anachronism of political debate in Britain: the issues of the 1970s and 1980s are debated passionately in the language of the 1930s.

To be concerned about the political control of knowledge is to assume that knowledge has more influence on action than is usually conceded in respectable academic thought. Such a revaluation calls into question a good deal of educational theory and research, including Jencks's impressive *Inequality* (London, Allen Lane, 1974). If we see education as working towards, rather than against, inequality in the distribution of knowledge – and hence in opportunity for political action – then we might also revise our assessment of educational success and failure.

2 Karl Marx and Friedrich Engels, *The German Ideology* (London, Lawrence & Wishart, 1965).

3. J. M. Goldstrom, *The Social Content of Education 1808-70* (Shannon. The Irish University Press, 1972). The quotations from nineteenth century texts, unless otherwise acknowledged, are all from this source.

4 Sarah Trimmer, *The Servant's Friend* . . . (London, 1824).

5 Sarah Trimmer, *The Two Farmers* . . . .(London, 1826).

6 William Allen, *Scripture Lessons for Schools on the British System of Mutual Instruction* (London, 1820).

7 *M. Arnold's Report,* P.P. 1867/8 XXV, p. 300. Quoted in J. Hurt, *Education in Evolution* (London, Paladin, 1972).

8 T. A. Cox and R. F. McDonald, *The Suggestive Handbook of Practical School Method* (Blackie, 1896). Quoted in David Steed, 'History as School Knowledge' (unpublished MA dissertation, University of London Institute of Education, 1974).

9 M. Lane, 'Books and their Publishers' in J. Tunstall (ed.), *Media Sociology* (London, Constable, 1970).

10 Marx and Engels, *The German Ideology*.

11 'Textbooks: A Look at the Industry' in *Educational Product Report,* EPIE IV/2 (1970).

12 Some of these conclusions are drawn from research for my unpublished doctoral thesis, 'Mediated Teaching 1960-72' (University of Sussex).

13 The two quotations, as well as the rather awkward term 'componentiality', are drawn from Peter Berger, Brigitte Berger and Hansfried Kellner,*The Homeless Mind* (Harmondsworth, Penguin, 1974).

14 The publications of Aaron Cicourel in the USA, and of Malcolm Parlett in this country, provide examples of useful evaluation.

15 I do not want to give the impression that there should be no academic contribution to such project teams; only that it should be countered by non-academic views. It is worth adding that these teams may be harder to establish in a few years' time. Apart from the possible lack of money, mentioned below, retrieval television (probably in the form of videodiscs) will eventually fulfil its promise, or threat, of making a radical change in educational publishing. The newer media have proved, on the whole, to be more entertaining, more powerful in communication, and more susceptible to political control, than the older medium of print.

Chapter 19

Conservative pupils ? Pupil resistance to curriculum innovation in mathematics

John Spradbery

Popular conceptions of school Mathematics tend to be dominated by rather static notions of its nature. The subject is seen to determine correct and, hence, incorrect pupil behaviour; there are 'right' methods of solving certain typical problems and 'wrong' ones which furnish unacceptable solutions. The postwar changes in school mathematics (notably the introduction of practical Mathematics and 'modern' or 'the New' Mathematics) have served only to increase the efficiency and range of Mathematics education. They have not challenged the established pattern of social relationships within the classroom: teachers and pupils continue to play the relatively passive role of reproducers, rather than producers, of knowledge.

Teachers appear to have accepted their role readily; most innovations in the content of school Mathematics syllabuses have followed the pattern of changes in university Mathematics and the opportunities for teacher involvement in curriculum reform have been limited in practice to making new topics 'relevant' and 'acceptable' to schoolchildren. There has been little consideration of what is Mathematics or how it reflects and maintains the interest of certain members of a set of competing social groups. Even the progressive 'discovery' methods of the primary school (which now feature in the Mathematics departments of most comprehensives) continue to maintain the traditional roles of, and divisions between, teacher and taught. What children 'discover' is not only predetermined *as* discoverable but is predetermined as being suitable for their age and 'ability'.

The change of emphasis in the Mathematics curriculum which has occurred with the advent of modern Mathematics, far from liberating the subject from the conception of it as a mechanical and abstract form of pre-existing knowledge, has simply diverted attention away from particular surface methods to underlying structures. Put metaphorically, children are not only expected to play a compendium of mathematical games (Algebra, Arithmetic, Geometry, etc.) according to specific rules, they are now expected to understand how the rules of each game have to conform to a more basic universal set of axiomatic rules. The body of mathematical knowledge is treated as though it has an existence which is independent of the knower. G. H. Hardy speaks of the subject in this way: 'I believe that mathematical reality lies outside us, that our function is to discover or observe it . . . ' [1]

In his criticism of Hardy, David Bloor suggests an alternative view of the subject by invoking Wittgenstein's argument that Mathematics is an invention, a collection of norms, and *not* a discovery. He suggests that 'there is a sense in which Mathematics comes into existence when and as it is done'. [2] A conception of Mathematics as existing only in social practice and, consequently, as changing with it creates two related possibilities: first, the content of the corpus of mathematical knowledge available at any time may be challenged and modified by the actions of people at that time: and, second, changes made to this corpus may effect wider social change. Such a conception of the subject suggests that teaching Mathematics is a political activity because of the nature of its 'content' and the routine practices of assessment and stratification within the classroom.

The current social organization of mathematical knowledge (skills and techniques) into a readily assessed hierarchy of abstractions and concepts inevitably leads to the measurement of schoolchildren *against* the subject. Margaret Hayman's claim that 'it is believed that only about 10 per cent of the population ever develop the capacity for abstract thought' [3] reflects this popular but uncritical acceptance of the subject as somehow 'reified'. Some brief observations of a group of London schoolchildren [4] demonstrate the absurdity of 'facts' such as those produced by Hayman and suggest that she has failed to consider both the social context of Mathematics teaching and its political importance.

The pupils, at sixteen years of age, had failed consistently to master anything but the most elementary aspects of school Mathematics. Every year they appeared in the bottom 20 per cent at examination time. Using Hayman's language, they had not developed the capacity for abstract thought. They had received, and remained unhelped by, considerable 'remedial' teaching and, finally, they left school 'hating everyfink what goes on in maffs'. Yet in their spare time some of these same young people kept and raced pigeons. They understood the intricacies of the racing rules as a part of the folklore of pigeon-keeping; what the expert mathematician would recognize as 'mathematical knowledge' featured in, though remaining undifferentiated from the rest of, this knowledge. Weighing, measuring, timing, using map scales, buying, selling, interpreting timetables, devising schedules, calculating probabilities and averages and applying the 'four rules' to numbers, measurements and money were a natural part of their stock of commonsense knowledge. They were learnt as such without the rituals of the classroom. These pupils were their own teachers, learning as they went, assessing and filling the gaps in their knowledge.

Although the mathematician may regard certain aspects of pigeon-keeping (along with many of the other daily activities of children) as being 'mathematical', such knowledge appears to have little value or status in the classroom. For 'Maths' to be 'Maths' (or 'proper Maths', as a number of children described it) it has to be separated from other everyday knowledge. In schools, Mathematics is rarely used naturally as a way of making sense of, and solving the problems of, the world. Usually, the converse is true; selected phenomena are reshaped in order to make sense of mathematical 'concepts'. Artificial problems are created by teachers and the writers of textbooks to test the abilities of pupils to reconstruct mathematical rules. Pupils and Mathematics are placed in opposition to one another.

An attractive and currently popular supposition is that suitably enlightened curriculum reforms can liberate pupils from the constraints imposed by subjects and school assessment procedures. Mathematics could, perhaps, be reunited with other knowledge and come to be a part of a wide-ranging, meaningful, interesting, useful and popular set of experiences shared by all, or at least most, pupils.

Any such liberalizing reforms can expect to face opposition from those whose academic, financial, commercial or industrial interests are maintained by the present state of Mathematics education. 'Standards' must be maintained and the 'purity' of the subject preserved. Somewhat surprisingly, the trials of a pre-publication pack of non-academic teaching material in Mathematics suggest that considerable opposition to any liberalization of the subject may also come from those who benefit *least* from the present organization of Mathematics education: the pupils who fail at, or are failed by, school Mathematics.

The *Mathematics for the Majority Continuation Project* [5] promises to provide 'a wide variety of most stimulating material in Mathematics' specifically written for pupils of 'less than average ability'. [6] The MMCP advertising literature claims that 'there are many non-academic manifestations of Mathematics which the pupil understands in an intuitive or physical way, such as in sport or in thinking about strategies of games, and arguments. The materials (the MMCP packs) present to pupils situations in which their own intuitive resources are brought into play and can be used and developed'. [7] Theoretically, at least, the packs should offer the possibilities of liberating children from a conception of the subject as pregiven and constraining and of freeing them from the painful experience of being assessed and pronounced failures.

A study of the trials of a pre-publication pack of MMCP materials, entitled *Machines and Factories,* [8] suggests that, however attractive this type of liberal innovation may appear to be, it is almost certain to be rejected by the pupils that it is designed to 'help'. *Machines and Factories* was given to a fourth-year secondary school class (including the pupils who raced pigeons) after more conventional materials had apparently failed to teach them anything but the most simple mathematical processes. The pack was welcomed with enthusiasm and excitement. After a few weeks of using the materials, however, the pupils rejected them and demanded a return to 'proper Maths'. They refused to continue with the assignments on the grounds that they were 'childish' and 'slowing' them down. Their reaction contradicted both the intentions of the producers of the pack and the suggestion that pupils will welcome less alienating activities in school.

Two important questions are raised by the pupils' actions: First, why did they reject something which appeared to offer a liberalizing alternative to a subject in which their only prospect was of continued failure? And, second, did their reaction reflect an attitude which has wider social and political implications? In an attempt to account for the pupils' rejection of the pack, a series of tape-recordings was made of the pupils talking about their work on the assignment . [9]

In nearly every recording the pupils complained that they should not have to waste their time on anything that is not 'proper' or 'general' Maths. By this they appeared to mean what teachers mean when they talk about traditional Mathematics – the topics which the pupils had been taught (and failed to learn) in their secondary school. One of the pupils, Sid, suggested that normal Maths is 'metric with, er, adding up, take-away, multiplying, dividing, averages, algebra, and all sort of stuff like that'.

In contrast to the topics which the pupils saw as constituting proper Mathematics they spoke of the activities demanded by the MMCP assignments as being inappropriate to Mathematics lessons because they were considered to be features of other, non-mathematical, situations. The following extract of a conversation with some of the pupils gives an indication of the boundary which is perceived to exist around Mathematics:

T/R: What do you, er, what do you think you should be learning in Maths?

Sid: Well, really learning about gears, car gears, gearboxes and things like that, that ain't really nothing to do with school, you're going to learn that when you leave school, if you know what I mean.

T/R: So what do you want to learn in maths?

Wally: (Untranscribable).

T/R: Eh?

Wally: About gearboxes, you're going to learn that in motor mechanics, that's all, but not in Maths.

T/R: So?

Sid: I think you should do general Maths.

T/R: Such as . . . ?

Sid: Averages, equations, and things like that.

Sid and 'Wally' each answered the question 'What do you think you should be learning in Maths?' with a criticism of the cards: they were learning about the *wrong* things. Sid again mentions particular topics as characterizing 'general Maths' but both he and Wally label topics which featured in the assignments as 'nothing to do with school' and which should not be learnt 'in Maths'. These topics, it seems, were appropriate only to other parts of the pupils' worlds, 'in motor mechanics' or 'after you leave school'. Later in the conversation Sid complained that 'we done all the gearbox in science' and, while talking about a card which 'shows you how to put a car together', one of the girls in the group suggested that 'that one was really stupid, that's more like, to do like, you'd like to do that in your careers lesson'.

As well as criticizing the pack for containing the wrong content, several pupils suggested that it retarded their 'progress' because it did not demand enough written work and because it was too 'babyish'. On one occasion Sid complained 'mainly they're [the assignments] just games, you know, and you don't hardly get any work done, like this week I've only done one page'. [10] On another occasion he described the assignments as 'not a bad card, like, but I think they're a bit childish for a person of our age, you know, and our ability'.[11]

The transcripts of the pupils' talk suggest that the pack was rejected largely because it was seen as an obstacle to their progress *in the subject*. Sid spoke of this progress as a movement towards the goal of obtaining a CSE pass in Mathematics and complained that the pack was slowing him down: 'If I am going to take CSE Maths it ain't going the, doing me the good way taking it like this is it, you know, like I can't, like, you know, take it if all I'm doing is this silly little cards that's going to give me a couple of good weeks blinking slowing me down'. Several other pupils also spoke about not 'doing well' in their examinations. Others were concerned that they should leave school with a sufficiently clear understanding of the subject to get and cope with a 'good job'. Some of the girls suggested that the pack was a 'waste of time for when we could be doing more worthwhile work, such as coping with money, when you leave school, working in a bank, explaining VAT, its a bit silly for a fifteen-year-old to be playing with silly scissors . . . ' [12]

From the way in which most pupils spoke about the pack and their work with it, it is clear thet they saw themselves as capable of making progress in Mathematics in spite of having failed at it throughout their school careers. It is equally clear that their optimism was not shared by those who wrote and introduced the *Machines and Factories* pack. The normal, highly structured, consecutive presentation of the subject was abandoned, the cards dealt with isolated everyday topics and concepts, and it was not easy for either teacher or pupil to assess the pupils' work.

Although the pack reflected teachers' notions of the 'less able' pupil, its style of presentation was unlike that of the other 'remedial' books and workcards which had been used with this group. The pack exposed the teachers' low expectations by presenting the subject in such a way that those who worked from it realized that they were being denied the chance to compete in Mathematics on the same terms as 'more academic' pupils. The pack presented material which did not correspond with the reified typification of Mathematics which teachers and pupils appear to share; it presented material whose status was only that of everyday, or even inappropriate, knowledge. Such knowledge was rejected because it was not seen as examinable or useful in future employment.

The rejection of the pack demonstrates an unwillingness of the pupils to challenge the constraints of the subject even though their actions [13] challenged the constraints of the school. We may conclude that the coercive power of this institutionalized school knowledge was greater than that of the school itself. [14] Pupils may disrupt the routines of the school organization, vandalize materials and premises, and even defy their teachers. But Mathematics could not be questioned.

This case study in a school is only an example of a much broader problem: the reluctance of those who benefit least from any body of institutionalized knowledge to question it or to accept changes which could liberate them from its constraints. Mathematics, like other institutionalized knowledge, has come to be seen 'as a body of generally valid truths [and] any radical departure from the institutional order appears as a departure from reality'. [15] The pupils' stated concern with examination success and their desire to learn about commercial topics suggest that the reality of the subject was reinforced by the strong relationship which was perceived by the pupils to exist between Mathematics and post-school institutions. Wally summarized the views of many when he stated, 'Maths can always come in handy . . .'cos most jobs it's Maths you want'. An implication of statements such as this (and of the pupils' general concern about future employment and promotion) is that Mathematics is closely related to those institutions which feature in our present mode of production. [16]

Neugebauer suggests that the domination of mathematical and scientific thought is a comparatively recent phenomenon: 'Mathematics and Astronomy had practically no effect on the realities of life in the ancient civilization' and 'It is only since the Renaissance that the practical aspects of mathematical discoveries and the theoretical consequences of Astronomy theory have become a vital component in human life'. [17]

By doing Mathematics in school, pupils not only sustain 'Mathematics', they also create a surplus of skills within themselves. As this surplus is of 'proper Maths' it has hardly any use value to the child outside of the classroom. It becomes of value to him only when, after leaving school, he uses it in employment. The argument behind statements such as 'doing well in Maths will help me get a better job' is that of what Paulo Freire calls 'the banking concept of education'. [18] Surplus knowledge, or surplus skills, are deposited by pupils within themselves to be used in later production.

Just as the increase of the surplus for appropriation ('profit') becomes a major instigator of advance in commodity production, so the increase of surplus skills can be seen as a major instigator of advance in Mathematics education. The two trends of postwar changes in School Mathematics have increased the value of the surplus of mathematical knowledge in school leavers. At the 'low ability' end of the spectrum the practical and remedial reforms have had − or should have had − the effect of raising the educational standards of, and hence widening the range of activities which can be performed by, future 'unskilled' workers. At the other end of the spectrum, the introduction of modern Mathematics can be seen as having the effect of ensuring that future 'professionals' are able to cope with and develop the increasingly systematized and integrated uses of Mathematics in industry and commerce that have been made possible by widespread computerization.

In his criticism of 'modern' mathematics being introduced into United States high schools, Morris Kline suggests that the subject is based upon 'a sophisticated, rigorously logical approach that was never intended for pedagogic purposes but was created to satisfy specialized and other esoteric professional interests'. [19] In order that these interests are satisfied new topics in Mathematics have to be

241

taught, learnt, practised and finally reproduced in the production process without change. Creativity and inventiveness in Mathematics are thus restricted to choosing between alternative but predetermined methods. It is these highly specialized skills that are used in later production, not as natural resources, but as tools in the production process.

But the manufacture of tools requires the consumption, transformation and manipulation of nature. The passive roles of teachers and taught as reproducers of knowledge require a denial of individual and collective responsibility for actually producing knowledge. The preoccupation with Science and Mathematics in our schools is a political preoccupation; a preoccupation with a materialism which denies the individual the opportunity to define his world, to act independently and responsibly and to express himself without the imposition of certain institutionalized contraints.

If there are to be changes in Mathematics education which will effect wider social change, teachers and taught must share in a united aim. Their goal may not be achieved in the isolation of the school. It may require wider institutional change. It is almost certain that it cannot be achieved by liberal curriculum 'reforms' being imposed upon reluctant pupils.

Acknowledgements

I am indebted to the teachers and pupils of the school for their encouragement and forthrightness. I am especially grateful to Michael Young who spent many hours helping and encouraging me; his detailed and perceptive comments have been an invaluable source of ideas and inspiration.

Notes

1 G. H. Hardy, *A Mathematician's Apology* (London, Cambridge University Press, 1967), p. 123.

2 D. Bloor, 'Wittgenstein and Mannheim on the Sociology of Mathematics', *Studies in the History and Philosophy of Science* (9 April 1973), p. 188.

3 M. Hoyman, 'Cause for Concern', *Times Educational Supplement,* (3 October 1975).

4 J. Spradbery, 'Mathematics in a School' (MA Dissertation, University of London, Institute of Education, 1975).

5 Sponsored by the Schools Council, published by Schofield & Sims.

6 Publisher's advertising leaflet and Schools Council brief to the Mathematics for the Majority Project.

7 Publishers' advertising leaflet.

8 I am not concerned in this essay with a criticism of the Project's published materials, but am interested in using the trial situation to explore some social constraints within the classroom.

9 The recordings were made by the pupils themselves (usually in groups of three or four) knowing that they would be heard by strangers and by me, their Mathematics teacher. As such, the recordings constitute semi-public documents which contain only those utterances which the pupils were prepared to let me and strangers hear.

10 It is not possible to say whether the production of written work was seen as being a characteristic of a body of context-free mathematical knowledge, or as simply related to doing Maths in school. In any case the pack was spoken of as denying the pupils the chance to make progress in the classroom.

11 The pupils spoke of 'age and ability' together – as one category. There was no suggestion that, in spite of their age, some pupils might not be able to cope with more difficult work.

12 A group of girls who were not satisfied with their recording presented me with a written document containing their opinions of the pack.

13 In rejecting the cards the pupils met with teacher opposition. They responded by vandalizing materials, congregating into large groups and ignoring teacher requests.

14 The distinction between school and institutionalized knowledge is somewhat artificial since each relies upon and nurtures the other.

15 P. Berger and T. Luckman, *The Social Construction of Reality* (Harmondsworth, Penguin 1967), p. 83.

16 The school was situated in an area of relatively high employment.

17 O. Neugebauer, *The Exact Sciences in Antiquity,* (Princeton, Princeton University Press, 1952), pp. 71, 72.

18 P. Freire, *Pedagogy of the Oppressed* (Harmondsworth, Penguin, 1972) ch.2.

19 M. Kline, 'Intellectuals and the Schools: A Case History', *Harvard Educational Review,* vol. 36, No. 4 (1966), p. 508.

Chapter 20

Teacher politics and educational change

Nigel Wright

How do we set about changing what goes on in schools?

So many people are having ideas about how schools might be changed, and so few people are having success in putting such ideas into practice, that an answer to the question is most urgently needed. There is so much resistance to change; we must start out with an awareness of the need for positive strategies for *making* change happen.

There are, of course, the 'usual channels'. Through the political parties, through the LEAs, through governing bodies. Or by sitting for twenty years, keeping your nose clean till they make you a headteacher. But seven years as a teacher left me with nothing but contempt for the usual channels. It is clearer than ever that those of us who desire change must learn to take matters into our own hands.

But how to do it? A good deal can be learned from the recent past: the last few years have seen unprecedented interest in education, and there has been plenty of radical activity. This paper sets itself the modest aim of examining the experience of one small but significant group of radical teachers. This experience is worth sharing because it can teach us a good deal about what *not* to do, and a little about what *is* worth doing.

Rank and File

Rank and File is a group of left wing teachers, formed in 1968, which set out to stir up the National Union of Teachers. The group was never big (at its peak it never had much above 1000 members) but it was vociferous, attracted a lot of attention and turned over some interesting stones. I do not intend here to record the history of Rank and File (though such a history would be valuable); I propose simply to present a string of ideas which Rank and File threw up and which I think can be helpful.

Amongst radical teachers there have always been two distinct ideas of how educational changes are made. [1] On the one hand are those who work by the slogan 'do it'. For them, the paramount task is to beaver away to provide some kind of alternative education *here and now* for the children they encounter. Apart from Countesthorpe and the few Free Schools, most such radicals operate in awful isolation. Only the periodic sacking (Duane, McKenzie, Gregory, Searle, German, Moreno: I name only a few cases which have received national publicity), or the occasional article (see, for example, the journal *Teaching London Kids*) remind us that they're there. [2]

244

On the other hand are those who feel that change will only be won by *collective* or political action of one kind or another. For these, the key activity is seeking out others who would be prepared to act with them.

In fact the two approaches are not necessarily mutually exclusive. But competition is never so fierce as between those who declare that cooperation is the milk of human existence. The two camps have never really worked closely together.

Rank and File's founding statement, in April 1968, put it firmly in the 'collectivist' camp:

> *Rank and File* is [a journal] produced by left wing teachers within the NUT, who believe that the Union could, and should, be the most important and effective factor in forcing change and progress, not only in the general sociological-educational field, but also − and most especially − in the struggle for better salaries and conditions for all teachers.

The vision was enticing. Picture, if you can (a fair amount of imagination may be needed), the huge NUT membership growing gradually more progressive in outlook, more committed to substantial changes in education, and at the same time becoming more active in their determination to achieve these changes. Such a thing − if it could happen − really would be an 'effective factor in forcing change and progress'.

The NUT was seen as a suitable framework within which progressive teachers could come together, both to fight for the changes they sought and to find defence from individual victimization. There was, however, an obvious difficulty: the NUT membership − anything but radical in outlook or militant in style. What was the point of 'linking up' with them?

The central tenet of Rank and File's strategy was *change through struggle,* the idea that changes arise out of conflict, and that people are themselves changed by *actions* which involve them in conflict. Militant forms of action, for example, would, by taking teachers out of their normal niche in society, by putting them in command − albeit temporarily − of their own activities, open up their minds to worlds of new ideas. Even if, before the action, they had conservative attitudes, the act of engaging in struggle would first make them susceptible to new ideas and at the same time increase their sense of independence and self-confidence so that they would end up more willing and able to countenance radical changes in education.

Events since 1968 have given this theory some credibility, though with a number of crucial difficulties which I hope to make clear in due course.

To get the strategy working, then, you need something to mount a collective struggle over. It was inevitable that teachers' pay should emerge as a suitable issue. In 1969 teachers all over the country were enthused by a campaign (the so-called 'interim award' campaign) for a £135 salary increase. It led to the first ever national strikes by teachers, who displayed unprecedented militancy. The successful conclusion (£120) was a vindication of militant tactics.[3]

The 1969-70 strikes were described by Enoch Powell as 'anarchy' and certainly they had an enormous impact on the attitudes of teachers. They showed us that when we acted together teachers could force even the notorious baddy Sir William Alexander (leader of the management), even the government of the land, to eat their words and give us what we demanded.

The strikes also brought many young teachers into contact with Rank and File. Strikes, demonstrations and meetings, as well as having their own psychological impact, bring people together in large numbers, and this presents a rare opportunity to speak to them, to get ideas across to them. Perhaps the biggest problem facing any teachers' movement is the simple difficulty of bringing itself and its ideas to the attention of other teachers. On the whole teachers don't go to meetings or look at the educational literature. They work in small units and communication between the units is negligible. Only an exceptional affair – like a strike – provides opportunities for the communication and spreading of ideas.

Collective struggle and educational change

The events of 1969-70 gave us the belief that the NUT *could* achieve things when it had a mind to do so. The subsequent years saw the extension of militant action by teachers. In 1968 the idea of teachers taking unofficial strike action was unthinkable. Now it is commonplace.

It is not my purpose here to review the use of strike action by teachers in pursuit of economic demands. Since 1970 there have been successes and failures. But I do want to examine what happened to Rank and File's scheme for *educational change* by collective struggle. For the fact is that with a few notable exceptions, it didn't happen. But the reasons *why* there was no collective action in pursuit of educational demands are instructive.

The problem of getting started

There were, right from the start, those who didn't want Rank and File to be preoccupied with economic matters – salaries and conditions. Although there was an intention that Rank and File should act as an educational ginger group. But the nature of Rank and File's strategy tended to subvert this. What we sought was the development of teachers' political consciousness, and awareness of their own collective power. It was the experience of collective struggle that was to bring about this development. And such a development was a necessary precondition for any assault on the educational *status quo*. The question was, 'How do we get started?', and the commonsense answer: take up whatever issue most teachers happen to be concerned about at this moment.

On this there was a distinct division of opinion. There were those of us who felt that teachers were most worried about the day-to-day anxieties thrown up by 'the crisis in the classroom'. Others, in contrast, argued that teachers were most worried about economic matters, especially their salaries.

In the event, the latter view prevailed: largely because it was not at all clear what we could do, in the short term, about teachers' day-to-day anxieties about their work. Educational issues were not yet suitable as a starting point for collective struggle because there was no widespread agreement amongst teachers about what needed to be done.

Thus it was that we educationists agreed to bide our time, awaiting the moment when teachers' consciousness, built up by a history of economic struggles, burst into the field of education.

It never happened; the economic struggles were never that intense, never that successful, and they usually only involved those who already had a radical outlook; we found there was no automatic spin-off from economic militancy into progressive thinking about education. Indeed, the most militant section of teachers – the National Association of Schoolmasters – was educationally the most reactionary.

Ambivalence within Rank and File

Within Rank and File (reflecting the left wing as a whole) there was a fundamental ambivalence about education. The *'quantitative'* view is that nothing much is wrong with education that a massive injection of resources can't cure. This, allied with a number of changes in the organization of education – particularly comprehensive schooling – could provide a 'first rate' education for the working class child. This view accepts the consensus view of what a 'first rate' education consists of. If only working class children were given the material opportunities, at home as well as at school, that middle class children enjoy, they could perform just as well academically. [4]

This view sees a great danger in the utterances of radicals who seem intent on snatching a proper education away from under the noses of working class children just as they are about to receive it for the first time in history.

The *'qualitative'* view (a very heterogeneous bunch) demands a fundamental review of what education really is for and how it should be done. They see it as fruitless – even harmful – to get working class children to take the diet that middle class children have successfully thrived on for so long.

Rank and File was more or less permanently crippled because it couldn't decide which of these two camps it belonged to. It ended up coming down in neither.

Politics

Many people active in Rank and File saw it just as a vehicle for revolutionary politics. Someone posed it, at a conference in 1969, as a choice between education with a little politics or politics with a little education. Rank and File tended towards the latter; and thus it was necessary to adjust Rank and File's programme to the needs of current revolutionary theorizing. One characteristic of such theorizing, at least over the past decade in England, is that it ignores (on the whole) the ideological sector and concentrates on the economic sector. Capitalism is to be overthrown on the economic front, so that's where the action's got to be. It follows that the best struggles are those that pose a threat to the capitalist economy.

There is plenty of doctrine to prove that pay claims – demands for more resources – pose a problem for the capitalist economy. But there's no doctrine to show that that abolition of caning or the introduction of mixed ability classes

247

(or anything more daring) poses any threat to bourgeois ideology (indeed, that such reforms could be advocated by very unrevolutionary people was seen as proof that such reforms could only reinforce the *status quo*). Faced with this doctrinal difficulty, I remember one session when we searched the scriptures for some illumination on educational questions. We didn't find much except a warning (Marx, *Critique of the Gotha Programme*) not to let the state get its hands on to the education of children. [5] Since this was clearly anarchy, it must have been an oversight on the part of the GOM, and we disregarded it.

There is no coherent Marxist theory of education. Given this, it's hardly surprising that Marxists, especially the most fundamentalist varieties, have no strategy for education. As it is, Marxists end up tail-ending the ready-made philosophies of non-Marxist – and even anti-Marxist – thinkers. [6]

Not only did Rank and File fail to come to grips with this difficulty: it never even spotted it.

The consequent duality in Rank and File's educational position, which I have already mentioned, had an unfortunate effect. Rank and File was continually alienating its potential supporters. Thus it repeatedly drove away the libertarians (quite a strong tradition on the fringe of English education) by its actions and statements: a refusal in 1971 to hold a joint conference with the Libertarian Teachers' Association; repeated attacks by Rank and File speakers on Free Schools and free schoolers; a decision in 1972 to reject a 'too libertarian' interview conducted exclusively for Rank and File with John Holt, the American writer.

And yet, at the same time, Rank and File was scaring off teachers at the other end of the spectrum. These people saw Rank and File as too long-haired, too libertarian, too professionally irresponsible.

In fact this latter group was crucial to Rank and File. It consisted of the traditional trade unionists in the NUT, the kind of people who might be expected to support Rank and File as a movement for trade union consciousness, for labour militancy, in a soft and feeble teachers' union. If Rank and File was to succeed in its economic strategies, it *had* to win over these trade unionists – of the 'old left'. It is ironic that they were put off by Rank and File's educational attitudes, inconsistent and ill-thought-out as they were.

The National Union of Teachers

Rank and File committed itself to work in, and through, the NUT. This meant accepting, at least in the short term, the NUT's own idea of what it is about. In effect, the NUT laid down parameters for Rank and File's activities and, subtly, thinking. On pay and conditions the NUT is a trade union. But on educational matters it is a professional association (written in Gothic script). Any attempt to raise educational matters in the NUT is circumscribed by the brick wall of 'professionalism': what goes on inside a school is the absolute prerogative of the headteacher; and what goes on inside the classroom is the absolute prerogative of the teacher. For this reason, any position taken by the NUT about what is going on in schools tends to be judiciously worded and highly generalized. No

248

conceivable criticism of teachers may be implied. Teachers are doing a marvellous job and the NUT will stand no criticism of them or their work. On the whole the NUT confines itself to macro-questions which are almost invariably organizational: comprehensive schools, nursery schools, examination systems class sizes, the James Report and so forth.

In fact, the NUT does play a part in curriculum questions: for example, through its seats on the Schools Council, and on the various examining boards. As far as one can judge (a proper investigation is needed) its influence here tends to be cautiously liberal. But the NUT's representatives on these bodies go as 'professionals'. There's no simple apparatus by which NUT members can control them.

Being a 'professional association' also has implications for the tactics which may be used to pursue educational objectives. Primarily, these must be non-coercive: committee work, polite press statements — the genteel techniques of a middle class pressure group. What this means, of course, is that on educational matters the NUT is usually ignored unless, by chance, it happens to be saying something which a significant power group is already thinking. In such situations one sees a sort of holy alliance — as with the Labour Party on comprehensive schooling.

If Rank and File succeeded in making a dent in the way the NUT dealt with trade union matters, it failed to make any impression at all on its educational decorum. Whether or not it is possible to raise radical educational ideas in the NUT remains a largely unanswered question. The annual Conference of the NUT is certainly no place to go if you're intent on questioning any taken-for-granted assumptions about the world.

One avenue we did explore was the Young Teachers' Conference of the NUT. This annual event was supposed to be a 'junior' version of the main Union conference. It was for the under-35-year-olds only, and had no decision making power. It was partly a 'training ground' and partly a chance for the younger half of the NUT to air their views which always received wide press publicity. In 1972 we raised a mild resolution which suggested that violence in schools had social causes and could be mollified by progressive reform inside schools (streaming, exams and corporal punishment were mentioned as being fit for 'reappraisal').

This resolution· was passed by a substantial majority of the conference. How representative that conference was is open to doubt. The NUT Executive took the view that the conference delegates (elected by local associations) who supported the resolution and another one which called for an end to salary differentials were a 'lunatic fringe'. The Executive decided never to hold another Conference for Young Teachers. Such a furious response to any questioning of conventional wisdom was quite typical of the NUT hierarchy. Their enthusiastic opposition to anything new was, of course, a reason for the slow progress of Rank and File.

Any attempt to change NUT policy requires the formulation of a precisely worded resolution. You cannot reasonably ask a union to adopt a new way of thinking, or a book, unless you can express it in a concise formula. This presents considerable problems if you want to raise a radically new idea: it just won't fit into a few words. Furthermore, since conference debates are rarely more than rituals, there would seem to be very little joy to be had from trying to raise new ideas about education that way. Only an idea that has already been in wide-spread currency, whose implications have to some extent been understood, can be put in the form of a resolution at a conference. On the other hand, raising an idea at a conference, even if it gets ridiculed, is one way of starting to put it into circulation. This may have been the extent of the value of a number of Rank and File's activities in the NUT.

Rank and File and professionalism

Although continually mocking the NUT's obsession with 'professionalism', the trouble was that Rank and File fell prey to the same syndrome. Its very strate-gies, its policies, its activities, were based on the premise that education is *something done by teachers*. If education was to be transformed, it would be teachers who would do the transforming. There were, it is true, a few dissenters from this view, but by and large Rank and File teachers – on educational matters – fell into the trap of seeing themselves as the suppliers of a commodity, and in this sense as professionals. To question this is of course to threaten many notions which are most important to teacher trade unionism: 'We ought to be well paid because we're doing a useful job which no one else could do', 'You can't have unqualified people doing the job', 'Our collective voice must be listened to because we are the experts', and so forth.

In fact there are many points at which teacher trade unionism will find itself, in the interests of *teachers,* opposed to progressive reforms in education. Rank and File never resolved the paradox involved in being left wing teacher trade unionists.

The problem of practice

In 1972 and 1973 Rank and File grew rapidly. The September 1972 issue of the journal sold 9000 copies. With the aid of charismatic speakers (especially Michael Duane and Chris Searle) meetings were organized all over the country which attracted large numbers of young teachers who were looking for new directions in their day-to-day practice. For a while it looked as though the 1968 generation was coming through, as though the cultural revolutions of the 1960s might begin to make a significant impact on education. Rank and File was starting to articu-late, at its meetings, if not in its journal, these beginnings of a movement. But hopes were not fulfilled; for the problem we never solved was 'What is to be done?'

On matters of salaries, working conditions and so forth it was easy to see what had to be done. Demands were clear and specific; other workers gave us precedents. We organized for trade union action.

But for educational change there was no such simple plan of action. It was far from obvious what had to be done and how to set about it. You couldn't put up a resolution to your NUT branch declaring that working class culture was a valuable thing or that knowledge was socially constructed. Even if resolutions on the content and method of education *were* adopted, it was difficult to see how a trade union could act on them. While you might, just conceivably, conduct a militant campaign for the abolition of the eleven-plus exam, or for the abolition of streaming (both organizational questions, though of course with deeper implications), it is just not possible to envisage such a campaign over, say, the myth of cultural deprivation or the need for oral history.

There are two important conclusions. One is that the educational theoreticians who pose radical ideas have failed to present practical strategies for action. Ideas are worthless if they don't include a plan for their application – not an idealistic one, but a practical one which takes account of the concrete situation that teachers find themselves in here and how. 'He who desires but acts not, breeds pestilence'.

The other conclusion is that Rank and File developed forms of action, and opened up paths of influence, which were ultimately unsuitable for making the fundamental shifts in education practice which some of us were groping for. It was the realization of this disillusioning fact which, amongst other things, led after 1973 to an exodus from Rank and File of the broad spectrum of radicals who were interested in 'education with a little politics'. Rank and File was eventually left as an out-of-touch rump with a narrow, economistic, view of the world.

The achievement of Rank and File

I want now to describe the area in which Rank and File *was* successful: the area in which, hopefully, history will give Rank and File a mention, at least in a footnote. This was Rank and File's assault on hierarchy.

To point to the hierarchical structure of education now, of course, is to point to something like pollution: you would be hard pressed to find anyone prepared publicly to defend it, although no one seems to be doing much to get rid of it. But in 1968 to point out and criticize education's hierarchical structure was virtually a sackable offence. Rank and File played a major part in bringing the matter to the attention of ordinary teachers.

Democracy in schools

In 1969 Rank and File published *The Teachers Charter,* a document which included a call for teacher participation in school decision making. It called for 'a shift of power from the minority, authoritarian position of the head and education authorities, to the full participation by the parents, staff, students and the community at large, in all decisions taken in an educational context'.

This was a radical thing for a group of teachers to be saying in 1969, and it was greeted with predictable horror by the educational establishment.

In 1971 these ideas were expanded into the pamphlet *Democracy in Schools.* [7] Despite many weaknesses, this is still a very interesting pamphlet, and its central proposition, the democratic control of schools by teachers, parents and pupils, in conjunction with the LEA, remains anathema to the powers that be in education (indeed, in some ways hierarchy is more firmly entrenched now than it was then).

My conviction is that such a democratization of the schools is the absolutely essential precondition for other qualitative changes in education. In fact, this is what 'the problem of practice' I have discussed above boils down to. We could not put ideas into practice because we had no power in our schools. Unless we could get the sympathy of the headteacher, nothing could be changed. Furthermore, we could not practise with ideas that we were only half sure of. To make a change in schools as they are presently arranged is regarded as such a momentous thing to do that only projects that seem certain to succeed are undertaken. A failed experiment is seen as something terrible: the hierarchical power structure reinforces this.

The *Democracy in Schools* policy fitted into Rank and File's strategy because it could be raised, as a resolution, in the NUT. The long-term aim was to get the NUT — through a conference resolution — committed to a policy of democratic schools and then use the resources of the Union to campaign for this policy.

At the 1971 Conference of the NUT a resolution on 'teacher participation' was debated. The resolution made the limited suggestion that certain school decisions might be taken by a staff council rather than by the headteacher. The NUT Executive, consisting almost entirely of headteachers horrified at the prospect of some diminution in their powers, managed to get the resolution sidestepped by proposing, instead, that a Union working party should examine the matter. The working party was eventually constituted with a distinctly conservative bias. Yet to the extreme vexation of the Executive, the working party report did recommend a limited amount of collective decision making on specific issues. [8] Sanity was, however, preserved; a leading communist, in a brilliant speech in which he attacked the notion of workers' control, helped the Executive persuade Conference delegates to throw out the report of their own working party. Subsequent attempts to raise teacher participation at NUT Conferences have been unsuccessful.

Rank and File's part had been, and went on being, to put the idea of democratic schools onto the map. It was able to do this because it had a country-wide organization, a magazine with a relatively wide circulation, and facilities for getting literature to teachers round the country. The value of such an apparatus should not be underestimated. It is still needed. The conventional media were never prepared to allow much time or space for the propagation of genuinely radical ideas like the democratization of schools. We had to do it ourselves.

Teachers' salaries

The most striking outward sign of hierarchy in education is the teachers' salary structure. By 1971, salary differentials between different positions on the teacher's promotion ladder had become so enormous that Rank and File could no longer simply align itself with others who called for 'more pay for teachers'. The distribution of monies gained in any salary award became the overriding issue. 'We are egalitarians', the editorial of *Rank and File No. 16* declared, and the question of an egalitarian salary structure became an indissoluble part of the democracy in schools policy. Rank and File became a crusader for the underdogs in teaching — those deprived of decision making power and paid the lowest salaries. These too are the very people who actually teach the kids. Promotion up the salary, power and decision making ladder takes the most experienced teachers away from the children and into the administrative 'managerial' work.

If we thought the downtrodden masses would flock to the banner, we were wrong for several reasons. First, more and more teachers were being put off Rank and File because of its domination by one particular left wing group (the International Socialists); not only put off Rank and File, but also put off Rank and File's ideas. Second, our literature remained didactic and jargon ridden. Thirdly, we badly underestimated the amount of time it would take for new ideas to seep in; ideas we put about in 1971 are still working their way into the consciousness of teachers. Fourthly, it became apparent that many teachers feel happy with their present lot; they prefer the security of knowing their place in an established hierarchy; they revel in getting orders from above and giving them to the children — 'ragged trousered professionalists', they were called in *Rank and File No. 6*. Internalizing and rationalizing their own subservience, they use it to justify the domination they exert — intellectually and physically — over their pupils.

Rank and File never sorted out what to do about those teachers who didn't seem to *want* the goodies that it hoped its policies would win for them. For Rank and File to appeal, there had to be an incipient, and widespread, desire for change. Amongst teachers, an overwhelmingly conservative profession (and maybe that is the only fact that matters), Rank and File was on to a hiding to nothing. Perhaps Rank and File was in the wrong place at the wrong time. It never seemed to gain much support beyond the young and open minded, especially those who entered teaching after 1968.

Rank and File's salary policy never got anywhere at NUT Conferences. A salary policy which is not adopted by the Union is, of course, no salary policy at all. But Rank and File, by challenging pay differentials, did pose a real challenge to some of the most deeply seated assumptions about school organization. Rank and File's enduring contribution was to put such ideas into widespread circulation. We have not heard the end of them.

Conclusions

Rank and File brought people together. The isolation which radical teachers can feel can be quite crushing. A teacher with unconventional ideas who finds himself without allies may be led by the sheer weight of hostility to start questioning his own sanity. Many, perhaps most, young teachers in this situation simply abandon teaching (this is one reason why radicals are so few in number amongst teachers).

If you can understand the horror of isolation, you can understand the euphoria, the tangible sense of solidarity, which some gatherings, especially national gatherings, of Rank and File teachers managed to inspire. Suddenly we realized that it was *their* sanity, not ours, which was in question. Suddenly we became aware of the possibility of change, because there were lots of us who felt the same things.

While Rank and File was sometimes inspiring, its dogged sectarianism, its devotion to doctrine and jargon, and its utter inability to make any compromise, meant that all the time it was making more enemies than friends, even amongst people who could so easily have been its allies.

Despite this, Rank and File did build a nationwide network of left wing teachers. Although the 'paid up' membership never rose much above 1000, the network probably loosely embraced several thousand teachers at one time. As an evangelical apparatus, this was fairly effective. Two or three thousand teachers can do a lot of talking. People whose business is to have ideas but not act upon them usually grossly underestimate the supreme importance of propagation. I suspect that most new ideas never get propagated at all, unless they appeal to some significant power group.

A third function of Rank and File was the confidence it gave, to young teachers especially, to begin to assert themselves, and particularly to do so collectively. It did a lot to break down the belief that innovation can only come from the top downwards. People with good ideas no longer see it as necessary to cringe and crawl to get a headship before their ideas can be put into practice.

A significant development of the past two or three years has been the emergence in a number of schools of groupings of progressive teachers who are prepared to stand together, and act together, to try and make changes in their schools. Sometimes these groupings have formed under the umbrella of the school NUT branch; occasionally they have been Rank and File groups. But usually they have had no external status.

This seems to me to be one of the most promising ways forward. In a way they are going back to the idea that Rank and File floated in its earlier days: that by getting together and acting collectively, much can be achieved. A lot will depend on the balance of power within a school – the flexibility of the head and the numerical strength of the progressive group. A good deal may be achieved by talk, by persuasion. But the William Tyndale case gave us a sharp indication of the constraints – in normal times invisible – on changes that might be made within a school. It is certain that these progressive groupings within schools will need to be strengthened by a link-up beyond schools: to provide moral and material support, to exchange experience and ideas. To some extent the journals *Teaching London Kids* and *Radical Education* supply this link-up. [9] But an organization, a movement, is needed. Not least is the need for a defence system for those who get into trouble. Let us be clear that there will be trouble. There is a deep-seated need for the education system to be committed to the *status quo,* whether intellectual, ideological, social, political or economic. To attempt change is to tread not only a difficult, but a dangerous path, as the William Tyndale teachers, whatever the mistakes they may have made, found to their cost.

Of course, the defence of teachers in trouble should be a function of the NUT.

But experience has shown us that the NUT bureaucracy, with its batteries of full-time officials, lawyers and experts, will wriggle out of having to defend a teacher if he gets victimized for some radical action. [10] Of the teachers I listed in the opening section of this paper, only Chris Searle got any effective backing from the Union. The William Tyndale teachers, all NUT members, were given virtually no help by the Union.[11] So we need, pending the transformation of the NUT (which would certainly be welcome), our own defence organization. Perhaps what I am suggesting is a Union of Radical Educators.

Rank and File was only one of a large number of groups that sprung up in the world of education in the late 1960s and early 1970s. Each has its own tale to tell. If we can learn from each, we can discover ways of making our dismal education system lurch a little nearer the true needs of its learners. Philosophers have merely interpreted the world . . . .

Notes

1 No matter what indicators you use, I don't think that more than 5000 teachers, out of the total force of 500,000, would actively question the broad consensus view of what education is and how it should be done.

2 *Teaching London Kids,* 79 Ronald's Road, London N5. Started October 1973. Published termly.

3 Described in Vincent Burke, *Teachers In Turmoil* (Harmondsworth, Penguin, 1971).

4 For a clear statement of this position, see *School Does Matter: Organisation for Achievement in the Inner City* published by the 'Right to Learn' group in 1974.

5 Marx observed drily that the people were in no need of education from the state; on the contrary, the state was in need of a stern lesson from the people.

6 See, for example, Maurice Levitas, *Marxist Perspectives in the Sociology of Education* (London, Routledge & Kegan Paul, 1974).

7 The pamphlet, although largely based on a draft by Eric Peagam and Dave Picton, was produced by a remarkable, and lengthy, process of collective writing involving hundreds of people.

8 *Teacher Participation: Report of the National Working Party* (London, NUT, 1973).

9 *Radical Education,* 86 Eleanor Road, London E8. Started September 1974. Published termly.

10 Whereas NUT officials will trip over themselves to assist a member who gets into trouble for, for example, breaking a pupil's jaw in a fit of temper.

11 See *William Tyndale: The Teachers' Story* (London, Writers and Readers Cooperative, 1976).

255

Notes on contributors

John Bartholomew teaches Sociology in the Department of Teaching Studies, Polytechnic of North London.

Richard Collins teaches Media Studies in the School of Communication, Polytechnic of Central London.

Denis Gleeson taught Sociology and Liberal Studies in a Further Education College and now teaches Sociology of Education at the University of Keele.

Ivor Goodson taught at Countesthorpe College, Leicestershire, and Stantonbury Campus, Milton Keynes, and is currently carrying out research into Environmental Studies at the University of Sussex.

Nigel Hand taught in secondary and middle schools and currently lectures in English at the College of St Mark and St John, Plymouth.

Jan Hardy taught Chemistry at Alperton Comprehensive School and now lectures in Education at Homerton College, Cambridge.

Ian Hextall taught Geography and Economics in secondary schools and currently lectures in the School of Education at Goldsmiths' College.

Anthony Hoskyns taught Physics at Holland Park School and is now Head of Physics at Sir Williams Collins School, London.

Gerard Macdonald works for the Inner London Education Authority's Learning Materials Service.

John Spradbery teaches Mathematics and is Acting Deputy Headmaster of a secondary school in Essex.

John Tulloch has worked in Journalism and Adult Education and currently teaches in the School of Communication, Polytechnic of Central London.

Graham Vulliamy taught Sociology and Liberal Studies in Further Education and now lectures in Sociology of Education at the University of York.

Chris Webb was Head of Humanities at Sir William Collins School, and later Education Officer for Shelter. He now directs the Nottingdale Urban Studies Centre in London.

The White Lion Street Free School opened in Islington in 1972 and is a non-fee-paying independent foundation run by the parents, pupils and workers involved.

257

Geoff Whitty taught History and Social Studies in comprehensive schools and now teaches in the School of Education at the University of Bath.

Richard Winter taught English in Further Education, was lecturer in English and Education, University of Malawi, and now teaches at Colchester Institute of Higher Education.

Nigel Wright taught Economics and Mathematics in London comprehensive schools.

Michael Young taught Chemistry in London secondary schools and now lectures in Sociology of Education at the University of London Institute of Education.

Author index

Subject index

National Union of Teachers (NUT): and Rank and File, 5, 190, 245 ff.; and the Schools Council, 194, 198

parents: involvement in Free School curricula, 184-5; resistance to change, 190, 191

physics teaching, *see* school physics

pupils: boredom in school physics, 157; choice in a Free School, 182; and curriculum change, 4; gaining confidence and understanding, 160; pupil centred learning, 131; secondary school pupils as primary school teachers, 147; writing in school physics, 161, 162

quiz programmes: and educational values, 110; and views of knowledge, 99 ff.

radical teachers, 1, 45, 224 ff.

Rank and File, 5, 6; and the NUT, 5, 190, 245 ff.; and school democracy, 190, 251

school English (English teaching), 9; and children's literature, 12; creative writing, 16-17; and drama, 17; and the high culture tradition, 9; and the Newsom Report, 13; and poetry, 11; and reading, 13

school mathematics (mathematics teaching), 236; and the division of labour, 241; and school and non-school knowledge, 237; and teacher-pupil relations, 238; Mathematics for the Majority Continuation Project, 238

school music (music teaching): traditional conceptions, 19-20; and Afro-American music, 19-21; and alternative music traditions, 20 ff.; changes in, 29-31; and ideology, 22-3; and the sociology of knowledge, 29

school physics (physics teaching), 150; community centres and, 151; electronics and, 153; heat and energy in, 154; Nuffield Physics for all abilities, 152; optics in, 152; pupil boredom, 157; pupil confidence and understanding in, 160; pupil writing in, 161-2; and school organization, 163-4; technology in, 156

school records, 75; and the division of labour, 85; and IQ tests, 79-80; and politics, 85; and teacher-pupil relations, 76

school science (science teaching), 47 ff.; and everyday life, 53; historical emergence of, 47-8; and learning theories, 50; mathematical abstraction in, 57; relevance of, 49; and scientific illiteracy, 51; and socialism, 60; and technology, 50

schooling, the political economy of, 3

Schools Council, 192 ff., 226, . 232-3, 242; *see also* Humanities Curriculum Project *and* Social Education Project

social control: 'good teaching' and, 141; social studies teaching and, 35

Social Education Project, 43-5, 210

social studies teaching, 35; and academic sociology, 36-7; and curriculum 'theory', 37; and discovery methods, 38; 'new' social studies, 35 ff.; and the Newsom Report, 35; radical social studies, 42-3; sexist assumptions in, 35; and social control, 35 ff.; and the sociology of knowledge, 41-2; and worksheets, 39

sociology of education, 1, 19; 'new' directions in, 2; systems models and, 2; Marxist perspectives and, 2-3, 6

sociology of knowledge: and school music, 29; and social studies, 41-2

teachers, autonomy of, 191; and educational change, 244; training of, 114

teaching, alternative models of, 129-30; changing concepts of, 134 ff., 142; 'good' teaching and social control, 141; as transmission, 128

television in schools, 166 ff.

textbooks and curriculum change, 87; and school knowledge, 87 ff.; and theories of knowledge, 97

William Tyndale School, 5, 6, 190, 191, 254, 255